Class and Community
in Frontier Colorado

Studies in Historical Social Change

SCOTT G. McNALL AND JILL S. QUADAGNO, EDITORS

Social Change in the Southwest, 1350–1880, Thomas D. Hall

Class Struggle and the New Deal: Industrial Labor, Industrial Capital, and the State, Rhonda F. Levine

Slave Women in the New World: Gender Stratification in the Caribbean, Marietta Morrissey

Old Age in the Welfare State: The Political Economy of Public Pensions, John Myles

The Social Origins of Democratic Collapse: The First Portuguese Republic in the Global Economy, Kathleen C. Schwartzman

Class and Community in Frontier Colorado, Richard Hogan

Class and Community in Frontier Colorado

Richard Hogan

 University Press of Kansas

© 1990 by the University Press of Kansas
All rights reserved
First Published 1990. Reissued 2020.

The text of this book is licensed under a Creative Commons Attribution-NonCommercial-NoDerivatives 4.0 International Public License (https://creativecommons.org/licenses/by-nc-nd/4.0).

Published by the University Press of Kansas (Lawrence, Kansas 66045), which was organized by the Kansas Board of Regents and is operated and funded by Emporia State University, Fort Hays State University, Kansas State University, Pittsburg State University, the University of Kansas, and Wichita State University.

Open access edition funded by the National Endowment for Humanities and the Andrew W. Mellon Foundation Humanities Open Book Program.

Typographical errors may have been introduced in the digitization process.

Library of Congress Cataloging-in-Publication Data
Hogan, Richard.
Class and community in frontier Colorado / Richard Hogan.
p. cm — (studies in historical social change)
Includes bibliographical references (p.).
ISBN 978-0-7006-0462-3 (cloth : alk. paper)
ISBN 978-0-7006-3155-1 (pbk. : alk. paper)
ISBN 978-0-7006-3099-8 (ebook)
1. Colorado—Social conditions. 2. Colorado—Economic conditions. 3. Colorado—Politics and government—To 1876. 4. Colorado—Politics and government—1876–1950. 5. Frontier and pioneer life—Colorado. I. Title. II. Series.
Classification: LLC: HN79.C6H64 1990 | DDC: 306′ .09788—dc20 89-28317
LC record available at https://lccn.loc.gov/89028317.

The paper used in this publication meets the minimum requirements of the American National Standard for Permanence of Paper for Printed Library Materials Z39.48-1984.

CONTENTS

List of Illustrations and Tables	vii
Preface to Kansas Open Books Edition	ix
Preface	xiii
1. Class Structure and Conflict in Frontier Colorado	1
PART ONE: CARNIVAL TOWNS OF COLORADO	17
2. Denver: The Carnival Capital	19
3. Central City: Supply Town for the Mines	49
4. Greeley: Dry Farming and Utopian Capitalism	79
PART TWO: CAUCUS TOWNS OF COLORADO	119
5. Golden: Denver's Western Rival	121
6. Pueblo: Skins, Steers, and Steel Center	151
7. Canon City: Gateway to the Southern Rockies	179
8. The Enduring Legacy of the American Frontier	207
Notes	221
Bibliography	241
Index	247

LIST OF ILLUSTRATIONS AND TABLES

Illustrations

Denver, 1858–1860	20
A wagon train arrives in Denver, ca. 1860	21
Denver in the 1870s	42
First National Bank, Denver, 1870s	43
Denver in the 1880s	47
Downtown Central City in the 1860s	50
Central City in the 1870s	67
Early Greeley	80
West's circular on Union Colony operations	87
Downtown Greeley	105
Golden in the 1860s	122
Golden in the 1880s	150
Pueblo in 1868	160
Pueblo in the 1880s	175
Downtown Cañon City	189
The railroad depot at Cañon City	204

Tables

1.1	Classifying Frontier Political Economies	10
2.1	Wealth by Class Category for Households in Denver, 1860	22
2.2	Distribution of Political Actions in Denver, by Issue Orientation by Identity of Party Claiming Governing Authority	29
2.3	Distribution of Political Events in Denver, by Issue, by Authority's Use of Coercive Violence	30

2.4	Distribution of Political Events in Denver by Season by Issue	34
2.5	Wealth by Class Category for Households in Denver, 1870	41
2.6	Criminal Cases in the Denver Courts, by Court by Offense for 1860–1864, 1868–1873, and 1880	44
3.1	Wealth by Class Category for Central City, 1860	55
3.2	Value of Mineral Production from Gregory Lode, 1859–1879	62
3.3	Wealth by Class Category for Central City, 1870	68
3.4	Criminal Cases in Gilpin County by Court by Offense for 1860–1862, 1869–1871, and 1880	76
4.1	Wealth by Class Category for Households in Greeley, 1870	92
4.2	Criminal Cases by Court by Offense for Weld County, 1871–1876	101
4.3	Criminal Cases in Weld County Courts, by Court by Offense for 1871–1876 and 1877–1880	115
5.1	Wealth by Class Category for Households in Golden, 1860	125
5.2	Political Actions in Golden by Issue by Governing Authority	130
5.3	Political Actions in Golden by Issue by Authority's Use of Violence	131
5.4	Votes Cast by Candidate by Precinct for Jefferson County Election of 1860	134
5.5	Wealth by Class Category for Households in Golden, 1870	141
5.6	Criminal Cases in Jefferson County by Offense by Court, 1862–1867 and 1869–1872	144
6.1	Products of Industry in Pueblo County, 1869	160
6.2	Wealth by Class Category for Households in Pueblo, 1870	162
6.3	Criminal Cases by Offense in the Pueblo District Court, 1864–1866, 1869–1871, and 1880	165
6.4	Pueblo City and County Vote in the 1870 Territorial Election	167
7.1	Wealth by Class Category for Households in Cañon City, 1870	190
7.2	Criminal Cases by Type of Offense for the Territorial District Court in Fremont County, 1862–1880	194
7.3	Cañon City and Fremont County Vote in Railroad Bond Election of 1873	198

KANSAS OPEN BOOKS PREFACE

When asked to write this new preface for my old book—my first book, published thirty years ago—I immediately thought of the preface of my (hopefully) forthcoming third book. My Georgia book will be something of a sequel to this book, moving from West to South but continuing with the comparative and historical perspective on local political economy in late nineteenth-century US communities. In fact, in the mid-1990s I was presenting papers at Social Science History meetings that compared third-party political movements in Colorado, Georgia, and Kansas.

To better appreciate the continuity and change in my approach to local history and community studies, I first turned to the original preface of this 1990 book and then to what I had already said in the notes of my second book, *The Failure of Planning: Permitting Sprawl in San Diego Suburbs, 1970–1999*, published in 2003. Then I looked at the penultimate draft of the aforementioned third book's preface, which helped me to think about the thirty years of scholarship since this first book. How I felt in 1990 has been preserved in the first preface. Here I will focus instead on how my thinking about doing local history has changed.

Today, as professor emeritus of sociology, I am not inclined to criticize the doctoral candidate of 1982 or the soon-to-be-tenured assistant professor of 1990. The original preface was fine, as was (and is) the book and even the dissertation that provided much of the theory and data. I will add, with thanks to my old friend Tom Noel, the world's foremost authority on Denver saloons, one correction that he pointed out in a review of this book. On page 21, Thomas Wildman is referenced as Wilder—in an unconscious reference to Laura Ingalls Wilder. When Tom pointed out that error (after the book was published) I was upset. Despite our best efforts, this typo lurks in silent witness to the fact that you cannot really trust sociologists to get the names and dates right. In fact, when I tried to find this typo, I realized that there was no reference to Wildman in the index, and the bibliographic reference to his letters, cited under Hafen, Leroy R. (editor), omits the name of Ann W. Hafen (his coeditor). Clearly, the young sociologist was not as sensitive as he might have been to the conventions of history. He was also unaware of the forthcoming rise of a decidedly feminist New Western History, announced by Patricia Nelson Limerick in "What on Earth Is the New Western History?" (in Limerick,

Clyde A. Milner II, and Charles E. Rankin, eds., *Trails: Toward a New Western History*). This book was, indeed, one of the last of the "New Social History" books of the seventies and eighties that used historical data to test sociological theories—most notably here, the theory of public and private government, which is the centerpiece of this analysis.

As I said in my last book, *The Failure of Planning*, this theory holds up well, but it tends to ignore the extent to which there are public and private faces of government in all localities, states, and even in the federal government. That said, the base in local frontier political economy and the implications for inter- and intra-class conflict, as the frontier is incorporated into the national and international political economy, remain worthy of the time invested in developing and testing this theory. If the form is a bit too social science dissertation–like, even after being completely rewritten as a book, the content is still worth preserving. The thesis is still defensible and potentially enlightening—even now that we have, apparently, transcended the New Western History in a fit of postmodern whimsy.

Since writing this book I have completed a totally different sort of local history—using archival and oral history combined with nonparticipant observation—to compare the experience of San Diego suburbs with growth and growth control, habitat preservation, and affordable housing from 1970 to 1999. *The Failure of Planning* was intended to be my popular book, one without all the tables and with most of the theory buried in chapter notes—a large portion of which were deleted to keep the book short and relatively inexpensive. *The Failure of Planning* used maps in lieu of tables, but this was before I learned about geographic information systems. The maps in this 2003 book were hand drawn or modified by an illustrator.

It is hard to imagine this book without its tables, although I would, if writing this book today, have done much more with maps. There is one map in this book, just before the first chapter, locating the cities and the two major rivers while somewhat abstractly representing the Rocky Mountains. In my current work on Georgia towns and counties during Reconstruction (1868–1880), I do much more with railroads and rivers. That would be a welcome addition to the Colorado story presented here, particularly since the railroads figure prominently in the story. The Georgia book will also benefit from my realization that statistical analysis can reduce the number of tables and the somewhat tedious survey of descriptive statistics. It will likewise benefit from the understanding that figures as well as maps can replace tables with descriptive statistics, thereby setting up a more sophisticated analysis that predicts if not explains election results, among others.

There was a battle raging in sociology in the seventies on the general linear model, the new structural equation models, and the relative merits of quantitative and qualitative analyses. As a graduate student at Michigan, 1975–1982, my mantra was, *I crunch numbers for money as a research assistant for faculty who do survey research, but my work is historical and qualitative.* That was obviously not true of this 1990 book, and it was even less true of the 1982 dissertation (still available on microfilm), which had even more tables, plus thirty-eight pages of technical appendices on sampling, coding, and analysis of data from various sources. In the appendix (227–229), there was even a brief discussion of statistical tests, including some comparing proportions of wealth by class, industry, and bracket ($100–$199) in Golden and Denver. This exercise was included to indicate that the student eschewed quantitative research methods but was thoroughly trained in their use and abuse.

These traces of the student project are not preserved here in this 1990 publication, but it benefits from the sampling, coding, and analytical skills that the student learned from his professors in Ann Arbor. Fortunately, in the intervening years, while I might have lost some of my youthful enthusiasm and energy, I have managed to transcend the battle of the quantitative versus qualitative, survey versus archival, article versus book promoters. Only by achieving the status of emeritus professor have I been able to completely ignore the ways in which other people attempt to judge my effort or achievement. At this point, I can say that I sometimes am extremely pleased with the opportunity to read and think a bit more and even to rewrite what others have found less than compelling. Hopefully, the final review of my Georgia book (in which one reviewer has already uncovered one typo in the misspelling of a middle name) will not exhaust my efforts to model tolerance and patience. These qualities should help us all as we await the new normal.

The other thing that strikes me, in revisiting this manuscript today, is the extent to which flesh-and-blood humans are less important than classes and parties. The more recent search for missing voices is more apparent in my current work, where I trace the prehistory of my towns in considering the Native American chiefdoms along the rivers and in the coastal zone where the rivers met the sea. The anthropology of this prehistory is missing here, barely referenced in the Pueblo and Greeley chapters and in two short paragraphs on the Sand Creek Massacre (159). Still, my intent is not to criticize my earlier work but to recognize where it stands in the context of my intellectual development. Clearly the energy and enthusiasm of youth are in evidence here, in the hours, days, weeks, and months spent in the Colorado archives, gathering data that I would eventually manage to organize and analyze. At this point, I am grateful for the data and the theory. It was quite an ambitious effort, unlike anything that I have done before or since. This was my first comparative local history, which established the foundation for my more recent efforts, and which might yet interest others in this path toward understanding the present by exploring the past and understanding the global by focusing on the local.

As I look around me today I am keenly aware of the importance of class and community, in Colorado, in California, in Georgia, and, especially, here in the college town of West Lafayette, Indiana, where my neighbors and I are attempting to deal with the problems of government and economy, protest and participation, race and gender, as well as class and party. I remain cautiously optimistic on the prospects for brokering a coalition of people and organizations pursuing class, race, and gender justice, along with environmental stewardship, and teaching them to avoid past errors while attempting to fundamentally change the world. Clearly we can think globally, but we must act locally and hope that we will not be fooled again.

Richard Hogan
West LaFayette, Indiana
June 2020

PREFACE

Since perhaps 1968 I have been disturbed by the conventional wisdom regarding the nature of republican capitalism in the United States of America. Initially, I was convinced, as were at least some of my peers, that the then current crisis in American institutions was unprecedented and that we were uniquely qualified to provide the solution. Simply by rejecting the dominant culture, defying the instituted authorities, and refusing to conform to prevailing practices we might establish a new society in which individuals were more concerned with the quality of life than with material wealth.

Twenty years of life in the ivory tower may have stifled my youthful idealism. It has certainly impressed me with the depth of my ignorance and the complexity of relations among economic, political, cultural, and social institutions. Academic study has not, however, diminished my dissatisfaction with popular images of American economic and political institutions. For the past ten years I have been struggling with the myths and realities of the American frontier experience. In the process, I have come to appreciate the extent to which our contemporary problems, including capital flight and the declining position of the family farmer, are but the latest symptoms of the contradictions and crises that have plagued our efforts at economic and political development. At the same time, I have become convinced that the entrepreneurial "booster" efforts to revitalize American communities are, in essence, attempts to recapitulate the process that created these problems in the first place. Ultimately, the solutions are more complex than I might have anticipated at the outset. The challenge is to reorient our approach to the crises of the contemporary United States.

Most generally, we face the same challenge that all developing nations must confront. We must, first of all, focus our considerable institutional capacity on the problem of our collective survival. If we cannot meet the basic human needs of our citizens, most especially food and shelter, our economic development efforts will be of no avail. Nevertheless, we have traditionally oriented our economic and political development efforts toward the expanding national and international economy rather than focusing even local productive capacity on the needs of the local population. In this regard we have yet to learn the lesson of our frontier history. The pioneers who established economic and political institutions on the western frontier were, it appears, very much aware that they were building a national political economy. Ultimately, however, many of them came to realize that this national political economy was a threat to their control of local institutions and to their survival as relatively autonomous entrepreneurs.

This book is a preliminary effort at a reexamination of the American frontier experience, focusing on the development of local economic and political institutions, which fostered the growth of national monopoly capital and federal administrative control. I do not, however, propose a conspiracy theory. Frontier entrepreneurs were willing, indeed anxious, to orient their industrial production toward the developing national market in the interest of potential profits. Nevertheless, they actively resisted the intrusion of national capital and federal authority when their control of local institutions was challenged. They were not pawns in the hands of national actors but were instead self-consciously organized in the defense of their autonomy, through third-party electoral challenges or, in some cases, violent confrontation. Ultimately, however, they were conquered, as different fractions of laboring and nonlaboring classes fought distinctive battles against a common enemy. In this regard they were not so different from the oppressed classes of the contemporary United States. Hence, we should seek neither to romanticize nor to emulate the experience of the western pioneers. Their story is not a parable. It is, in fact, a tragedy, and we are now performing Act III.

Despite my critical perspective on American economic and political development efforts, I have tried to avoid moralizing and sarcasm. I will apologize at the outset to historians and others who might be disturbed by my use of "Carnival" in reference to public, democratic government. In chapter 1, I offer a rationale and an explanation of how this differs from the way that European scholars use that term. Aside from the implications associated with my choice of this term, I have, I hope, purged the text of distracting sarcasm and expressions of moral outrage.

I have attempted to provide a clearly stated theory, in the first chapter, with a minimal amount of obscure theoretical debate and literature review. In the brief section on "Caucus Towns of Colorado" (part 2) and in the conclusion (chapter 8), there is a more self-conscious effort to speak to the literatures and address the concerns of my colleagues in social history and related fields, particularly in the notes.

Both in the initial research and in the production of this manuscript, I have incurred more debts than I can acknowledge, much less repay. Faculty and students in the Department of Sociology and Anthropology at Purdue University contributed many ideas that have influenced this book in a variety of ways. Ongoing discussions with members of the Social Science History Association and the Sorrento seminar have further shaped these efforts, as have comments by John Larson, Hal Woodman, Jon Teaford, Nancy Gabin, and other colleagues in the Purdue History Department.

Much of the theory and some of the analyses presented in the following chapters were developed in "Carnival and Caucus: A Typology for Comparative Frontier History," published in *Social Science History* in 1987. The editors and reviewers of that article offered valuable suggestions that have certainly shaped this book as well. Similarly, editors and reviewers from *Theory and Society* helped me to clarify my thinking on the frontier experience more generally. Their efforts are also much appreciated.

Various archivists, librarians, and clerks have offered invaluable service in locating documents. City and county officials from all six localities were more than helpful. The staff at the Western History Department of the Denver Public Library and at the Colorado State Historical Society were especially helpful in this regard. Various members of the Departments of History and Sociology at the University of Denver, the University of Colorado, Boulder, and the University of Northern Colorado, Greeley, were most gracious in offering assistance. Lyle Dorsett and John Livingston offered critical advice and encouragement, while William Key and Wilbert Moore offered valuable assistance in providing office space and access to the libraries at the University of Denver.

A National Science Foundation dissertation grant (SES80-02004) and a similar grant from the University of Michigan provided funding for my initial analysis of Colorado frontier towns. This allowed me to travel to the archives, to hire assistants, and to complete my doctoral dissertation. The staff at the Center for Research on Social Organization (University of Michigan) was indispensable, particularly Sheila Wilder, who taught me how to administer a grant and supervise student workers. Chuck Tilly, Bill Gamson, Jeff Paige, Shaw Livermore, and Andy Modigliana all suffered through my earliest efforts and helped me to finish my dissertation. Without their help, this book would have been impossible.

Both the National Institute of Mental Health and the Mental Health Research Program at Rutgers/Princeton provided me with two years of support and allowed me to move on to new and different projects after the dissertation was completed. Aside from whatever value my research on community reaction to group homes might contribute, the three-year respite from frontier politics made it possible for me to forget my dissertation and write my book. That, combined with the support and encouragement from my colleagues at Purdue and David Greenberg's initial interest in my work, has greatly facilitated this effort. Bob Perrucci offered both concern and encouragement to this young assistant professor intent on writing a book. Reece McGee was instrumental in getting me a one-semester research leave so that I could complete this project before my tenure review. He also read the penultimate draft, offering valuable editorial comments.

Comments and suggestions by Scott McNall and the anonymous reviewers selected by the University Press of Kansas were most helpful in pointing to potential problems and suggesting ways to avoid them. Scott McNall in particular and the entire staff of the University Press of Kansas were extremely encouraging and, at times, listened patiently as I recited my tale of woe. All of these people did their best to ensure that this would be the best book that I could write. For those problems that remain, I must take full responsibility.

Kay Solomon deserves special thanks for her services in word processing this manuscript. Most important, however, my wife and my friends and family have put up with me and accepted the fact that I have been living in the nineteenth century for what seems like a lifetime.

Class and Community
in Frontier Colorado

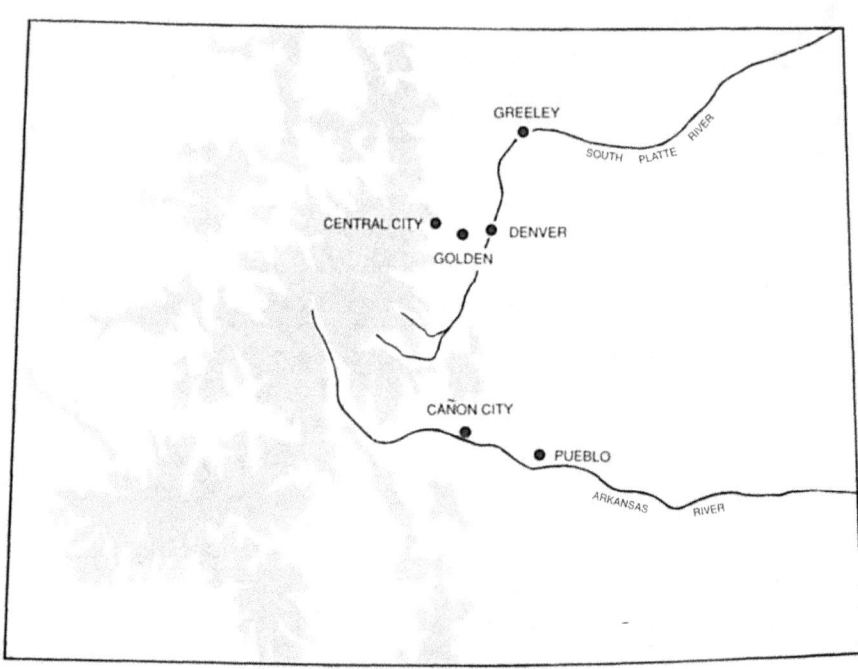

CHAPTER ONE

Class Structure and Conflict in Frontier Colorado

In 1876, Colorado was admitted to the union. Then, as the nation recovered from the economic depression of 1873 and the Colorado silver mines attracted eastern capital investment, it seemed that economic prosperity would be achieved. Prosperity did not bring domestic tranquility, however. In northern Colorado, first Grangers and then Greenbackers were organizing in opposition to monopoly capital, and competing farming settlements were fighting to secure water rights. In 1880, there were strikes in the coal mines of Erie (in largely agrarian Weld County), and a strike in the silver mines of Leadville inspired the governor to declare martial law. In Denver, the bricklayers, carpenters, and printers were on strike, and there was some concern that they might follow the example of the Leadville miners and attempt to enforce collective bargaining rights.[1]

The political struggles of the early statehood period were not simply labor's response to proletarianization. Local capitalists were also involved in resistance to national monopoly capital and to the imposition of federal authority. In 1876, W.A.H. Loveland and his associates defied the Union Pacific and even kidnapped a federal judge in their efforts to retain control of the Colorado Central Railroad. A similar railroad war was raging in 1879, as a large deputation of "peace officers" met armed resistance when they attempted to seize the South Pueblo depot of the Denver and Rio Grande. At the same time, federal efforts to reclaim public-domain lands by cutting illegal fences and investigating the validity of large land grants, particularly in southern Colorado, inspired considerable if less spectacular forms of local resistance to federal authority.[2]

Thus both capital and labor were resisting the intrusion of national monopoly capital and the imposition of federal authority as the newly established State of Colorado institutionalized its relations with the national political economy. Ultimately, we must find an explanation for these political struggles not only in Colorado but in the United States more generally. The simple explanation is that the political struggles of early statehood were a response to the closing of the Colorado frontier. Frederick Jackson Turner argued that the frontier offered economic opportunity and the experience of establishing democratic institutions, which combined to mold the distinctively American character and to forestall the economic and political crises that had plagued western Europe in the mid nineteenth century.[3] Thus the closing of the Colorado frontier, like the closing of the American frontier more generally, produced alienation and conflict as the opportunities for entrepreneurial economic development and grass-roots political action declined.

The frontier experience did not forestall the crises of American republican capitalism, however; to a large extent, it produced them. The frontier experience facilitated capital penetration and territorial expansion, thus fostering the development of a national monopoly capitalist class and a centrally administered federal government. At the same time, it provided frontier residents with the tradition of local control and the experience of collective political struggle. Consequently, frontier settlers offered intense, sometimes violent opposition to the growing power of national capital and federal authority. Thus the frontier experience generated both interclass and intraclass conflict in the struggle between local and national interests.

When the Thirteen Colonies successfully rebelled against the authority of the British Empire, the new American nation had neither a strong central government nor a national monopoly capitalist class. Neither the merchants and industrialists of New England nor the merchants and planters of the South were capable of extending their control beyond their regional political economies. Even in confederation, they were unable to challenge Britain's control of international trade.[4] Ultimately, however, they were able to secure control of the North American continent, largely on the basis of squatter's rights.

Lacking centralized economic and political control, mid-nineteenth-century eastern investors and politicians could, at best, facilitate the efforts of western entrepreneurs, who provided the basis for capital penetration and territorial expansion. Frontier settlers absorbed the risks of economic and political development and were granted autonomy, more or less by default. If they were able to establish government and produce reliable profits in local industry, they could attract eastern capital investment and secure political status as a member of the union. At that point, the frontier settler might expect to reap handsome profits by selling local property to eastern investors. Then the pioneer could retire or go off in search of a new frontier.

In the process, however, classes were forming in both East and West through an ongoing struggle to control industrial production. Frontier classes formed in the struggle to establish local enterprise and to claim a share of the surplus. Those who were successful were thereby capable of defending their class-based interests in local government. Thus Rocky Mountain miners were able to defend usage rights in the gold mines, backed up by mining district law and later sanctioned by the federal government. In a similar vein, farmers were able to secure homesteading rights, defended by claim clubs and later sanctioned by the federal Homestead Act of 1862.[5] Merchants, shopkeepers, and real estate speculators were able to defend their claims to city lots by authority of their town companies. Thus the various fractions of frontier classes were politically organized in defense of their class-based interests.

Since federal authority did not provide an adequate basis for establishing frontier government, the various fractions of laboring and nonlaboring classes struggled to protect their interests and cooperated in varying degrees in establishing local and regional governments that were capable of defending their persons and property against competing claims. The merchants, shopkeepers, and speculators (the "boosters") were the prime movers in establishing political institutions, since public order facilitated their efforts to attract labor and capital to the frontier community, enabling them to profit from increased trade in the commodities, service, and real estate markets.

If they were to succeed, however, the boosters had to court the interests of local industrial classes and convince them that local government would protect their persons and property. Consequently, local government represented the interests of the classes that controlled local industry. When the laboring classes were economically independent and politically organized, as were the gold miners and the small-scale family farmers in northern Colorado, local government was dedicated to the defense of personal liberty as well as public order. The dignity of labor was celebrated and the rights of persons were defended in public, "Carnival" government. When the laboring classes were not economically independent and politically organized, as in the ranching and transportation industries or in the large-scale farming enterprises of southern Colorado, the rights of persons were subservient to the rights of property and private, "Caucus" government prevailed.

In either case the development of a national monopoly capitalist class and a centrally administered federal government undermined local control of the economy and government and inspired local resistance to the intrusion of national actors. As the frontier government institutionalized relations with state and national authorities, local defense of persons and property was all but abandoned. Local authorities focused attention on maintaining public order by prosecuting drunks, gamblers, and prostitutes; crimes against persons and property were adjudicated by state and federal courts. At the same time, eastern capital investment established monopoly capital's control of local industry, with the aid of federal authority, including at times military force. Thus local labor and capital could quite rightly conclude that the government was no longer willing to defend their interests.

Consequently, local resistance to federal authority and national monopoly capital emerged in proportion to the degree of local class-based political organization and the extent to which national actors were undermining local control of industry and government. When laboring classes were accustomed to defending their economic independence through participation in public, Carnival government, local resistance took the form of labor-capital conflict, as in the mining strikes of 1880. Where local capitalists were accustomed to unchallenged control of local industry and government, resistance took the form of conflict between local and national capital, as in the railroad wars. In either case, however, local actors, whether labor or capital, were responding to the threat of national capital penetration and the imposition of federal authority.

The nature and extent of this conflict depended upon the willingness and capacity of local actors to accommodate capital investment or survive capital flight. Skilled trades workers, merchants, and shopkeepers in Denver, for example, were able to accommodate national capital investment in railroads, mining, and manufacturing so long as this did not interfere with local trade. Conflicts focused on wholesale and shipping prices were relatively minor concerns, so long as the added costs could be passed on to the consumers. In this regard, family farmers in northern Colorado and capitalist farmers in southern Colorado were also engaged in a running battle with railroads and wholesale dealers. The most protracted struggles, however, were in the railroad industry and in the mines, where local capitalists and local workers directly confronted the emerging national capitalist class.

Political parties, particularly the Democrats and the Greenbackers, attempted to exploit local resistance to national capital and federal authority by claiming that the Republicans were conspiring with the monopoly capitalists. In this regard, the opposition parties were increasingly successful between 1876 and 1896. Nevertheless, they were ultimately defeated by the growing power of the national Republican Party, which retained the loyalty of the wealthy farmers and those skilled trades workers who were convinced that they might maintain their privileged status by supporting national capital in the interest of economic growth. In the medium run, the skilled trades workers were accommodated in trade unions that eschewed radical politics, while the reform efforts of the farmers were preempted by the progressive platform of the Republicans. Western miners were repressed, and small-scale capitalists were driven from the market by cutthroat competition. Thus was local resistance conquered.

The frontier experience fostered the development of western industrial classes with the economic resources and political experience required for class-based conflict. At the same time, the frontier experience fostered the development of a national monopoly capitalist class that undermined local control and inspired protracted conflicts between labor and capital and between local and national capital. This enduring legacy of the American frontier experience is based on the contradictory interests of local autonomy and national incorporation that continue to plague the American nation. To understand the nature and significance of this conflict, it is necessary to trace its roots to the nineteenth century. In so doing one can appreciate how dependence on federal authority and monopoly capital was established initially in cooperation with local industrial classes but was ultimately sustained despite vigorous local resistance. Then, perhaps, one might appreciate the empty promise of contemporary booster efforts.

PERSPECTIVES ON THE AMERICAN FRONTIER

The academic literature on the American frontier can be categorized by a local-versus-national focus, on the one hand, and by a consensus-versus-conflict perspective, on the other. The consensus perspective on local history focuses on booster efforts to promote economic growth, which is viewed as the collective interest. Frontier communities were capable of collective action in progrowth, "booster" coalitions if they were relatively homogeneous settlements or were able to overcome internal divisions by establishing community-based voluntary associations. Thus the success of the community was contingent on the perspicacity and unity of local elites and their ability to mobilize the population by appealing to collective interests that transcended religious, ethnic, or social class differences.[6]

The consensus perspective on national development focuses on the economic and political institutions established during the early constitutional period, and it evaluates the capacity of western settlers to adapt these institutions to the distinctive conditions that obtained on the frontier. Such analyses provide the basis for connecting the efforts of local boosters with the more or less adaptable institutions imported from the east. Boorstin can thereby explain "how the planter lost his versatility," while Abbott can explain how the boosters of Chicago were more successful than their Cincinnati counterparts.[7] Thus the consensus perspective offers a comprehensive theory of local and national development, based on the self-interested problem-solving efforts of the pioneers in interaction with the development of American institutions.

This consensus perspective has been challenged by local historians who argue that economic development policies were contested by conflicting local interests. In addition, revisionist, "world system" development theorists argue that national policy was disputed by conflicting regional and sectional interests. Viewed from this perspective, the frontier experience involved local conflicts over economic development strategies that were confounded by sectional conflicts as the commercial-industrial Northeast attempted to exploit the agricultural and ore-producing South and West. Ultimately, this conflict destroyed the institutional structure of American republican capitalism and established, in its place, the modern, bureaucratic state and the modern, monopoly capitalist system.[8]

One might argue that this conflict perspective does not form a logical whole, due to ideological rifts within critical and neo-Marxist theory. Nevertheless, it stands as the revisionist opposition to the conventional account, both in local history and in the economic and political development literature.[9] Thus the terms of the debate are reduced to "conflict versus consensus" in local development planning and "facilitation and adaptation versus exploitation and crisis" in national institutional development.

The consensus perspective has, quite rightly, focused attention on the town boosters who promoted economic and political development in the interest of personal profit, realized through increased commodity trade or inflated prices for local property. The booster attempted, in essence, to effect the marriage of frontier industrial classes and eastern commercial and financial interests. The incentive was profit. Local entrepreneurs established the basis for eastern capital investment, absorbing the risk and claiming a substantial profit in return. Eastern capitalists were ensured that their investments were secure, because the frontier entrepreneurs had established the reliability of profits.[10]

The essential problem with this model of frontier political economy is that it ignores class formation. In the course of economic development, frontier industrial classes were formed through a process of political struggle focused on the appropriation of the industrial surplus. Consequently, these classes became increasingly interested not simply in potential profits but in control of industrial production. At the same time, a national monopoly capitalist class was forming in the struggle to expand productive capacity and capture new markets through a process of cutthroat competition and cooperation among the survivors.[11] Ultimately, the marriage of eastern capital and frontier industrial classes was destroyed in the struggle to control local industry.

In this regard, the conflict perspective and especially the "new class theory" of the neo-Marxists have exaggerated the extent to which class relations can be reduced to a simple process of exploitation. To argue that the frontier industrial classes were exploited by the merchant and the eastern capitalist is to impose a deterministic, static, structural analysis on a problematic, dynamic struggle. The frontier industrial classes, whether they physically labored in productive enterprise or hired the labor of others, were not generally exploited by a hegemonic merchant-capitalist class (the exception being southern debt peonage, which was not generally a frontier institution).[12] Like the merchant, members of the frontier industrial class were entrepreneurs, investing in economic development in pursuit of profit. In addition, they were often capable of challenging the merchant's control of commodity prices. In short, they were profit-oriented entrepreneurs who jealously guarded their share of the industrial surplus against unreasonable claims by the merchant. If anything, the merchant, as town booster, courted the interests of the frontier industrial classes in efforts to sustain economic and political development.

This does not imply that frontier settlers formed a single homogeneous class. Not only did commercial and industrial classes emerge as distinctive interests, but industrial classes were divided through the struggle to control the available surplus. Classes formed as frontier actors organized in defense of their economic resources and clashed with opposing interests. On the Colorado frontier, for example, the owners of city lots and farm lands organized town companies and claim clubs while the gold miners organized mining districts. In their initial organization, these class-based political organizations might seem similar, but in the course of political struggle they diverged sharply in form and content.

COLORADO FRONTIER POLITICAL ECONOMY

The town companies in Denver and elsewhere in frontier Colorado were joint-stock ventures representing the interests of real estate speculators who hoped to prosper from the appreciation of municipal properties. Consequently, the companies donated lots (and shares of stock) to prospective businesses on the stipulation that the property be improved and that the lot-holder pay periodic assessments toward civic improvements, which might further increase property values. The Auraria Town Company required that members build a house "sixteen feet square, and comfortable to live in" as the minimum required improvement, but most lots were donated contingent upon establishing a particular type of business, notably hotels and newspapers.[13]

The claim clubs represented the interests of the farmers and sanctioned claims by homesteaders so long as they engaged in agricultural enterprise. The Arapahoe County Land Claim Club specified, in its constitution, the terms for appropriating 160 acres. The claim had to be occupied by the claimant (or designated agent), five acres of land were to be fenced, and one acre plowed "for agricultural purposes" within sixty days of filing the claim.[14] Once the claim was filed and the stipulated improvements verified, the claimant's property rights (including the right to sell the property) were sanctioned by the club. There were no assessments, and no shares of stock were issued. The clubs were not joint-stock ventures. They merely represented the claim-holders' commitment to recognize each others' claim.

The mining districts, like the claim clubs, did not issue shares of stock or collect property assessments. They merely specified the laws governing the appropriation, use, and sale of claims. Unlike the claim clubs, mining camps did not require that a claim be filed with the district, so long as the miner marked the boundaries of the claim and engaged in more or less continuous production. The purchase or sale of claims had to be registered, for a nominal fee, but usage rights were free and unencumbered so long as there were no competing claims.[15]

Thus, in frontier Colorado the basic structure of the frontier economy was reproduced in the political structure, as separate governments represented the interests of three distinct actors—miners, farmers, and lot-owners. The relations between these actors shaped the interests of the various classes as they struggled to appropriate a share of the available surplus.

The lot-owners defended property rights, in general, and the corporation's claim to municipal properties, in particular. The miners defended the rights of persons, specifically the right to physically labor in productive enterprise, seizing natural resources and claiming the product as the property of the laborer. The farmer, like the miners, defended the right to appropriate natural resources on the basis of invested labor but also claimed a proprietary right to the land. Thus the lot-owners defended property rights while the miners defended the rights of persons. The farmers defended both property and personal rights, in keeping with their interests as laboring proprietors.

As the frontier economy developed, finer class distinctions emerged. There were laboring lot-owners (butchers and bakers, for example) and nonlaboring lot-owners, including merchants and local businesspersons who invested in road and irrigation companies, employing wage labor in industrial enterprise. There were laboring farmers, who relied on family labor, and nonlaboring farmers, who employed more labor than their families provided. Within the laboring classes, there were independent "artisans" (including miners and farmers) and wage workers. Initially, however, the major frontier interests were lot-owners (including speculators, merchants, shopkeepers, and businesspersons), miners, and farmers.

These actors began to define their interests and thereby came to define themselves as classes through conflict with opposing classes that threatened to undermine their position in the frontier economy. The owners of city lots had a long-term interest in economic development, which would increase the value of their property. Nevertheless, their short-term survival was contingent on the sale of goods and services to local industrial classes. Consequently, class formation began with disputes in the commodity market. In 1859, gold miners opposed price fixing by the Denver merchants as "an effort not only mean and unjust but derogatory to the dearest interests of every working man in the Rocky Mountains." The merchants had attempted to reduce the price paid for locally produced gold, but the miners, by threatening to establish independent commercial connections to the east, were able to maintain the traditional price. At the same time, Denver blacksmiths, printers, and bakers were able to cooperate in establishing standard price lists.[16]

Thus the commodity producers of frontier Colorado organized to defend their control of local industry, much as the Colorado farmers did in 1873, when the farmers organized Grange cooperatives. In the process, they came to recognize their interests and antagonists and thereby came to identify themselves as a class. This was the opening battle in the struggle against republican capitalism, which included violent labor uprisings and third-party electoral challenges, between 1876 and 1914. This was not, however, simply labor-capital conflict in response to proletarianization. Colorado capitalists also developed class-based political organization.

The Denver Town Company, after fighting lot-jumpers between 1858 and 1860, in 1864 faced homesteaders who were armed with federal law and county government sanction. In Golden, Colorado, local businesspersons were able to control the "provisional" county government in 1859, but they were opposed by regional claim clubs that defended competing town companies and wagon roads. Although members of the Golden town company were able to accommodate regional opposition under territorial government in 1861, they later faced competition from national capitalists, defended by federal authority, in the railroad wars of the 1870s.[17] Thus local resistance to federal authority and national monopoly capital was not, as some Marxist theories might suggest, simply labor's response to proletarianization.

One might characterize the economic development of the nineteenth century as a process of proletarianization, in which independent artisans (yeoman farmers, craft workers, or miners) were gradually reduced to the status of wage workers. In some industries, however (notably cotton production, cattle ranching, and coal mining), laborers did not, to any appreciable extent, enjoy the status of independent artisan, even prior to the Civil War. In each of these industries, frontier labor was exploited by frontier capital, often through employment. Consequently, the nature of industrial-commercial and local-national alliance and cleavage was distinctive in these industries simply because laboring classes were not formed through struggles between merchants and artisans.

FRONTIER CARNIVAL AND CAUCUS TOWNS

When frontier laboring classes controlled the essential means of production, merchants and town boosters courted labor in efforts to stimulate production and trade and establish local government. In these artisanal, petty-commodity-production economies, the booster alternated between excoriating the laboring classes for their indolence and vice and promising untold riches as the reward for diligent labor. The political representation of the booster alliance with labor was almost a parody of democratic government—a mixture of New England town meeting and evangelical revival, appropriately termed "Carnival." It was, however, unlike the western European "Carnival" in which commoners subjected their leaders to symbolic ridicule. In the American Carnival tradition, the leaders made fools of themselves, through rhetorical flourishes in symbolic mass appeals, attempting to reaffirm their commitment to the people much as presidential candidates do today. These Carnival governments were, above all, public spectacles, with frequent elections, parades, and public meetings.

Carnival governance is distinguished in both the form and content of frontier governing authority. In frontier Denver, for example, where local boosters spared no efforts in courting the economically independent and politically organized laboring classes, the coercive power of government was clearly in the hands of the popular tribunal and was used primarily in defense of persons rather than property. The People's Court held open-air meetings of the assembled citizens and specialized in the protection of persons, publicly executing convicted murderers but never convicting a person accused of horse theft. Even the county commissioners, who tended to specialize in property rights, met frequently in public session and routinely received communications from constituents. In cases where considerable controversy might be expected, as in decisions to issue railroad bonds, the question would be debated in a meeting of the assembled citizens, rather than in council chambers.[18]

Finally, Carnival governance, as indicated in newspaper reports, explicitly defended popular sovereignty even at the expense of legal technicality. The municipal government of Denver was called "the People's Government of Denver as ordained and established by the Miners' government of Jefferson Territory." There was, in fact, no such territorial authority, but the rhetoric explicitly recognized the fact that the miners controlled the frontier political economy.[19]

When frontier laboring classes were not economically independent and politically organized, as in the railroad town of Golden, the boosters courted local business interests. Local government, in these towns, was a decidedly private, corporate enterprise, appropriately termed "Caucus." The Golden City Association (the local town company) was a corporate governing body, concerned primarily with the rights of property. There was, for all intents and purposes, no municipal government in frontier Golden, and the county government was dominated by the local business community, particularly by members of the Association. In fact, even the People's Court of Golden was primarily concerned with punishing persons accused of stealing from local businesses. There were relatively few elections and public meetings, and the bulk of local political actions was focused on the protection of property rights.[20]

Denver and Golden approximated the ideal types of Carnival and Caucus towns (see Table 1.1) and thus indicate the political consequences of artisanal versus wage-labor production. In both cases and in Colorado more generally, local actors struggled to defend their control of local industry. Independent artisans and local businesspersons organized in opposition to antagonistic interests and ultimately in opposition to monopoly capital investment. Where laboring classes were economically independent, politically organized, and accustomed to defending their class-based interest through public Carnival government, these conflicts divided labor and capital. Where nonlaboring classes enjoyed a tradition of unchallenged control, through private Caucus

Table 1.1 Classifying Frontier Political Economies

Class That Controls Local Industry	Predominant Political Interest	Form of Local Government	Type of Local Government
Artisans	Persons	Democratic	Carnival
Employers	Property	Corporate	Caucus

governance, the struggles were primarily between local and regional or between local and national capital.

What Follows

In the chapters that follow, this general perspective on the American frontier experience will be specified and defended in the analysis of six Colorado settlements. My objective is to illustrate the conflicts rooted in the contradictory goals of local autonomy and national incorporation as institutionalized in the American approach to its western frontier. Before proceeding, it will be helpful to briefly summarize the theory that guides this analysis, since it differs markedly from prevailing perspectives on the American frontier.

Contrary to the consensus perspective, it is here asserted that local autonomy and incorporation into the national political economy were contradictory goals, dialectically interrelated in the institutionalized approach to American economic and political development. The lack of capital accumulation and political centralization created the possibility for relatively autonomous frontier settlements, but it was only through local struggle against eastern speculators and federal Land Office policies that the western settlements were finally granted the opportunity to appropriate the resources of the western territories and to establish frontier political economy on that basis.

Under the Articles of Confederation and the early years of the Constitution, federal land policy was designed to raise revenues and promote economic development through the sale of large sections of the public domain. The roots of the ongoing struggle between western frontier settlers and eastern capitalists or government officials can thus be traced to actions that predate the Constitution of 1787. Land speculators gained control of the Northwest Territory as the federal government attempted to pay Revolutionary War debts by selling western lands. It was only through the political struggles of squatters and debtors that the federal government was finally convinced to facilitate homesteading efforts. In fact, the legal basis for appropriating 160-acre homesteads was not established until 1862, when the Republicans made good on their campaign promise designed to gain western support for the northern Republican cause.[21]

Ultimately, a weak and divided set of eastern capitalists and federal politicians granted de facto autonomy to the western entrepreneurs as the only viable basis for fostering capital penetration and territorial expansion. The American approach to economic and political development thus institutionalized the contradictory interests of local autonomy and national incorporation. The growth of a national monopoly capitalist class and a centrally administered federal government was predicated on the relatively autonomous entrepreneurial efforts of western pioneers. In the course of economic and political development, frontier industrial classes developed in defense of their control of local industry. At the same time a national monopoly capitalist class and a federal government developed the capacity to undermine local autonomy through capital investment and the imposition of federal authority.

In contrast to some versions of the conflict perspective, it is here asserted that neither federal nor local government was the instrument of the capitalist class, used to exploit the agricultural and ore-producing South and West for the benefit of northeastern industrial capitalists. Neither were the laboring classes of the western frontier exploited by a hegemonic merchant-capitalist class. Merchants and industrialists were not sufficiently powerful to control the federal government, and the federal government was incapable of controlling the western territories. Except for the southern cotton industry, in which first slavery and then the crop lien system were sustained by restrictive emigration laws, neither eastern capitalists nor federal officials could prevent western settlers from escaping beyond the boundary of social control, into the western frontier.[22]

In fact, it was necessary to induce rather than coerce the prospective settler to absorb the risk in developing western economic and political institutions that might then be incorporated into the national political economy.[23] Although there might well have been considerable incentive to migrate in search of adventure, the predominant inducement was the prospect of reaping the profit that would be available when frontier industries attracted capital investment. In this regard, one might argue that the frontier settlers formed a relatively homogeneous class of entrepreneurial laborers and capitalists, but distinctive classes were formed as frontier economic relations were established and various fractions of local classes organized in defense of class-based interests.

In the following analysis of frontier political economies, three general class-based interests will be distinguished: (1) merchants and speculators, (2) laboring classes, and (3) nonlaboring classes. The merchants and speculators will be distinguished as commercial (as opposed to industrial) interests. This is appropriate in keeping with the consensus tradition of focusing on the town boosters, and it also distinguishes those classes that extracted a share of the industrial surplus on the basis of commerce rather than industry. Among the industrial classes, laboring and nonlaboring classes will be distinguished as those who physically labored in production versus those who employed the labor of others. The economic and political relations between these three distinct interests essentially shaped the process of class formation.

The commercial classes defended public order and economic growth in the interest of attracting labor and capital and thereby expanding commerce and reaping the benefits of real estate appreciation. They were the boosters and the prime movers in local "law and order" campaigns and progrowth, economic development initiatives. They were not, however, directly involved in economic development and could not sustain themselves without the efforts of the industrial classes. Consequently, they actively recruited the support of the industrial classes, offering protection for property and persons as the incentive for supporting local government and offering potential profits as the incentive for economic development efforts.

The interests of laboring and nonlaboring classes were diametrically opposed, since each sought to control the available industrial surplus by controlling productive enterprise. The laboring classes defended their rights to the surplus on the basis of their invested labor. The entrepreneurial laborer (or independent "artisan") claimed the right to appropriate natural resources and invest labor in petty-commodity production, claiming the full value of the product, be it gold, wheat, or bread. This generated petty squabbles with the commercial classes regarding the fair price of products, but the merchant did not generally attempt to seize control of the natural resources or to control the production process.

The nonlaboring industrial classes, however, did challenge the artisans' right to natural resources and the products of industry. This challenge was based on property rights and the right of the property holder to claim a return on the investment in property, including purchased labor. In general, when the profits available in local production were sufficiently reliable to entice capital investment, nonlaboring classes would invest in the purchase of property and the employment of labor. With sufficient capital accumulation, the independent artisan could be driven from the market by the economies of scale that nonlaboring employers could institute. The falling rate of profit thus forced the artisan to choose between wage labor or movement to a new industry or locality.

In this regard, the legal defense of property versus persons corresponded to the opposing interests of nonlaboring versus laboring classes, each of which defended the basis for its class-based control of local industry. The rights of persons in general and labor in particular represented the legal basis for the artisans' claim to both natural resources and the labor-value represented in the artisan's product. The rights of property similarly represented the legal basis for purchasing natural resources and labor and thereby establishing control of local enterprise. Thus the relative importance of crimes against persons versus property indicates the extent to which local "law and order" was committed to protecting the interests of laboring versus nonlaboring industrial classes. Similarly, resistance to the intrusion of national capital was couched in the rhetoric of persons versus property rights, as local laboring and nonlaboring classes attempted to secure their basis for control of local enterprise.

At least initially, frontier industries were plagued by unreliable profits and a lack of capital accumulation. Independent gold miners moved freely between artisanal production, wage labor, and prospecting. In fact, the successful prospector was able to employ wage labor or to sell his discovery for a handsome profit. Consequently, the struggle between employers and laborers tended to occur fairly late in the process of frontier class formation, after entrepreneurial efforts had demonstrated the reliability of profits and thus attracted eastern capital investment. Hence the struggle between labor and capital for control of local industry was generally confounded with the struggle between local and national interests, as eastern capital invaded the frontier economy.

In some cases, however, frontier nonlaboring classes were able to secure control of industries that promised reliable profits with minimal capital investment. The construction of wagon roads, for example, required little capital investment beyond daily wages for the construction crews. The companies did not have to purchase right-of-way and could anticipate reliable profits so long as the mining and milling enterprises could sustain the demand for transport. Similarly, cattle raising required minimal investment beyond the price of wage labor so long as the rancher could claim a sufficiently large parcel of land to justify the investment in importing cattle from Texas and then driving the herds to market.

Nonlaboring classes consequently controlled local industry in the frontier ranching settlements and in the transportation centers, and laboring classes had neither the economic independence nor the political organization required to defend their personal rights. Nonlaboring classes were thus able to establish private Caucus governance, in defense of property and public order, and the laboring population was effectively excluded from political participation.

When labor was economically independent and politically organized, as were the Colorado gold miners and the farmers of northern Colorado, boosters courted the interests of labor, defending the rights of persons in public Carnival government. When nonlaboring classes controlled frontier industry, as in the transportation and southern Colorado farming and ranching settlements, local government was a private, corporate, affair in which nonlaboring industrial and commercial classes united in the defense of property and public order. Thus the form and content of local government was, at least initially, largely determined by the organization of frontier industry. In any case, the boosters were able to establish public order and to cooperate with local industrial classes in promoting economic development in the pursuit of wealth.

Ironically, the success of economic and political development efforts undermined the alliance of commerce and industry, as booster efforts to attract labor and capital threatened the autonomy of local industrial classes. Where laboring classes were accustomed to defending their economic independence through participation in public Carnival government, the intrusion of eastern capital inspired labor-capital conflict, and the likely resolution was to repress, coopt, and preempt labor. Where nonlaboring classes were accustomed to unchallenged control of the local political economy, eastern capital investment and the imposition of federal authority inspired conflict between local and national capital. Local capitalists willing and able to accommodate national interests were facilitated in their efforts, but protracted resistance from other local capitalists was ultimately crushed.

Local-national conflict was not simply labor's response to proletarianization but was, in fact, a more general conflict between national monopoly capital and local industrial classes that had developed political organization in defense of their control of frontier industries. In this context, "monopoly capital" refers to large-scale corporate enterprise and the concentration of assets in a few firms that claimed the bulk of the regional and national trade. Generally, monopoly capital investment foreclosed the opportunities for the small-scale entrepreneurs who had traditionally controlled frontier enterprise.

These local actors generally resisted monopoly capital penetration, but the nature and extent of local resistance varied not only across Carnival and Caucus towns but across fractions of laboring and nonlaboring classes that were differentially threatened by national capital and federal authority. In Colorado, the mining, cattle, and railroad industries were the major targets for eastern capital investment. Given their distinctive traditions as Carnival and Caucus towns, the mining towns experienced the most rancorous labor-capital disputes while the railroad and cattle towns were the site of the most protracted struggles between local and national capital.

Local resistance was predicated on opportunity as well as threat. The factory workers and coal miners of southern Colorado were equally threatened by monopoly capital investment, but they were not mobilized in opposition in the early years of statehood. In general, the southern Colorado laboring classes had neither the tradition of class-based political struggle nor the opportunity to participate in public Carnival government. The labor uprisings of 1880 were concentrated in those towns and counties where local laboring classes had a tradition of popular participation in Carnival governance and where the Republican Party had been most successful in promoting economic development as the collective interest that united labor and capital. Even in these settings, however, the wealthiest and most privileged segment of the laboring classes tended to remain faithful to the Republican Party.

The more proletarianized segments of the Colorado laboring classes rebelled in response to the threat of monopoly capital investment and the opportunity for political participation based on the tradition of public Carnival governance. In a similar vein, the most threatened segments of the nonlaboring classes (railroad builders and ranchers in particular) rebelled in response to the threat of monopoly capital investment and the opportunity to circumvent instituted legal procedures based on the tradition of private Caucus government. Thus a coalition of laboring and nonlaboring classes joined forces in efforts to oppose the intrusion of monopoly capital and the imposition of federal authority promoted by the Republican Party.

The lines of alliance and cleavage that developed between 1876 (when statehood was proclaimed) and 1896 (when the Silver Democrat–Populist alliance carried Colorado) will be traced to the process of class formation in the struggles between commercial and industrial classes in the six local histories that follow. In Denver, the relations between artisan-shopkeepers (such as butchers and bakers) and merchants shaped the formation of laboring and nonlaboring classes, whose interests were defended in public Carnival government. In Central City, it was the relations between miners and merchants, and in Greeley the relations between farmers and merchants. In all three towns the economic independence and political organization of laboring industrial classes (artisan-shopkeepers, miners, and farmers) provided the basis for public Carnival governance and prepared labor for subsequent battles with capital.

In the Caucus towns of Golden, Pueblo, and Cañon City, nonlaboring classes enjoyed unchallenged control of transportation, ranching, and farming industries. Unlike the farmers of Greeley, the farmers of Pueblo and Cañon City employed wage labor and effectively exploited ethnic and kinship ties to sustain a population of Hispanic laborers and more privileged Anglo workers. Neither the Anglo nor the Hispanic laboring classes had the economic independence or political organization to defend their personal rights. Consequently, the factory workers, at the turn of the century, did not have the tradition of public Carnival governance, which offered the opportunity to resist the intrusion of monopoly capital. In these Caucus towns, traditionally governed by the nonlaboring classes and faithful to the Democratic Party, resistance to national capital was primarily a struggle between local and national capital.

The process of class formation and political organization will be analyzed in each of these towns. Each town will be treated in a separate chapter to familiarize the reader with each of the local histories. To emphasize the distinctions between the two types of towns, the Carnival towns will be presented first (part one), followed by a brief recapitulation of the Carnival-Caucus distinction and its significance in shaping class formation and resistance to national capital and federal authority (part two). After the three histories of Caucus towns, the concluding chapter will return to the electoral politics of early statehood and the interclass and intraclass conflicts of 1880. The failure of the Greenback-Labor Party and the Silver Democrat–Populist alliance will be considered in the context of the ultimate defeat of local resistance to incorporation into the national political economy. In this context, the lessons of this frontier history will be considered.

PART ONE

Carnival Towns of Colorado

Each frontier community was in some sense unique, so efforts to typify or classify tend to blur important distinctions. Consequently, local histories often focus on a particular type of town and analyze conditions that might explain variation within a general category distinguished by time, place, and industry. Thus Chicago might be compared to other midwestern commercial centers or Abilene compared to other Kansas cattle towns.

The following analysis differs markedly from this general model for comparative local history. The communities were selected not on the basis of similarities but on the basis of interesting differences. Furthermore, the most general distinction between these towns is based not on industry, region, or period of initial settlement but on the nature of the economic and political institutions established in each locality. The Carnival towns that are analyzed in the next three chapters include a commercial and financial center (Denver), a mining-supply town (Central City), and a farming town (Greeley). Denver was founded in 1858 and Central in 1859, but Greeley was not established until 1870. On the basis of time, place, and particularly industry, it might seem that these towns do not belong in the same category. In each of these towns, however, the frontier laboring classes were economically independent and politically organized. Consequently, local boosters courted the interests of labor, protecting the rights of persons in public Carnival government. Hence each is considered a Carnival town, despite other important differences.

The next three chapters will not ignore these differences but will focus on the parallel experience of artisan-shopkeepers, miners, and farmers, each of whom established a tradition of class-based political struggle in opposition to nonlaboring classes. The significance of this experience will become more apparent in the concluding chapter, after the Caucus town histories.

CHAPTER TWO

Denver: The Carnival Capital

The history of Denver is that of the challenge faced by town boosters attempting to institutionalize relations with national actors while accommodating the interests of local laboring classes. After attracting entrepreneurial labor and capital to the goldfields, the town boosters struggled to establish public order and were thus forced to court the interests of the economically independent and politically organized laboring classes. Consequently, public Carnival government was established. Artisans and merchants cooperated in defending the rights of persons and in maintaining public order while promoting economic development in the pursuit of potential profit.

Once the boosters had succeeded in attracting monopoly capital investment and achieving federal government sanction under statehood, Denver laboring classes discovered that local government was no longer defending their interests. As Denver made the transition from frontier mining-supply town to financial and commercial center of the territory and then to economic and political capital of the state, local actors, especially laborers, gradually lost control of local economic and political institutions. The boosters then faced the challenge of preempting or repressing laboring-class opposition to monopoly capital and federal authority. This was the ultimate challenge for the Denver boosters.

THE SUPPLY TOWN FOR THE MINES

Denver was established in the fall of 1858 by three town companies that claimed land still occupied by the Cheyenne and Arapaho nations but nominally under the control of the Kansas Territory. The Saint Charles, the first and only claim to be sanctioned by the territorial legislature, was usurped by the Denver Town Company while the Saint Charles party was in Kansas, seeking a territorial charter. The boosters of the Auraria and Denver town companies, having thus dispossessed the previous claimants in defiance of Kansas authorities, established competing settlements at the confluence of Cherry Creek and the South Platte River and attempted to attract labor and capital with the promise of a new El Dorado. By the spring of 1859, successful prospecting ventures inspired an army of immigrants seeking their fortunes in the Rocky Mountain mining camps.[1]

Denver, 1858–1860. Courtesy Colorado Historical Society (F-42989)

The speculators and merchants of both Denver and Auraria responded by establishing banks, stage coach and express companies, milling and manufacturing enterprises, and a variety of hotels, restaurants, and local services. Gambling halls and saloons were among the most popular amenities provided for the immigrants. There were thirty-five saloons in 1860, or one for every 136 residents.[2] Denver was not only the commercial but also the entertainment center of the Rocky Mountain mining industry, and so the town thrived on the gold dust that was harvested daily by an army of independent placer miners. On that basis, the merchants, shopkeepers, and speculators were able to sustain the local economy.

The Denver economy of 1860 was dominated by the mines and by the service industry supported by miners. Banking, real estate, insurance, and other forms of speculation accounted for less than 5 percent of the population and only 6.6 percent of local wealth. Given the rapid population growth, construction trades provided employment for roughly 8 percent of Denver households (that figure should perhaps be inflated to include some "laborers" who could not be identified with a specific sector). Nevertheless, not even 3 percent of local wealth was invested in construction, and even fewer people and dollars were invested in milling, manufacturing, and transportation.

Most of Denver's wealth came from outside the community. In fact, the influence of mining, farming, and ranching was underestimated in these census data, since people thus employed did not work in Denver but merely came into town for provisions. Some farmers might have maintained a Denver residence, but only two farming households were identified in these 1860 data. There were, however, 132 mining households, despite the fact that the productive gold mines were located some thirty miles west of Denver (near Central City). It is possible that the enumerator included persons who were merely in town for provisions, who wintered in Denver, or who were

A wagon train arrives in Denver, ca. 1860. Courtesy Colorado Historical Society (F-21977)

among the many persons who moved freely from prospecting and mining in the mountains to commercial and industrial pursuits in Denver.

Thomas Wildman, for example, arrived in Denver in June 1859, spent some time panning for gold, and then returned to Denver, where he worked as a clerk and bought four city lots (for fifteen dollars). He also hauled lumber for a local mill, receiving five dollars per day toward the purchase of an ox team. Wilder may not have been representative, since he was literate and was the son of a New England capitalist. Nevertheless, his correspondence suggests that like many residents of Denver he had little money but many prospects. He noted that there was a local market for almost anything that an artisan might manufacture. Had he been a hatter, like his grandfather, he would have been more secure in his financial status.[3]

Despite the questionable status of Denver residents enumerated as "miners" by the census, these data do not exaggerate Denver's dependence on mining. Even those miners who bought supplies in the mountains were, in fact, dealing with the Denver merchants who had supplied the mountain traders. In any case, mining absorbed 35 percent of the households and 28 percent of the wealth. Service industries, including shopkeepers (including saloonkeepers) and professionals (including gamblers), accounted for an additional 16 percent of the households and 24 percent of the wealth. Those who provided services greatly outnumbered the commodity traders, who accounted for less than 6 percent of the households and 12 percent of the wealth. In addition, nearly a quarter of the population and just over 20 percent of the wealth was divided between common laborers and persons without a declared occupation. These persons and dollars were available for investment in some form of local enterprise, but they were not yet committed to a specific industry.

As shown by the data in Table 2.1, artisans (including "craftworkers," miners, and farmers) constituted 44 percent of the households in Denver and controlled nearly 40 percent of local wealth. The craftworkers included those in construction trades (brick masons and carpenters, for example), traditional crafts (bakers and cobblers, for example), musicians, artists, and teamsters. Since it is impossible from census data to determine whether these craftworkers were self-employed or working for others, only those reporting some wealth were included as artisans, on the assumption that independent artisanal status was based on owning one's shop and one's tools, which implies some real and personal wealth.

Table 2.1 Wealth by Class Category for Households in Denver, 1860

Class Category	Total Wealth	Percentage of Wealth	Number of Households	Percentage of Households
Nonlaboring classes	$131,900	55.90	162	43.32
Financier	7,200	3.05	8	2.14
Businessman	8,425	3.57	9	2.41
Owner	7,400	3.14	8	2.14
Professional	22,600	9.58	10	2.67
Merchant	44,300	18.78	49	13.10
None	37,975	16.09	78	20.86
Laboring classes	108,045	45.79	212	56.68
Artisan	94,005	39.84	165	44.12
Worker	14,040	5.95	47	12.57
Total	235,945		374	

Source: U.S. Bureau of Census (1860) Population Schedules for Arapahoe County, Kansas Territory.

Data come from a 10 percent systematic sample of occupied dwelling units, aggregated to household level and collapsed into class categories based on occupation. Miners and farmers are "artisans." Otherwise, "artisan" includes all craft titles, except households reporting no wealth (classified as "worker").

Miners and farmers were classified as artisans because those who physically labored in these industries were primarily independent commodity producers. One might argue that the miners enumerated in the Denver census were not independent artisans but were more likely to be working for wages. Nevertheless, their reported wealth and their opportunities for artisanal labor in the mountains suggest that they were not reduced to wage labor. Sixty-eight percent claimed between $100 and $1,000 in wealth, and 12 percent claimed over $1,000. In this regard, they resembled the craftworkers.

"Workers" (presumably wage workers) constituted less than 13 percent of the households and claimed nearly 6 percent of the wealth. Many of these workers had nothing to sell but their labor, but these data do not indicate widespread employment, which requires both wealthy employers and laborers without the opportunity for independent subsistence. On the first count, Denver lacked a critical mass of wealthy employers. Merchants (including noncraft shopkeepers, such as hotel and saloon keepers) were the most numerous fraction of the nonlaboring class, and they controlled the largest share of nonlaboring class wealth. On a per capita basis, the professionals were the wealthiest, but they (like the merchants) did not employ many workers. The largest employers were those classified as "owners," including the owners of lumber and ore-reduction mills, a freighter, and a contractor, but these actors controlled less than $1,000 each, so it is unlikely that they were major employers. The businesspersons (enumerated as "traders" but more appropriately considered "investors") were involved in a number of enterprises (gold mines, toll roads, and irrigation ditches) that did employ labor, but they also controlled less than $1,000 each in real and personal wealth. Those who reported no occupation reported, on average, only $487, which suggests that they were not major employers either. In fact, forty-nine of them reported no wealth, and only five reported over $1,000. There was, however, one household reporting no occupation but $15,000 in wealth. This exceptional case was a wouldbe capitalist, prepared to invest in something but not yet employing anyone other than domestic servants. Overall, these data indicate a dearth of employers.

Second, and equally important, these data indicate a lack of propertyless workers who depended upon wage labor. There were nineteen craft-title households (such as "brick makers" and "plasterers") that reported no wealth and were thereby classified as "workers." These, along with clerks and other service workers, probably worked for wages in local shops. It is unlikely, however, that most of the laboring population worked for wages. It has been estimated that common laborers earned from $1.50 to $3.50 per day, or $10.00 to $20.00 per week. These were fairly high wages for the period, but the cost of living was incredibly inflated. In the fall of 1859, flour sold for $40 a barrel (196 pounds), bacon was $.50 to $.60 per pound, eggs were $2 a dozen, and corn $4 a bushel. Food was expensive and so was shelter, since housebuilders charged $5 to $8 per day (more than twice the wage for common labor).[4] The laboring classes in the Denver of 1860 controlled, on average, over $500 per household. This was more wealth than they might have been able to save by earning these wages and paying these prices.

Even if one includes, as laborers, all households reporting no occupation and no wealth, average laboring-class wealth would still exceed $400.[5]

Somewhere between one-tenth and one-third of the Denver population worked for wages in 1860, but many of these persons were at least semi-autonomous workers who tried their hand at prospecting before coming back to work in Denver. On average, the artisans reported on by the census claimed $569.73 in real and personal wealth. That was more than sufficient to purchase a city lot, have a residence-workshop constructed, and set oneself up as an independent artisan-shopkeeper. The more popular choice was to go into the mountains in search of fortune, but in either case the artisan was economically independent. Hence one can characterize the Denver economy of 1860 by the relations between independent artisans (miners, farmers, and crafts) and merchants (including noncraft shopkeepers, such as saloonkeepers). Denver was the commercial center for an artisanal petty-commodity-production economy.

THE STRUGGLE FOR POLITICAL CONTROL: 1859–1861

The economic independence of the Denver laboring classes was a major factor in provoking the political crisis that emerged in 1859. Denver was governed by town companies, corporate creatures of the propertied classes, but it was virtually impossible to exclude labor from local governance, given the economic resources and developing political organization of the laboring classes.

In April 1859 Denver citizens established the People's Court, which became the symbol of popular justice, modeled on the miners' courts (see chapter 3). The People's Court held impromptu public trials. Assembled citizens elected twelve jurors, selected local attorneys to serve as judge and as counsel for the defense, and then proceeded with a public trial, often held out of doors. If the accused was convicted, the trial was followed by a public execution, but the People's Court was not a vigilante gang and was, in fact, inclined toward acquittal when the evidence was not overwhelming. Generally, the popular tribunal specialized in hanging confessed murderers.[6] Of the ten trials held by the People's Court from 1859 to 1860, nine were murder trials.

Consequently, the boosters of Denver and Auraria tried to establish some form of government that might protect property as well as persons and thereby facilitate efforts to attract eastern capital investment. At the same time, the boosters hoped to establish public order by imposing some restraints on the rather raucous entertainment industry. In March 1859 the voters of Arapahoe County, Kansas Territory, had elected county officers to replace those appointed by the Kansas governor, but Denver and Auraria boosters were not satisfied with local government that was sanctioned by the distant power of

Kansas Territory. They held a meeting, on 11 April 1859, and E. P. Stout, the president of the Denver Town Company, offered the following resolution:

> Resolved: That the various precincts be requested to appoint delegates to meet in convention on the 15th inst., to take into consideration the propriety of organizing a new State or Territory."

This resolution was unanimously adopted and the convention was held in Auraria, as scheduled. The Denver and Auraria boosters carried the convention and adopted the following resolution:

> Resolved—That the discussions of this convention shall have but one object, viz.: The formation of a new and independent State of the Union."

In the ensuing deliberations, the delegates arranged for additional meetings to draft a constitution, prepare a slate of officers, schedule a local election, and memorialize Congress.

These activities occupied the time and energy of the lawyers and businesspersons of Denver and Auraria through the spring and summer of 1859, but they were largely ignored by the authorities in Kansas and in Washington and, to a large extent, by the laboring classes in Denver. Meanwhile, however, the farmers residing in the vicinity of Denver organized a land claim club and thereby defended their homestead claims.[9] The club also recorded the claim of the Denver Town Company, thus providing a "legal" basis for a claim that had never been sanctioned by Kansas Territory.[10] Despite the organization of new "governments," however, the People's Court remained the effective governing authority, routinely using the coercive power of government to punish crimes against persons and basing its authority on the expressed will of the assembled citizens.

It proved less than satisfactory, however, in punishing crimes against property, as the following episode points out. The People's Court convened in May to hear the case against James Hanna, accused of stealing horses. The *Rocky Mountain News* reported the story as follows.

> HORSE THIEF—On Friday night last a man by the name of James Hanna, formerly of Ohio, was caught in the pineries, about 30 miles from this place, with five ponies and a mule in his possession. On Saturday he was brought to town and the animals were identified and claimed by their respective owners. The people held a court, for the purpose of trying the offender, by appointing a president, clerk, and twelve jurymen. After hearing the evidence, which was of an indefinite character, the jury pronounced it not sufficient to convict him, and he was accordingly released.[11]

That was not the end of the matter, however, since some citizens remained convinced of Hanna's guilt. They threatened him with hanging, thereby eliciting his confession and his promise to lead the vigilante posse to his associates. After a lengthy but unsuccessful search for the remainder of the horse-thieving gang, the vigilantes hanged Hanna but did not kill him. Instead, they gave him fifty lashes and made him promise that he would never return to the Rocky Mountain region. In closing his report of the incident, William Byers added this editorial comment.

> We hope this will be a warning to all who may feel disposed to take horses without leave, for depend upon it, the next one caught will not be dealt with so leniently. Forbearance has ceased to be a virtue where so many horses are being stolen.[12]

Despite this warning, however, the theft of livestock continued. On 23 May, only three days after the Hanna incident, a couple of new faces appeared before the Probate Judge. They were accused of stealing horses but were released for lack of evidence.[13]

The theft of horses and the general lack of effective governing authority committed to the defense of property and public order continued to plague the Denver boosters through the summer of 1859. Thomas Wildman reports as follows in his letter of 8 September 1859:

> There was a man killed in Auraria last week, and the people hung one night before last in Golden City, which is about 12 miles from here, for shooting at another man. There is to be a Vigilance Committee organized in this town this evening. All the leading men of town have signed the Constitution, and its object is a good one. We have no jail here and no laws in fact, and the object of the committee is to give all persons accused of crime a fair trial and punish them according to their deserts. It is thought that stabbing and drunkenness will be rampant here this winter, and we think that the rowdies and gamblers will be more careful if they find out that the first men of the town are determined to punish crime.[14]

Nevertheless, local authorities remained incapable of securing private property, and William Byers warned that vigilante justice would be employed if the horsethieving did not stop. "The light fingered gentry had better look out, or some of them will be suddenly called upon to perform on a tight rope."[15]

In November 1859, after the voters of Colorado (including the voters of Denver and Auraria) had overwhelmingly defeated the statehood movement, the Provisional Government of Jefferson Territory was organized. This territorial government was not recognized by federal authorities and enjoyed, at best, limited popular support. Nevertheless, it sanctioned the organization of county and municipal governments in Denver and elsewhere in Colorado. The miners refused to recognize the authority of the Provisional Government and continued to operate their mining district courts (see Central City history, in chapter 3). Even in Denver, the organization of "legal" governments did not preclude the actions of frontier authorities, who continued to defend their narrowly defined, class-based interests in property or persons. Nevertheless, the municipal government of Denver was established in December 1859, after voters approved the municipal charter by margin of merely 65 votes (367 to 302).[16] This was a booster's government, committed to the defense of public order and operated by and for the merchants, shopkeepers, and real estate speculators. Twelve of the 13 elected officers were identified in local business directories. Of these 12, 2 were lawyers, 2 were merchants, 4 were realtors or bankers, and 4 were shopkeepers or clerks.[17] Thus the local boosters were organized in their effort to establish public order.

While newly elected city and county officers were preparing to take office, a paramilitary force, called the Jefferson Rangers, was organized in Auraria to provide the coercive violence that might sustain the Provisional Government of Jefferson Territory. Convinced that the people were prepared to combat lawlessness, the newly elected mayor offered an optimistic appraisal of the prospects for law and order:

> It is surely a matter of rejoicing that the two chief cities of the Territory of Jefferson [Denver and Auraria] . . . have at last come together in friendly accord; that all harsh feeling and bitter bickering will henceforth cease, and together they will emerge from the discord and anarchy, and that together they will assume a position, at once creditable to themselves and greatly to the advantage of all commercial relations and social enjoyments.[18]

Within ten days of this speech, however, there was violent resistance to local governing authorities, in defiance of the mayor. First, on 30 January 1860, a group of Denver settlers began construction on a city lot that had been claimed but not "improved" according to the rules of the Denver Town Company. Representatives of the town company attempted to reclaim the lot, with the support of the claim club and the newly elected mayor, who personally entreated the "lot-jumpers" to cease and desist. Meeting armed resistance, the mayor retreated to a series of public meetings, which proved incapable of generating a consensus. Then, under the cover of darkness, someone destroyed the lot-jumpers' building. The following day, there were armed confrontations, as the lot-jumpers prepared for retribution. Ultimately, however, the Denver Town Company paid $100 for the property destroyed and, in return, the lot-jumpers relinquished their claim.[19]

Meanwhile, in Auraria, denizens of the local saloons and gambling halls, referred to collectively as "Bummers," were accused of stealing a wagonload of turkeys. Rather than calling upon the municipal or county officials or convening a session of the People's Court, concerned citizens held a meeting and appointed a committee of five (including W. H. Middaugh, the county sheriff) to investigate the allegations. The committee interviewed witnesses, including some of its own members, and then reported that they had reached a verdict of guilty. The citizens then ordered the Bummers to leave town within five days, under penalty of death. They were not able to enforce this order, however, and the Bummers paraded through town, armed to the teeth, in defiance of the citizens' judgement.[20]

Sheriff Middaugh was unable to enforce the order, but Thomas Pollock was more successful, since he managed to disarm one of the Bummers by striking him with his rifle. William Byers praised Pollock's bravery but suggested that if the blacksmith "had given him the contents of his rifle, in a vulnerable place, it would, no doubt, have terminated the trouble, and, as everybody says, served him right."[21]

Instead, the Jefferson Rangers convinced the Bummers to leave town, at least temporarily, but a trial before "concerned citizens" finally settled the issue. Byers reports as follows:

> The expelled of last week have been lurking around in and near town for several days past. Night before last a descent was made upon a cabin about a mile or two below town, and Wm. Harvey was captured. Yesterday, at 11 o'clock he was put on trial before a jury of six men, upon the charge of assault with intent to kill W. H. Middaugh [the sheriff]. . . . The prisoner plead guilty to the charge under extenuating circumstances. His counsel . . . argued . . . that the prisoner, at the time of committing the act, was under the influence of liquor, and consequently not in his right mind—that he harbored no ill feeling toward any one. . . . In half an hour the jury came in, and, with some good advice and caution, discharged the prisoner. . . . And here rests the turkey war, Vigilance Committee, &c., for the present.[22]

It is not clear that the Denver Vigilance Committee was responsible for this trial, but it seems that the case was not tried before the People's Court. The People's Court continued to claim original jurisdiction in homicides, but it never rendered judgement on assault charges.[23] Thus it seems likely that the trial was held before a committee of concerned citizens who did not claim the authority of the People's Court.

Between January and September 1860 the situation in Denver was turbulent, with the town companies, the claim club, the county governments of Jefferson and Kansas Territories, the municipal government of Denver, and the People's Court all attempting to govern (see Table 2.2). Their efforts were supplemented by the coercive power of vigilantes, the Denver Vigilance committee, the Jefferson Rangers, and various groups of "concerned citizens." Nevertheless, none of these governments were both willing and able to exercise general governing authority[24]—instead they tended to focus on narrowly defined, class-based issues that represented the interests of their constituents.

Table 2.2 Distribution of Political Actions in Denver, by Issue Orientation by Identity of Party Claiming Governing Authority

Authority	Issue				
	Property	Persons	Government	Class	Total
Town company	16 (1.0)	0	0	0	16
Claim club	5 (1.0)	0	0	0	5
County government	14 (.88)	0	2 (.12)	0	16
Vigilantes	3 (1.0)	0	0	0	3
People's government	11 (.28)	17 (.44)	11 (.28)	0	39
City government	2 (.13)	5 (.31)	9 (.56)	0	16
Defy government	2 (.50)	1 (.25)	1 (.25)	0	4
Class	0	0	0	4 (1.0)	4
Party	0	0	1 (1.0)	0	1
Unknown	3 (.75)	1 (.25)	0	0	4
Total	56 (.52)	24 (.22)	24 (.22)	4 (.04)	108

Source: *Rocky Mountain News*, April 1859–March 1860; *Western Mountaineer*, December 1859–November 1860.

"Political action" is defined as an action that involved three or more people defending a collective interest by making claims on, to, or in defiance of local (municipal or county) governing authority. It includes legislative, enforcement, and judicial actions by local authorities.

Proportion of row total is to the right of the frequency.

There were, in fact, three Denver governments. One represented the propertied interests; a second, the rights of persons; and a third attempted to sustain public order (or "government") and to accommodate the often contradictory interests of property and persons. The town companies and the county officials constituted the government of property, and the claim club and the vigilantes were their allies. The "People's Government" (including meetings of concerned citizens and actions by the People's Court or the Denver Vigilance Committee) was both the most active and the most diverse, but it tended to concentrate on crimes against persons, especially murder.[25] Denver's third local government, the municipal government, was the government of public order. It represented the interests of merchants and shopkeepers, who were attempting to sustain trade with the miners and to entice eastern capital and labor to develop the regional economy. In this regard, they were in competition with the local saloons and gambling halls, which absorbed an inordinate share of the local gold dust and also undermined the claim that Denver was a safe place for the investment of capital and labor. There were, in addition, groups that defied local government and classes that acted largely in opposition to each other. The "party" government was the Denver Republican Party, and the unknown governments were referenced in reports indicating that the suspects were seized and turned over to "the proper authorities."

Despite periodic vigilante lynchings, the People's Court, in particular, and the "People's Government," more generally, controlled the coercive power of government and used coercion primarily in defense of persons, mostly in the arrest and execution of alleged murderers. The town companies, claim club, county government, and city government rarely used violence. Vigilantes and parties who defied the government always used violence, but they acted only upon occasion, whereas the People's Court began routinely prosecuting criminals in April 1859.

Vigilante efforts and similar ad hoc versions of government were generally initiated only when the appropriate (or routine) procedures were deemed inadequate. Neither the People's Court nor the county judge was particularly effective in convicting crimes against property, for example. In fact, as indicated by the information in Table 2.3, local authorities rarely employed coercive violence in the defense of property but usually responded violently to crimes against persons, most especially homicide. Thus the People's Court was not adequate to defend the interests of the property holders or the boosters' interest in public order. Consequently, vigilantes supplemented efforts to defend property, and the Denver Vigilance Committee was organized to supplement efforts to maintain public order.

Table 2.3 Distribution of Political Events in Denver by Issue, by Authority's Use of Coercive Violence

Issue	No Violence Employed	Violence Employed	Total
Property	41 (.73)	15 (.27)	56
Persons	9 (.38)	15 (.63)	24
Government	21 (.88)	3 (.13)	24
Class	4 (1.0)	0	4
Total	75 (.69)	33 (.31)	N=108

Source: *Rocky Mountain News*, April 1859–March 1860; *Western Mountaineer*, December 1859–November 1860.

"Coercive violence" is defined as physically seizing, harming, or destroying either property or persons under the claim of governing authority. It can include arrest and imprisonment as well as eviction or demolition.

Proportion of row total is to the right of the frequency.

After a series of homicides and lesser crimes that scarcely commanded attention in the local press, William Byers declared that the People's Court no longer represented the interest of the people but had been perverted by the gamblers and cutthroats who found refuge in the saloons and gambling halls.[26] In response, Thomas Gibson, editor of the *Rocky Mountain Herald,* launched a public attack on the Denver Vigilance Committee and its supporters (including Byers), who refused to hold public trials and to provide the newspapers with the names of the judge and jurors. As the editorial debate continued, there were meetings to deal with the problem of livestock theft, trials by the Denver Vigilance Committee, lynchings by the vigilantes, public trials and executions by the People's Court, and meetings to denounce the undemocratic and secretive operations of the vigilantes.[27]

On 1 September 1860, nine men formed a posse to pursue livestock thieves. They reported that they were unsuccessful, but within the next few days Black Hawk, John Shear, and A. C. Ford were executed by "unknown parties," who claimed that these men were the leaders of the local horse-thieving ring. Smiley explained the mystery surrounding these lynchings, based on his interview with one of the vigilantes.

> Who constituted the grim tribunal that condemned and executed these three alleged members of the alleged great western association of horse-thieves, no one undertook to inquire. Many could have closely guessed, and of course, some certainly knew. However, it was then sharply understood to be a forbidden topic, and no one cared to disregard that understanding. These circumstantial details were related to the writer by a low-voiced gentle-mannered pioneer, of those times, who is still [in 1901] a well-known and much esteemed citizen of Denver, and is the only one of Ford's four executioners now living.[28]

Both the alleged horse-thief association and the posse organized to pursue them contained lawyers and politicians who had been actively involved in local government. Shear (who was hanged as a horse thief) was a member of the city council, as was Thomas Pollock, the leader of the posse. Ford (who was seized from the Kansas stage and unceremoniously shot) was active in the People's Court and had often served as counsel for the defense. Most members of the posse had similar experience.[29]

Somewhat ironically, at least two members of the posse later attended a meeting to protest vigilante justice and signed a petition of protest published in the *Rocky Mountain Herald.* Furthermore, at least four of the protesters were identified at various times with the Denver Vigilance Committee.[30] The boosters of Denver were attempting to defend public order in whatever manner might be most effective. A legally constituted government was preferable, but the established government was inadequate. Consequently, the boosters were engaged in a debate over tactics, in which some argued for expedience while others demanded democratic due process.

There has been much confusion regarding the debate between Byers and Gibson and the connection between the vigilantes, the Denver Vigilance Committee, and the People's Court.[31] Byers and Gibson were both good Republicans and champions of the "class harmony" platform. If Byers supported public order while Gibson supported popular participation, both were accommodated in the government of labor and trade, the second municipal government established in October 1860. In the interim, their struggle was focused on the relative importance of public order and public government. Byers defended public order, even if that required private justice. Gibson maintained that public government was necessary if public order was to be achieved. Given the economic independence of Denver's laboring classes and the tradition of popular government established by the People's Court, Gibson was correct in his assessment. In the short run, however, it seems that Byers was successful in promoting private solutions to the problem of public order, relying on vigilantes and on the Denver Vigilance Committee.

This short-term solution was necessary, because the laboring classes did not recognize the legitimacy of "legal" governments established by the boosters. The People's Court was the only legitimate government, but as we have seen, it was not dedicated to the defense of property and public order. Although the "People's Government" was actively involved in defending property and public order (see Table 2.2), the People's Court focused almost exclusively on executing confessed murderers.

Other trials, such as the trial of the Bummers on the charge of turkey theft or the trial of Harvey for assault with intent to kill, did not involve twelve jurors and appointed counsel and did not claim the authority of the People's Court. In this regard, the trials by concerned citizens were indistinguishable from the trials before the Denver Vigilance Committee. Both were distinguished from the People's Court, however, by the form and content of criminal proceedings. The People's Court operated according to the laws of the regional mining districts (see chapter 3) and defended the rights of persons, executing convicted murderers but refusing to punish persons accused of crimes against property or public order.

Thus the People's Court became subject to attack by the boosters who wanted to control the decidedly raucous entertainment industry and the petty thefts and general disorder associated with the gambling halls and the saloons. William Byers led the attack on the People's Court, and he explained the problem as follows:

> Recent events in and around Denver have shown the great necessity for some kind of government and law. . . . For several weeks the mania

has been for stealing, and then retaliation has commenced in a most serious and terrible manner. . . .

Had the Provisional Government been recognized and properly carried on, we might now enjoy almost as much security for person and property as is enjoyed in any new country. . . . But in Denver where the Provisional organization had its earliest and most active friends, it can hardly find a supporter.[32]

As the citizens of Denver debated the issue of local government, a mechanic explained the problem as follows.

Now sir as a Mechanic and representing a laboring class of this community, I wish to be heard for a moment. I cannot get up in public meetings and express my views intelligibly, neither can many of the laboring class among us, nevertheless we have our notions of things, and are a numerous class and have as good a right to be heard as the Lawyers and others who get up at public meetings and consume all the time. . . .
[The current plan for a municipal government] . . . appears to be a very acceptable plan to the committe who framed it, as well as to all the business and laboring men of that meeting. The only ones who made any objection were the Lawyers—who took sides for and against the plan and consumed the whole evening gassing over it. Now sir as a laboring man and mechanic, I protest to having our time consumed by any such a notoriously gassing fraternity as the Lawyers.[33]

After nine months of ineffective government culminating in the lynching of a city councilman, the people of Denver were prepared to establish a new municipal government, but they demanded that it be a government of the people. Like the miners in the mountains, they would not submit to government by lawyers and businesspersons and would not accept the Provisional Government for that reason. Thus the lawyers, perhaps deservedly, became the symbol of everything that was wrong with the government of property and order. Local merchants and shopkeepers, as well as William Byers, joined the miners and mechanics in their condemnation of lawyers and repudiated their ties with the Provisional Government.

On the first of October 1860, "the People's Government of Denver City, established and conducted by the Miners' Government of Jefferson Territory" was elected by an overwhelming majority. This was truly a merchant and shopkeeper government, whose officers included six merchants, four shopkeepers, only one realtor, and no lawyers. As its name implies, the municipal government had repudiated its connection to the Provisional Government. When the voters of Colorado were polled on 22 October, the majority voted against the continuation of the Provisional Government. Two days later,

William Byers published the following: "We were told on Saturday evening that the Provisional Government had come into contact with our city government, to which we replied, 'if so, we are henceforth opposed to it.' "[34] Denver boosters thus established municipal government by repudiating connections to the Provisional Government and pledging allegiance to the miners, as the supreme authority of Jefferson Territory, and to "the people" as the local sovereign. The battle for local control was finally settled in October 1860.

As can be seen from Table 2.4, this battle involved not simply multiple authorities but shifting class-based concerns, which indicates the capacity of frontier classes to fight for their interests in local governance. In the fall of 1858, the town companies were the representatives of property, and local governance was limited to struggles within the propertied class. With the gold rush, in the spring and summer of 1859, the People's Court and the vigilantes were organized to protect persons and property, and elections were held in efforts to organize a more effective regional government. In the fall of 1859, Denver and Auraria merchants attempted to control the price paid for locally produced gold, which inspired retaliation from the mines, convincing the merchants to restore the traditional price (see chapter 3). Thus the merchants offered the first two instances of class-based efforts to control the Denver commodities market, inspiring resistance from the miners.

Table 2.4 Distribution of Political Events in Denver by Season by Issue

Season	Issue				
	Property	Persons	Government	Class	Total
Fall 1858	3 (1.0)	0	0	0	3
Spring 1859	7 (.58)	3 (.25)	2 (.17)	0	12
Summer 1859	7 (.78)	1 (.11)	1 (.11)	0	9
Fall 1859	11 (.68)	3 (.19)	0	2 (.13)	16
Winter 1860	18 (.72)	0	7 (.28)	0	25
Spring 1860	3 (.30)	2 (.20)	4 (.40)	1 (.10)	10
Summer 1860	2 (.14)	9 (.64)	2 (.14)	1 (.07)	14
Fall 1860	5 (.26)	6 (.31)	8 (.42)	0	19
Total	56 (.52)	24 (.22)	24 (.22)	4 (.04)	N=108

Source: *Rocky Mountain News*, April 1859–March 1860; *Western Mountaineer*, December 1859–November 1860.

Proportion of row total is to the right of the frequency.

In the winter of 1860, both the Provisional Government and the first municipal government commenced operations as merchants and shopkeepers defended their interest in public order (or "government") and Colorado landholders attempted to protect their property rights. This was the government of property and order, sustained by the town companies, claim clubs, and city and county governments. Its efforts inspired protracted political struggle as various groups attempted to establish or disestablish local governing authorities, and class actors began, once again, to organize.

This time, it was the skilled trades, artisans, and shopkeepers. The printers union was established in the spring and published a standard price list in the summer. Later, local blacksmiths and bakers also established standard prices for their goods and services.⁴⁵ In this regard, skilled trades, artisans, and shopkeepers were following the example of the Denver and Auraria merchants. Unlike the merchants, however, the printers, bakers, and blacksmiths physically controlled the production of commodities and services enumerated in their price lists. Hence they could claim to represent the laboring classes of Colorado. They were therefore riding the wave of popular discontent, fueled by the regional miners and aimed at the government of property and trade, which had been established in the winter of 1860 (December 1859–February 1860).

By the fall of 1860, labor had managed to fight its way into local government. Printers had established the first labor union, and the Denver commodity producers had organized in defense of their control of local commodity prices. Denver boosters then proclaimed their allegiance to the laboring classes, including the miners, and "the People's Government" was established. So long as this government did not interfere with the mining districts, it was tolerated as the legitimate government of Denver. Even the editor of the *Cañon City Times* reported that "the newly organized city government of Denver promises, from its present workings, to be the government for the people."³⁶ This was a Carnival government, dedicated to personal liberty as well as public order.

THE CHALLENGE OF NATIONAL INCORPORATION

After accommodating the demands of frontier laboring classes, Denver governing authorities faced the challenge of maintaining local control while institutionalizing relations with national actors. This required, first of all, that local government respond to the often contradictory interests of local landowners, artisans, and merchants, each of whom had been represented by a distinct frontier government. In addition, a new set of actors, including farmers, ranchers, and mining-claim speculators, brought new and sometimes conflicting demands that became more pressing as the industrial base of the Denver economy expanded. At the same time, local government had to accommodate the demands of national actors, choosing sides in the Civil War and in the economic struggles associated with national and international investment in railroads, irrigation, stock raising, and mining.

Upon taking office, in October 1860, the Denver City Council attempted above all to be responsive to the demands of constituents. They held fifty-seven meetings in the first calendar year and received thirty-four petitions from local residents. The first petition came from the merchants of Blake Street, who demanded that gambling and the sale of liquor be prohibited on public sidewalks; the next petition demanded that peddlers be licensed. In response to this popular demand, Ordinance Number One declared that it was illegal to gamble or to sell liquor or other merchandise in the streets and alleys and that peddlers must be licensed to sell from their wagons, the produce of the country excepted.[37] This exception is as interesting as the rule. Merchants and shopkeepers were protected from competition by peddlers, but local farmers were exempt from the tax on peddlers.

In a similar spirit of cooperation, Ordinance Number Two declared that the claims of the Arapahoe County Land Claim Club and the actions of the county courts (of Kansas or Jefferson) were legal, so long as they were recorded in the Court of Common Pleas. The new city government also attempted to replace the People's Court, but this proved to be a controversial issue. Initially, the city officials merely served as officers of the People's Court. When Charles Harrison (a saloon keeper) was accused of murder in December 1860, he was tried by "the people" before the judge of the City Appellate Court and was prosecuted by the City Attorney. The defense pleaded justifiable homicide, and the jury could not determine guilt, because of contradictory eyewitness accounts, so Harrison was freed. Shortly thereafter, the city council passed a resolution endorsing the city attorney's decision to drop the case.[38]

There were two more homicide trials in December 1860, but the city officials were not involved in the first case. The defendant, Patrick Waters, had fled prosecution but was pursued and captured not by the City Marshall but by the recently acquitted Charlie Harrison. The "people" met in Harrison's saloon, found the defendant guilty of murder, and hanged him on 21 December 1860. A few days later, Patrick Kelley was tried for murder before Judge William Slaughter, the Justice of the City Appellate Court. Slaughter determined that Kelley had not intentionally killed his victim, so the defendant was released, because manslaughter was not within the original jurisdiction of the city court, according to the laws of Kansas Territory.[39] Byers was enraged and offered the following editorial remarks on justice in the city court.

> Lawyers who are fattening themselves at the expense and jeopardy of the public weal will not long be allowed to jeopardize the public safety. "Self preservation" is a necessary law that all recognize, and the citizens of Denver will again return to the plan of disposing of desperate cases in the People's Court, as in days gone by—objectionable though it be.[40]

The city government was caught between the authority of Kansas Territory, the influence of Harrison and the local saloon keepers, and the "law and order" sentiments of Byers and his supporters. The "law and order" faction presented a petition to the Council, demanding that gambling be outlawed, but no such legislation was passed. Saloons and gambling halls were licensed, however, and in March 1861 the Council passed an ordinance barring houses of ill repute from "certain sections" of the city.[41] The city government thus attempted to contain and regulate vice but to tolerate the raucous entertainment industry as the price for continued trade with the mines. Serious attempts to control gambling, drinking, and related vices came only after the Civil War, when the Colorado Territorial Government was able to take the lead in local law and order campaigns.

Municipal authorities were more successful, at least initially, in cooperating with the town companies and in replacing the Arapahoe County Claim Club. After the Auraria and Denver companies merged in April 1860, the newly constituted Denver Town Company filed its claims with city authorities, who thus replaced the claim club in sanctioning the claims of the Denver Town Company. Later, however, when the city was defending preemption rights claimed under authority of the Homestead Act of 1862, the Denver Town Company launched a public attack on municipal authorities, who had allegedly betrayed the interests of the pioneer claimants.

The Homestead Act, in which the northern Republicans made good on their promise to trade farms for tariffs, provided virtually free land for the homesteader, which was a boon for the landless would-be farmer but a threat to the efforts of local real estate speculators. Legislation of 1864 specifically granted homestead rights in the Colorado region, and a number of settlers took advantage of the opportunities.[42]

Denver was expanding to the south and east, so in the spring of 1864 Henry C. Brown laid claim to a homestead that contained much of what is now called Capitol Hill. R. E. Whitsitt, of the Denver Town Company, rushed to the scene and demanded an explanation. Smiley reported as follows:

> R. E. Whitsitt ... demanded to know what he was doing there. "I seem to be building a house," replied Mr. Brown. "Well," exclaimed Mr. Whitsitt, "you've got no business to be building houses here; you get right out!" Mr. Brown, hatchet in hand, stepped forward as he answered: "Dick, this is my land. I'm not going to get out, and you can't make me."[43]

That was, essentially, the end of the matter, but the "Lot Question," which focused on allegations that local officials were not defending the claims of the pioneer settlers and were allowing squatters (or homesteaders) to appropriate claims that had been secured by authority of the Denver Town Company, continued to agitate the body politic and was a major partisan issue in the municipal elections of 1868. In fact, the city government had surrendered authority to the county, which granted pioneer settlers thirty days to document their claims before the land would be declared available for homesteaders. Allegedly, documents that were to secure prior appropriation rights were lost in the flood of 1864, which further complicated the issue.[44]

In any case, the lot-jumping allegations of 1864 suggest certain parallels to similar incidents in 1858 and 1860, but there was one important difference. In all of the lot-jumping cases, physical possession was the best guarantee of title. Even in 1864, those claimants who were not physically present were hard pressed to secure their claims within the required thirty days. In 1864, however, the city and county were cooperating with territorial and federal authorities, even though local actors—specifically, the town companies—were claiming prior appropriation. In the final analysis, settlers were able to sustain their claims based on federal authority, and local officials merely administered the details. Although local officials suffered the wrath of the dispossessed in the election of 1868, they could quite honestly claim that they were merely conforming to federal policy.

A similar shift was apparent in local government's response to the saloons and gambling halls of Denver. Once the territorial government was established in 1861, the territory took responsibility for licensing and regulating frontier vice. Gambling was legalized and taxed, at first, but new legislation was passed in 1866 outlawing all forms of gambling and specifically prohibiting municipal ordinances to the contrary. At this point, neither gambling nor saloons were eliminated, but they were no longer local problems. Violations of the ordinance were prosecuted in territorial district courts, which gradually assumed responsibility for protecting property, persons, and even public order. Territorial authority did not put an end to vigilantism, however, as Denver citizens organized a "Committee of Safety" to drive the gamblers out of town. Then in 1868 a "Vigilance Committee" hanged a prisoner who was already in the custody of the local marshal. The victim was alleged to have committed multiple murders and, most recently, to have assaulted and robbed the local Police Court judge.[45]

According to Smiley, however, these vigilante actions were not indicative of anarchy or disrespect for local authorities. Quite the contrary—the vigilantes were inspired by "the steady, quietly growing morality of the city," which motivated the boosters' efforts to eradicate the last vestiges of frontier vice and lawlessness: "If the new law proved incapable to deal with the evil, there were ways and means, concerning the effectiveness of which there was no difference of opinion; the same by which the community had several years before been rid of characters more dangerous to society than the reckless gamblers."[46] After the Civil War, Denver became the financial and commercial center for an increasingly differentiated Colorado economy. As will become apparent, it no longer served as the entertainment center for the Colorado mines and was no longer dependent on the local service industry to sustain the local economy.

ATTRACTING EASTERN CAPITAL

By 1868, Denver had become the regional commercial and financial center, connected to local industries through mining-supply towns like Central City, farming towns like Cañon City and Greeley, and cattle towns like Pueblo. Although these smaller towns were in competition with Denver, local politicians were often able to strike bargains in the territorial legislature. In this manner, Denver boosters obtained Cañon City support to move the state capital from Golden to Denver in 1867. In exchange, Cañon City was granted the Territorial Penitentiary.[47] Having thus outflanked their counterparts in Golden, Denver business leaders turned their attention to the transcontinental railroad, since the town that was able to establish centrality in the national railroad network would gain a tremendous advantage in the competition for commercial and financial control of the Colorado economy.

The major problem in attempting to establish a Denver connection to the transcontinental railroad was that national actors demanded local funds, but the farmers of the surrounding county refused to support county bond issues to raise funds for eastern capitalists. An additional problem was that Golden, located only fifteen miles west of Denver, was competing for the rail connection, and Golden residents took the lead by organizing the Colorado Central Railroad to serve the gold- and coal-mining region. In 1866, Governor John Evans convinced the Union Pacific (U.P.) to survey a route to Denver, but the U.P. was also interested in a connection to the Colorado Central. Hence the U.P. officials attempted to facilitate a cooperative venture in which rail connections from Denver to Cheyenne would be complemented by a Golden to Denver route.[48]

At a large public meeting held in Denver on 11 July 1867, the residents of the surrounding County of Arapahoe agreed to finance the project, so long as the Denver to Cheyenne route was completed first. Apparently, they did not trust the owners of the Golden railroad, and subsequent events suggested that this lack of trust was not without foundation (see Golden history, chapter 5). In any case, the plan for cooperation failed, but the plans to build a railroad continued.

Denverites next turned to the Kansas Pacific (K.P.), which was slowly approaching Denver from the east. Colonel James Archer, of the K.P., arrived in Denver on 8 November and met with Governor Evans and representatives of the local business community. He informed them that the K.P. would not come to Denver unless the city (or county) raised 2 million dollars, a prospect that seemed unlikely. Nevertheless, the boosters of Denver quickly organized themselves into the Denver Board of Trade and discussed plans to raise sufficient resources to establish a connection to the transcontinental rail.[49] After considering their prospects carefully, the board called a citizens meeting on 14 November and introduced Colonel Archer as the representative of the Kansas Pacific. When Archer repeated his demands to the citizens, he met with vociferous opposition from an audience that expected good news. Many had assumed that the railroad was on its way and that the meeting was called to announce that fact. In any case, the Board of Trade had prepared for the public outcry, having summoned George Francis Train for the occasion.

Train berated his listeners for their self-pity, reminding them that "God helps those that helps themselves." After Train had whipped the audience into a frenzy of public-spirited pride and distaste for eastern capitalists, it was suggested that Denver and Arapahoe County citizens might join together with local government and build a local railroad. The Board of Trade took the lead in this venture, securing local investment and convincing county voters to approve a $500,000 bond issue to finance the construction efforts. Thus the Denver Pacific Railroad was born of local opposition to national capital and cooperation between businesspersons and local government, with the support of the county voters.[50] This was but another instance of classic Carnival politics. Public meetings generated public outcry and, ultimately, the union of labor and capital in promoting economic development.

In 1870, both the Denver Pacific and the Kansas Pacific connected Denver to the transcontinental rail. Then, Denver businesspersons gracefully bowed out of the transportation industry and thereby avoided the battles with the national railroad companies.[51] Evans donated $500,000 worth of Denver Pacific stock to the County of Arapahoe in July 1870, and this stock was later sold to Jay Gould. Denver's business community was not unaffected by the railroad wars, but it was able to survive, because the local economy was based on control of finance and trade rather than transportation. Evans and other Denver businesspersons did invest in other railroads, but the Denver economy did not rise and fall with the local transportation industry. In general, Denver businesspersons merely required rail service and were willing to allow the national actors to control the transportation industry.[52]

The Denver economy of 1870 was dominated by banking and trade, which together claimed over 60 percent of local wealth, although they included less than 20 percent of the households. Manufacturing, transportation, and construction claimed 35 percent of the households but only 15 percent of local wealth; service industries claimed 22 percent of the households but only 5 percent of the wealth. By 1870, miners had abandoned Denver for the growing mining towns, but farmers replaced them to a certain extent. The few farming households enumerated in the 1870 Denver census were among the wealthier farmers of Arapahoe County, who could afford to maintain a town house. Nevertheless, these farmers did not support the frontier service sector (notably the saloons and gambling halls) that had catered to the Colorado miners. Hence the service sector declined, as trade and finance came to dominate the Denver economy.

By 1870 the nonlaboring classes of Denver, although they still constituted roughly 43 percent of the households, controlled 84 percent of local wealth (see Table 2.5). The owner-employer class (including contractors and manufacturers) controlled over $15,000 per household, more than enough to employ an army of laborers. Overall, the laboring classes constituted 57 percent of the households (as they had in 1860), but they now claimed only 16 percent of local wealth. In fact, if farmers were removed from the laboring classes (on the assumption that they employed more labor than their households provided), the laboring classes would then retain less than 10 percent of local wealth.

Table 2.5 Wealth by Class Category for Households in Denver, 1870

Class Category	Total Wealth	Percentage of Wealth	Number of Households	Percentage of Households
Nonlaboring classes	$555,770	83.93	83	42.56
Financier	144,570	21.83	2	1.03
Owner	61,500	9.29	4	2.05
Professional	23,100	3.49	14	7.18
Merchant	284,450	42.96	37	18.97
None	42,150	6.37	26	13.33
Laboring classes	106,400	16.07	112	57.44
Artisan	90,000	13.59	30	15.38
Worker	16,400	2.48	82	42.05
Total	662,170		195	

Source: U.S. Bureau of Census (1870) Population Schedules for Arapahoe County, Kansas Territory.

In contrast to 1860, wage workers in 1870 constituted 42 percent of the households but claimed less than 3 percent of the wealth. Most of this wealth was claimed by clerical workers, the privileged segment of the wage-working class. Service workers (including some craft-title households that reported no wealth) and common laborers constituted nearly 35 percent of the households but reported .41 percent of local wealth. These were the workers who had nothing to sell but their labor.

Thus the Denver economy of 1870 contained both wealthy employers and propertyless workers. Many skilled workers were working for wages, as the opportunities for independent subsistence declined. Labor was abundant

Denver in the 1870s. Courtesy Denver Public Library, Western History Department

and became even more plentiful when railroad construction was completed. Skilled trades workers and miners were then competing, as wage labor, with the immigrants who were released from the railroad construction crews. The artisans of Denver were still holding their own, reporting an average of $1,760 in wealth, and many were employing assistants, who were no longer able to sustain themselves as independent artisans. Nevertheless, Denver was no longer the commercial center of an artisanal petty-commodity-production economy. By 1870 it was the commercial and financial center of an increasingly diversified and highly capitalized Colorado economy.

LABOR-CAPITAL CONFLICT AND RESOLUTION

The proletarianization of Colorado labor created tremendous labor discipline problems that inspired political leaders to preempt or repress labor's opposition to the capitalization of the Colorado economy. By 1870, placer-mining claims were being reworked by mining companies that employed Chinese laborers. As the miners resisted the intrusion of capital and the use of Chinese labor, they gradually developed union organization. The early strikes were disputes between miners and a single employer, who could replace his recalcitrant workers without granting wage concessions. In March 1870, for example, miners in Clear Creek walked off the job to protest a reduction in wages. They were

First National Bank, Denver, 1870s. Courtesy Colorado Historical Society (F-7735)

soon replaced by workers who were willing to accept lower wages. This was, however, only the beginning of the war between miners and mine owners.[53]

Aside from labor discipline problems in the mines, the farmers of Colorado were actively opposing the Colorado boosters who organized the Board of Immigration in 1872 and attempted to attract investment in large-scale irrigation works. In October 1873, an irrigation conference was held in Denver, where William Byers and his allies advertised the tremendous opportunities for capital investment in Colorado irrigation companies. At that convention, J. Max Clark of Greeley argued against the Denver proponents of extensive irrigation projects and thereby inspired the wrath of the Denver boosters, including William Byers (see Greeley history, chapter 4). Gradually, the farmers were uniting in opposition to merchants and corporate capitalists. Nathan Meeker, editor of the *Greeley Tribune*, who tended to eschew political controversy, published a lengthy discussion of this battle between labor and capital:

> The Farmers' or laborers' party is achieving considerable success. . . . There are complaints of various kinds for which redress is sought, among them are those of the extortions of railroads, of money lenders and cap-

italists, and the corruption of congress. . . . My notion is, that there will be no remedy until the farmers and laborers unite, each class for itself, and do their own business, being their own managers, producers dealing with producers, exchanging for what each produces, and then the idlers will be choked off.[54]

The Colorado farmers were developing class consciousness, and they were beginning to define their interests as compatible with if not identical to the interests of the laboring classes. At the same time, miners were confronting monopoly capital investment and organizing labor unions that provided the organizational and political experience that the Western Federation of Miners and United Mine Workers would later exploit.[55] Nevertheless, these labor discipline problems affected the efforts of the Denver boosters only indirectly. The real threat was the possibility that the laboring classes of Colorado, including miners, farmers, and skilled trades workers, might unite in opposition to monopoly capital and the nationalist platform of the Republican Party.

As Denver made the transition from frontier mining-supply town to financial and commercial center of the territory and then to economic and political capital of the state, local actors, especially laborers, gradually lost control of local economic and political institutions. This is apparent in the criminal dockets of Denver courts (see Table 2.6.). Justice of the Peace Courts had been established by the Kansas Territory, by the Provisional Government, and by the Colorado Territory. Prior to the Civil War, when Denver boosters were courting the interests of local artisans and shopkeepers, the local Justice

Table 2.6 Criminal Cases in the Denver Courts, by Court by Offense for 1860–1864, 1868–1873, and 1880

Court	Offense against			
	Persons	Property	Government	Total
1860–1864				
J. P.	44 (.46)	45 (.47)	7 (.07)	96
District	12 (.11)	31 (.29)	65 (.60)	108
Total	56 (.27)	76 (.37)	72 (.35)	204
1868 to 1873				
Police	0	0	290 (1.0)	290
District	48 (.09)	149 (.28)	343 (.64)	540
Total	48 (.06)	149 (.18)	633 (.76)	830
1880				
District	27 (.04)	81 (.13)	507 (.82)	615

Source: J. P. and Police Court dockets: State Archives in Denver; Territorial District Court dockets: Denver Federal Center; State District Court docket (1880): State Archives

Proportion of row total is to the right of the frequency.

of the Peace Court was primarily concerned with crimes against persons and property (notably assault and larceny). During that time, the territorial district court was concerned with more serious crimes (robbery and murder) but was primarily involved in crimes against the state (nonpayment of taxes, licenses, or failure to appear).

After the Civil War, the territorial court assumed responsibility for most, if not all, crimes against persons and property. The local police court merely rousted drunks and prostitutes and left the more serious crimes to the territory. By 1880, even these misdemeanor cases were heard before the district (state) court, although there may have been a police court that was prosecuting persons for disturbing the peace.[56] Generally, as Denver became incorporated into the national political system, federal and state courts assumed responsibility for prosecuting criminals. Along with this shift toward central authority came a corresponding change in the types of crimes that were prosecuted. Concern with crimes against property and especially crimes against persons declined precipitously as the courts concentrated on crimes against government (or public order). Hence the laboring classes could, with justification, argue that the Denver government was no longer defending the rights of persons.

Faced with the growing discontent of Colorado laborers and the prospect of a unified laboring class, Denver party leaders presented themselves as the friends of labor. The Democratic newspaper blamed the Republicans for the problems faced by the silver miners and by the laboring classes more generally. The Democrats were the free trade, states rights, hard money, antiimmigrant party, who blamed all economic and political problems on the protectionist platform of the Republicans, who were allegedly conspiring with monopoly capital. As the Democratic editor explained, "The bullion value of a silver dollar is eighty seven cents and fifty-nine one hundredths of a cent. Free coinage, which the republican triumph last fall killed, would have given our miners the difference between this and par."[57]

That same Democratic editor did not support the right to organize labor unions, however. In fact, W.A.H. Loveland, who had purchased the *Rocky Mountain News* and converted that paper to his Democratic views, refused to negotiate with the Denver Printers Union, recognized as the legitimate bargaining unit since 1860, which thereupon went on strike. As Loveland explained, "It is an indisputable fact that no combination of men own a prescriptive right to the privileges of labor."[58] Loveland criticized the Republican governor, however, for imposing martial law on Leadville after violent confrontations in the wake of the silver miners' strike. He argued that the governor might have sent the militia but allowed local officials to continue to exercise their authority: "[Instead] he swept the law itself aside, deposed every officer connected with it, and established within our midst a military despotism which recognizes no law except the will of the commander, whose discretion he made the absolute governing power within this great country."[59]

The Denver Democratic Party generally blamed the Republicans and the Chinese for the low wages of the Leadville workers. The solution to the labor problem was the free coinage of silver, the abolition of all forms of protectionism, including unions, and the removal of the Chinese. As the November elections approached, the Denver editor fanned the flames of racial animosity, alleging that Garfield was involved in a Republican conspiracy to provide capitalists with an army of Chinese laborers.[60]

> If the martial law play which has been put on the boards of Colorado, of which the first act has been played, is applauded and called out again by a majority for Pitkin, it will become a precedent, and the state troops will be at the command of the capitalists, and the capitalists when they commence importing Chinamen to work for seventy-five cents per day, will call upon the governor in the name of this precedent to declare martial law and assist them to put the workingman's nose to the stone and grind the life out of him by degrees.[61]

As the appeals to bigotry became more intense, tempers flared. An argument over a laundry bill, or some similarly trivial dispute, inspired a wholesale attack on Denver's Chinatown on 2 November 1880. This racial pogrom, inappropriately termed the Chinese Riot, was celebrated by the Democratic editor in the headline, "Chinese Gone." Loveland blamed local officials for upsetting the Denver citizens and finished his report with the observation, "Washee washee is all cleaned out in Denver."[62]

Of course, Denver Republicans blamed the Democrats for the violence of class conflict that plagued Colorado in 1880. Like their opponents, the Republicans claimed to be the friends of the laboring classes, but they also attempted to divide the interests of labor by preaching class harmony. When the printers were organizing in opposition to the Democratic press, the *Denver Weekly Times* reported as follows, "Our first objection is that there can be no such thing as a war between capital and labor which will not be in the end detrimental to both."[63] The editor went on to explain that he also opposed monopolies and above all opposed the idea of organizing workers into a class of "mere wage-laborers, and taking away the ambition to become an owner or proprietor."[64]

As the party of class harmony and public order, the Republicans were alarmists, never missing the opportunity to reestablish order in the wake of Democratic efforts to incite class warfare. The Republican press presented the Leadville strike as "The Crisis at Hand," and it was a Republican governor who declared martial law and sent troops to protect the workers from intimidation at the hands of the union leaders. The Republican press also reported that the local authorities had already warned the striking Denver brick makers that intimidation tactics would not be tolerated.[65] Later, in another plea for public order, the Chinese Riot was reported as "Denver's Disgrace,"

Denver in the 1880s. Courtesy Colorado Historical Society (F-6856)

incited by the Democratic campaign of racial and class animosity: "Those whose business called them up late Saturday night were not slow to predict trouble from the drunken crowd of Democratic roughs who took part in the Saturday night demonstration and closed the night by parading the streets, making night hideous with their bachannalian revels."⁶⁶

Thus the Republicans were able to maintain their stance as the friends of labor and above all the party of order. When the coalition of farmers and silver miners threatened to unseat the Republican majority, the party adopted the free-silver issue and dedicated itself to responsible government after the chaos of Populism and Silver Democratic rule. As the party of class harmony and public order, the Republicans continued to dominate Denver politics. They catered to the silver interests and later supported the reforms proposed by the wealthy farmers. They tolerated the Denver skilled trades unions, which were later affiliated with the American Federation of Labor, but repeatedly repressed the miners.

In 1896, during a particularly rancorous mining strike in Cripple Creek, the state militia was dispatched to Cripple Creek to protect the strikebreakers from the Western Federation of Miners. This was but another battle in the antilabor "law and order" campaign that ultimately broke the back of the radical miners' unions after pitched battles in Cripple Creek, 1896–1904, and then at Ludlow Station in 1914. In the Ludlow Massacre, five miners and one militiaman died, along with two women and eleven children who were killed when the miners' tent colony was burned.⁶⁷

Thus the Denver boosters finally won their battle against the miners. The miners had controlled the frontier economy and in the short run had sustained their control of regional government. They won the opening battles yet lost the ultimate war—essentially the history of the Colorado labor movement. Its ultimate defeat was at Ludlow Station, but its roots can be traced to the frontier mining districts near Central City.

CHAPTER THREE

Central City: Supply Town for the Mines

Unlike Denver, Central City was not established by real estate speculators who claimed title to local lands and then attempted to attract productive labor. The Central City region was settled by gold miners and prospectors, whose entrepreneurial efforts attracted merchants and shopkeepers to the mountainous region west of Denver. Those miners and prospectors dominated the regional economy: They physically controlled local mineral production and organized district governments to defend their control of the mines and to accommodate the demands of the nonlaboring classes. Hence the merchants and shopkeepers of Central City did not challenge the miners and were content to operate under the authority of mining district law until the economic and political strength of the local miners was undermined by national economic and political actors.

Central City boosters did not face the labor discipline problems that plagued Denver authorities in 1880, largely because they were less successful in attracting eastern capital investment. Consequently, local laboring classes were not threatened by national monopoly capital. Merchants and artisan-shopkeepers survived capital flight first as a small-scale mining-supply town and later as a tourist town. Central City remains a merchant and artisan-shopkeeper town, continuing its Carnival town tradition, offering tourists a living monument to a time gone by, and supporting a few determined prospectors.

MINING DISTRICT GOVERNANCE

In February 1859, John H. Gregory followed Clear Creek far into the mountains, some thirty-five miles west of Denver, attempting to locate the source of the gold dust that he found in the creekbed. He followed the standard prospecting procedure of examining the gravel in each branch of the creek to determine which yielded the greatest concentration of gold. Thus he was able to trace the source of the ore to the north fork of Clear Creek, near the present location of Central City. A blizzard halted Gregory's prospecting efforts before he was able to locate the mother lode and forced him to seek shelter in the town of Arapahoe, near the present site of Golden. During the winter, however, Gregory was able to organize a prospecting party, composed of local residents who agreed to provide the requisite labor and capital. Thus equipped, the

Downtown Central City in the 1860s. Courtesy Colorado Historical Society (F-7270)

Gregory party left Arapahoe in May and proceeded to the north fork of Clear Creek, where their efforts were swiftly rewarded with the discovery of a rich vein of ore.[1]

The partners divided the vein of ore into "mountain" (or "lode") claims of one hundred by fifty feet, granted two claims to Gregory (as discovery claims), and granted one claim to each of the remaining members. No records of these actions have survived, but it seems that the Gregory party elected officers and established some general governing principles. In any case, as soon as the news of Gregory's discovery reached the settlements on the eastern plains, an army of would-be prospectors invaded Colorado. The gold rush of 1859 brought literally thousands of people to the Gregory Diggings, and these newcomers soon demanded their share of mining claims:

> The more recent arrivals began to murmur about the first comers—none of them had been here for a month yet—monopolizing everything; and contended for a redistribution of claims . . . cutting them down to twenty-five feet each. In consequence of this feeling a great meeting convened at Gregory Point, numbering some three thousand men.[2]

The newcomers in the Gregory Diggings complained that the old-timers monopolized the mountain (or lode) claims, which was probably true. The significance of this allegation deserves comment. Gregory had discovered a partially decomposed vein of ore that yielded a fairly high concentration of gold. One single pan of the gold and rock fragments could bring five dollars, and a small party of miners could produce $150 per day. The vein of ore, or lode, was located on the mountainside, hence the claims that encompassed the vein of ore were called mountain claims. Beneath the mountain claims, in the creek beds or dry gulches, gold dust accumulated as the mountainside eroded, and gold particles settled in the gravel deposits of the creeks and gulches—these gold deposits were called placers. Gulch claims could be worked by scraping the creek bed (or gulch) and washing the gold dust from the gravel. Panning for gold dust in this fashion was called placer (as opposed to lode) mining, and in the early years of placer mining, a good gulch claim could yield five dollars per day.[3]

Clearly, the mountain (or lode) claims were more valuable than the gulch (or placer) claims. A gulch claim could sustain a miner, or a couple of partners, who were willing to provide the physical labor themselves. A mountain claim could sustain a small number of employees and still yield handsome profits for the employer, or the claim could be sold or rented, if the claimant preferred not to engage in productive enterprise. Members of the original Gregory party did, in fact, take advantage of these possibilities for exploiting their mountain claims, but newcomers had only the two options of purchasing a mountain claim from the Gregory party or panning for gold in the gulches and creekbeds.

Faced with these limited opportunities, the newcomers attempted to accomplish two things in their legislative efforts of June and July. First, they attempted to increase the availability of mountain claims by stipulating that no person (except the discoverer) could claim more than one and that claims (except discovery claims) had to be worked or would be forfeit. The laws of June even specified that, for company claims, the name of each member had to appear on the claim. This was probably a response to the allegation that old-timers were using holding companies to extend their control over district mining claims. In any case, the goal was to expand the opportunities for newcomers to acquire mountain claims.[4]

A second agenda is likewise apparent in the July legislation. The amended laws recognized any claim that was being worked, whether recorded or not, and allowed for disputes to be settled in favor of the plaintiff when the defendant could not answer the summons and appear within three days. Taken together, these laws suggest that any abandoned claim could be appropriated, unless the absentee owner could return within three days to defend the disputed claim. Although it is not clear that there were large-scale appropriations during the summer of 1859, it does seem that the balance of power was swinging in the direction of those who physically labored.

The government of the mining camps displayed a classic irony. The local economic elite were the old-timers, who worked the mountain claims, but governance was subject to the will of the people, most of whom were newcomers who worked gulch claims. Thus the opening battle for control of the mines was an assault by newcomers on the monopoly of the old-timers with regard to the control of mountain claims. Nevertheless, the old-timers managed to sustain their position. Gregory, as the discoverer, was granted two claims, which were to be protected even if they were never worked. Also, there were no limits on the number of claims that might be purchased, so long as the purchase was recorded and the claims were worked.

The battle against the old-timers produced at best a hollow victory, but the precedents set were soon applied in the neighboring camps, where newcomers attempted to get in on the ground floor. Miners from Gregory and Jackson Diggings and newcomers to Colorado established a variety of new mining districts, including Tarryall in South Park. Some residents of that district, obviously disgusted with the distribution of claims, established Fairplay, perhaps as an explicit condemnation of the older districts. Those who remained in the vicinity of the Gregory Diggings established more than a dozen independent districts whose laws and general form of governance differed only slightly from the parent district.[5] The newcomers, in demanding a share of mountain claims, were defending a collective interest that they could not sustain, because their medium-run interest was to become old-timers. It was thus to their advantage to protect the rights of old-timers, so the newcomer–old-timer struggle was of limited intensity and duration as new districts were established and a new set of newcomers arrived. In all cases, the right to sell or purchase claims was defended, since newcomers desired the opportunity to purchase mountain claims and old-timers desired the right to sell their claims to the highest bidder.

In any case, working miners gained the experience of defending their class-based interest in controlling the production of gold. Through mining district government, they defended the rights of the working miner and established a tradition of public, democratic government. Through their participation in miners' courts and mass meetings of the assembled miners, they gained the organization and experience to respond effectively to any actor who might threaten the interests of the working miner.

The interests of the absentee owner were not particularly important in 1859, but the July legislation of the Gregory district specified the rights and obligations of several new actors, each of whom would become a more or less permanent resident. First, persons were allowed to claim a lot of forty by one hundred feet to erect a building, but such claims did not extend to mineral rights. Second, "homestead" preemption rights were recognized, so long as these did not interfere with mining claims. Third, persons were granted lots, in two hundred and fifty foot squares, to erect quartz mills (for ore reduction) and were granted water rights, so long as these did not interfere with previous claims. Fourth, irrigation ditch companies were granted right-of-way, so long as previous claims were not damaged. Finally, companies were allowed to claim two hundred and fifty feet on either side of a tunnel claim, when digging in search of a new vein of ore. All previous claims were to be respected, and tunneling could not cease for more than six days, or the claim would be forfeit.[6]

Recognition of these more permanent settlers marked the opening of a new chapter in mining camp law. Granting the right to build permanent structures provided for the establishment of commercial enterprise. Recognizing homestead rights provided for permanent settlers, notably farmers, although it is not clear that the rocky gorges allowed for anything more extensive than a vegetable garden. Quartz mills, irrigation companies, and tunneling ventures marked the capitalization of the mining industry. In general, these newcomers represented the penetration of commercial and industrial capital, which ultimately transformed the mining camp, although the process was slow and uneven.

Prior to the organization of the Colorado Territory, the mining camps continued to exercise governing authority, as miners maintained their physical control of the mines. Mining camp governance did seek to accommodate newcomers and thereby expanded the scope of governing authority to include what was, in Denver, the business of town companies, claim clubs, and other provisional authorities. To appreciate the extent of the miners' political control, it is useful to describe the extent to which they dominated the local economy, not only in the mines but also in the supply town of Central City.

THE MINERS' TOWN AND TERRITORY

Prior to territorial organization in 1861, the Colorado mining industry was decidedly undercapitalized, because the reliability of profits was insufficient to attract eastern capital. Potential investors could predict neither the location nor the extent of local mineral wealth, so the more conservative investors who had survived the financial crises of the mid-nineteenth century were more inclined to invest in agricultural lands, which might be expected to appreciate in value. In order to attract capital to the Rocky Mountain mining frontier, prospectors and miners had to absorb the risk in demonstrating the potential profits available in the Colorado mines. Once the reliability of profits was established, the entrepreneurs could sell to eastern capitalists who had the resources to exploit paying claims more effectively.[7]

Individuals like Gregory and his partners were able to locate a valuable claim and sell it for incredible sums (by 1859 standards). Gregory sold his claims for $21,000 and offered his services, as a prospector, for $200 per day, but his was clearly an exceptional case.[8] Most of the miners in the Gregory Diggings (in fact, in Colorado) earned subsistence by panning for gold in the creek beds. Placer mining was profitable for individuals or small groups of partners who could operate relatively simple mechanical devices that would separate gold dust from gravel.[9] Lode mining and ore-reduction companies did employ labor, but given the opportunities for independent subsistence and the limits on economies of scale, employment was rare. The mining and ore-reduction operations of 1860 were mostly small-scale enterprises. Twenty-eight (21 percent) of the 131 companies enumerated in the 1860 census had less than $1,000 of capital investment. Only thirty (22 percent) had invested over $5,000, and none had invested more than $12,000. Most (78 percent) did not employ more than half a dozen men. The employment of women was practically unknown.

In general, the material existence of the Central City region was based on the efforts of independent miners, who individually, or in partnerships, produced a steady stream of gold dust that was traded in Central City for the means of subsistence and production. The ore produced by lode mining companies sustained a small ore-reduction (milling) industry, but the bulk of local enterprise was financed and controlled by small-scale entrepreneurs, while most of the local wealth flowed directly from the independent placer miners.

Central City, although not yet chartered as a municipality, was both an artisanal production site and the commercial center of the local mining industry. It was the headquarters for local miners and provided bars and brothels as well as commercial connections to the Denver market. Mining was the basis for the local economy, contributing more than 30 percent of the households and 40 percent of the total wealth. The gold produced by local miners sustained the service industry, and the lode mining ventures provided the raw materials for the local quartz mills. There was a modest investment in construction, still less in manufactures, and only a few farming families that managed to sustain themselves as vegetable gardeners. The fact that only 7 percent of local wealth was invested in trade (as opposed to service industries) indicates the extent to which Denver and other larger supply towns controlled the regional market. To a certain extent, the merchants and shopkeepers of Central City provided convenience stores for the mines. The larger commercial and financial enterprises were located elsewhere. The laboring classes of Central City dominated the local economy in 1860, representing nearly 60 percent of the households and controlling almost 60 percent of local wealth. Of these, independent artisans (miners, farmers, and artisan-shopkeepers) controlled over 50 percent of total wealth and represented nearly 47 percent of local households. Some of the laborers worked for wages, but the data indicate a dearth of both propertyless workers and wealthy employers. The workers identified in Table 3.1. reported, on average, over $600 in real and personal wealth, and artisans (mostly miners) reported over $1,000 per household. Among the nonlaboring classes, the wealth of the business and professional classes, in general, was hardly staggering. Merchants (including noncraft shopkeepers, such as hotel and restaurant owners) accounted for a relatively small share of local wealth.

Table 3.1 Wealth by Class Category for Central City, 1860

Class Category	Total Wealth	Percentage of Wealth	Number of Households	Percentage of Households
Nonlaboring classes	$173,570	40.60	141	40.40
Financier	50	0.01	1	0.28
Owner	32,500	7.60	9	2.57
Professional	48,985	11.46	36	10.31
Merchant	56,560	13.23	55	15.75
None	35,475	8.29	40	11.46
Laboring classes	253,942	59.40	208	59.60
Artisan	224,557	52.53	164	46.99
Worker	29,385	6.87	44	12.60
Total	427,512		349	

Source: U.S. Bureau of the Census (1860) Population Schedules for Arapahoe County, Kansas Territory.

Data come from a 75% systematic sample of occupied dwelling units, aggregated to household level and collapsed into class categories based on occupation. Miners and farmers are "artisans." Otherwise, "artisan" includes all craft titles, except households reporting no wealth (classified as "worker").

Given the distribution of local wealth and the organization of mining district government, it seems reasonable to assert that local miners controlled Central City. It is true that they were a large and somewhat diverse class, but their mining-district organization provided a vehicle for exercising regional economic and political control. The miners ruled the mines and thereby controlled the regional frontier economy. On that basis, they controlled regional government and defended their collective interests in the face of challenges by merchants, lawyers, politicians, and business enterprises that attempted to gain control of the Colorado gold mines. Local business and commercial enterprises were sustained only as the servants of the miners. Clearly, the miners could afford to establish their own commercial connections to Denver or, as they threatened in 1859, could bypass the Denver market and establish independent connections to the East.

In the long run, as the mountain claims were sold and the opportunities for new discoveries diminished, control by those who physically labored in the mines was severely curtailed. By establishing the profitability of mining and securing the rights of property (as well as persons), miners established the conditions for capital penetration, but this was a slow and uneven process. It was facilitated by entrepreneurial labor and promoted by commercial and business classes, but capitalization proceeded at a snail's pace and met resistance at every turn. While the town boosters and politicians of Denver were anxious to attract eastern capital, the miners desired only a market for their gold. Most of them probably hoped that they would eventually locate a mountain claim that they could sell for a king's ransom, but their interest in economic development did not, generally, extend beyond the sale of a paying claim. In the short run, miners resisted the intrusion of any actor who might interfere with the production and sale of gold or who might claim an inordinate profit from the productive efforts of the miners.

Merchants were the most visible representatives of the nonlaboring classes, so they were the first antagonists faced by the regional miners. In October 1859, merchants of Denver and Auraria agreed to reduce the price paid for locally produced gold. The value of gulch gold (nuggets) was reduced from $18 to $17 per ounce, and the value of quicksilvered gold (dust) was reduced from $16 to $15. When the miners learned of this price-fixing conspiracy, they were prepared to retaliate.[10]

On 29 October 1859 there was a mass meeting in the Gregory Diggings to discuss the recent action by merchants of Denver and Auraria. The assembled miners unanimously approved five resolutions that were then published in the Denver newspapers. After expressing disapproval and willingness to take appropriate action (in resolution 1 and 2), the miners described their alliance with regional shopkeepers and the class-based interests that they represented:

> 3. Resolved, That we duly appreciate the action of our Mountain Traders in the aid and comfort they have extended to us in receiving our gold dust at the usual prices while they themselves are suffering from the changes lately affected.
>
> 4. Resolved, That in our efforts to render null and void the self constituted action of the Merchants and Traders of Denver and Auraria, relating to the value of gold dust, we will in no case lose sight of our own Mountain Traders who have, and still are, standing by us arm to arm and shoulder to shoulder in our endeavors to put down an effort not only mean and unjust but derogatory to the dearest interest of every working man in the Rocky Mountains."[11]

First, the miners claimed that mountain traders (in Central City and elsewhere) were still paying the standard price of $16 to $18 per ounce and were absorbing the cost of the Denver price reduction. Second, the miners claimed that miners and local traders were cooperating in opposition to the merchants of the Front Range. Third, miners claimed that they were representing the interests of productive labor. In short, they claimed to control the mines and the mining supply towns and to represent the interests of labor, in opposition to the merchants of Denver.

Denver and Auraria merchants had attempted to forge the alliance of land and trade as the basis for regional and municipal governance, under authority of the Provisional Government of Jefferson Territory. Hence, the miners seem particularly astute in their political analysis. In fact, one speaker at the miners' meeting noted that the alliance of Denver and Auraria merchants was an insufficient basis for regional control. He suggested that the miners could obtain better prices in Golden or could organize a transportation and trade cooperative. The message was clear. The miners did not rely on the merchants, but in fact the merchants were at the mercy of the miners. These sentiments were also expressed in a similar meeting at the Russell Diggings.[12] Miners were prepared to play merchant against merchant and town against town or to cooperate with local merchants and subsidize the development of the mountain trade.

The possibility of a producer cooperative must have seemed no idle threat to the Denver merchants. They reestablished the traditional price of gold and later explicitly recognized the authority of the Colorado miners and spared no effort in courting their favors. Nevertheless, the miners were not impressed by the efforts of the Denver boosters. Not only did the miners oppose the unnecessary expense and formality of statehood, but they had no use for a provisional government. One resident explained that the provisional authorities operated side by side, administering multiple remedies, while each collected a fee for services.[13]

The miners of the Central City region were impatient with the lawyers and politicians of Denver, but they were not blind to the increasing complexity of local governance and the variety of distinctive interests that were represented in the mining region. The laws adopted by the Gregory district in February 1860 were remarkably complete and well considered and might be deemed conventional in all but spelling. These laws specified the rights of farmers, ranchers, and irrigation and ore-reduction companies and also included laws of garnishment, mechanic's lien, and public nuisance. The mining camp was willing to accommodate new actors and to establish the necessary laws and elected officials. The miners would not, however, surrender their authority to a regional government.

Hence, mining camp law contained a variety of statutes that had nothing whatsoever to do with the control of mining claims. For example, in the Nevada district (just west of Central City), a miners' meeting of 28 April 1860 declared "bawdy houses, grog shops, [and] gambling saloons" a public nuisance, punishable by a fifty dollar fine and banishment from the district. In this regard, the miners, like the Denver boosters, promoted public order. Nevada miners also promoted economic development. They passed a law to grant right-of-way for railroad companies and had several laws relating to obstruction of public highways and public health dangers. Most interesting is the law that, in contrast to Denver's municipal government, forbade the licensing or taxation of peddlers selling provisions from their wagons.[14] Clearly these laws were written by those who produced gold and purchased food, not by the merchants who sold food to the miners. Thus the interest of the miners was distinguished from the interest of the merchants by the content of legislation.

The mining camp courts sustained a general governing authority that subsumed the concerns of land, trade, and labor. They claimed to represent the interest of productive labor but also established the rights of property, particularly the right to purchase or appropriate mineral claims. Nevertheless, the miners would not sacrifice their control to regional authorities, and they repeatedly expressed opposition to the Provisional Government of Jefferson Territory. In December 1859, correspondents from the Central City region informed the Denver press that the miners were united in opposition to the provisional government. There was, in fact, a general revolt of miners, who refused to pay taxes and repudiated the authority of the provisional government. A mountain correspondent claimed that only the politicians and businesspersons of the mountains supported the provisional government and the efforts to establish county governments that would, in essence, replace the mining district governments.

> There was an election held here on the 3rd inst., which tested, thoroughly, the feeling of the miners. It drew very nearly the entire vote. The question was "for" or "against" County organization. . . . For it, all that could be mustered were 95 votes, and nearly all of those live in and around "Wood"-ville, or are working on the ditch which is under the immediate supervision of J. M. Wood. The number of votes against it were 395, which proves my assertion—that the opposition is unanimous—to be correct.[15]

On the eve of the municipal election in Denver, 600–700 miners sent a petition of protest to the Provisional Government of Jefferson Territory. In September 1860, while Denver was struggling to establish its second municipal government, a mountain correspondent offered a solution to the problems of municipal governance in Denver:

> If the present state of affairs continue in your city, and if the people of Denver desire, we will be happy to extend the jurisdiction of Gregory district, so as to include your vicinity, and give to your people what they never have enjoyed, and what they do certainly need—a responsible and reliable government.[16]

Denver would not accept governance by the mining camps any more than the miners would accept government by Denver politicians. Hence, local authorities continued to operate without a regional government, which created problems not only in Denver but in the mining region. There was no mechanism for settling disputes between mining districts, and attempts to subdivide districts were at times hotly disputed. For example, the Spring Gulch district was organized in the fall of 1860, but when the officers attempted to carry out their duties, they were arrested and tried by the Nevada district court. The object of dispute was water. The miners of Spring Gulch were using hydraulic machinery that required control of substantial water rights, and the miners of the Nevada district were quick to recognize the threat to their control of the local mines. At a meeting on 28 September 1860, the Nevada district miners adopted the following resolution:

> Whereas we are informed that certain interested persons of Spring Gulch are desirous of obtaining a portion of this Nevada District it is thereby resolved—That the setting off of the portion of our District claimed by Spring Gulch would deprive us of one of the best portions of our District embarras our records oppress our miners by new records and laws and diminish our prosperity by losing control of the Gulch Stream on which we miners depend for success.
> Resolved that we miners and citizens of Nevada District will resist such invasion in any manner to the extreme of opposition.[17]

Aside from this interdistrict struggle, there was a controversy within the Nevada district between miners and mill owners who alleged misconduct in the election of January 1861.[18] Quite possibly the controversy was rooted in complaints surrounding the operation of the Consolidated Ditch Company. At least it seems that miners and mill operators expressed distinctive interests regarding what developed into "the ditch war" of 1861.

The Consolidated Ditch Company was organized in 1859 to provide water for the mining and milling operations in the Central City region and was chartered by the provisional government in January 1860. During the summer, a series of meetings was held in the Nevada district, in which miners protested that their claims were being flooded due to negligence on the part of the ditch company. In November, the local mill owners complained that they were still not receiving an adequate supply of water from the Consolidated ditch. Complaints regarding too much or too little water reflect, to some extent, seasonal variation, but more serious problems faced local residents.[19]

In the spring of 1861, the provisional government in Denver determined that the Consolidated Ditch Company was liable for damages suffered by the Black Hawk milling company, but a meeting in Central City attempted to overturn the decision of the Denver court. This inspired another mass meeting that supported the decision of the Denver authorities, suggesting that the participants at the Central City meeting had been misled. At this point, neither the mining districts nor the provisional government was able to resolve the dispute with the Consolidated Ditch Company. A running battle between mill owners and the ditch company produced considerable recrimination and not inconsequential property damage as the "ditch war" raged on through the fall of 1861.[20]

This case illustrates the problems of local control in the absence of either an umbrella government or a coalition between local authorities. The miners would not accept the provisional government, which was, as previously noted, based on the coalition of land and trade interests. Owners of ditch companies and quartz mills might be expected to have joined this coalition and to have allowed the provisional government to settle their disputes, but the miners would not accept this challenge to their control of the mines. The fact that miners depended on ditch companies and ore-reduction mills made the problem all the more serious. The solution was territorial governance, but the challenge was to establish a territorial authority that could encompass, yet not threaten, the local governing authorities.

Before the outbreak of the Civil War territorial governance was impossible. First of all, southern congressional leaders would not accept a new territory that was clearly aligned with the Republican Party. Equally important, the miners would not accept any regional authority that might threaten their control of the mines. The Civil War removed both barriers. The Southern Democrats withdrew from Congress, and the miners abandoned their claims as speculation became more profitable than productive enterprise.

The Civil War: Years of Transition

The speculative frenzy of the Civil War years was fostered by the combined effects of national inflation and regional depression. In order to finance the war effort, the federal government suspended specie payment and flooded the economy with paper, called greenbacks, thereby inspiring creditors to seek more secure investments. As federal currency was depreciating and gold was becoming a scarce and valuable commodity, eastern investors overcame their reluctance to speculate in the Colorado goldfields. Agricultural lands, which were the conservative investment of the mid-nineteenth century, were less attractive during the Civil War. Given the demand for food and the availability of cheap money, farmers could pay off their mortgages with inflated currency, thereby exchanging depreciated currency for valuable land. The mining frontier offered the opportunity to balance the trade deficit. In Colorado capitalists could exchange paper for gold, so Wall Street financiers, Boston merchants, and even humble mechanics seized the opportunity to secure their depreciating paper assets.[21]

The federal government would not trade gold for paper, but the Coloradans were anxious to do so. The miners sought windfall profits, and the merchants and real estate speculators sought capital investment that might facilitate economic development. Thus Colorado mining claims were routinely bought and sold, even before the speculative frenzy of the Civil War years. After Gregory had sold his claims for $21,000, the purchasers were able to produce $18,000 in profits almost immediately but were then discouraged by the difficulties in mining and milling the ore. Between 1859 and 1863, the Gregory lode was purchased or leased many times, but no one could overcome the problems of mining and milling the ore so as to realize a reliable profit. Coloradans claimed that the problem was insufficient capital, but there is no support for this assertion.[22]

In 1860, George Pullman (the railroad car magnate) and some Chicago investors commissioned a firm in Illinois to manufacture the Black Hawk ore-reduction mill. At tremendous expense, the mill was transported to the Russell Diggings, where Pullman attempted to establish an efficient milling operation. Within a year, however, Pullman was convinced that most of the local ore was practically worthless, since the best available milling procedure did not yield a fraction of the ore's assayed value. Pullman even leased the Gregory lode for a short while but was not able produce reliable profits and soon abandoned the claim. In fact, Pullman began to diversify his investments to include a ranch in Golden and a variety of less risky enterprises. Fully aware of the risks in mining ventures, Pullman charged exorbitant interest (25–50 percent per month) on loans to miners.[23]

Judd and Lee owned a part of the Gregory lode, which they tried, unsuccessfully, to sell for $6,000 in 1862. At the time they were operating at a loss, but subsequent digging uncovered a large vein of ore that produced $200,000 in profits by June 1864. At that point, the Black Hawk Mining Company was organized in New York, with Lee remaining as a major shareholder and local manager. The Consolidated Gregory Company purchased 500 feet of adjoining property at a total cost of $500,000.[24] Obviously, much money was to be made in the sale of mining claims, but could not the mine owner have realized even greater profits by working the mine? Apparently not. Available evidence suggests that more than half of the total yield of the Gregory lode was produced prior to June 1864, despite the fact that effective milling techniques were not developed until 1867. It would be difficult to determine exactly how much profit or loss accompanied the various mining enterprises associated with the Gregory Diggings, but the general picture is fairly clear. Fossett offers total production figures for the Gregory lode, from discovery until 1879 (see Table 3.2.).

These figures suggest first, that Gregory might have been a millionaire if he had retained possession of his claims; second, that 1864 was the time to sell; and third, that the sellers of the Civil War period generally did better than the buyers. Judd and Lee cleared $200,000 in 1863–1864 before organizing the Black Hawk Company. In the next six years, despite incredible capital investment and technological developments, the company did not average close to $200,000 per annum in total production. Obviously, profits did not approach the 1864 level. After Consolidated Gregory's $500,000 purchase in

Table 3.2 Value of Mineral Production from Gregory Lode, 1859–1879

Company	Years	Value of Production
Various operators[a]	(May) 1859–(June) 1864	$3,500,000
Black Hawk	1864–1869	936,654
Briggs	1864–1869	368,700
Briggs and Black Hawk	1869–1879	600,000
Consolidated Gregory	1864–1879	500,000
Smith and Parmalee	1864–1869	375,000
New York and Colorado[b]	1869–1879	450,000
Naragansett	1864–1879	100,000
Total		$6,830,354

[a]estimated
[b]includes what was Smith and Parmalee

Source: Frank Fossett, *Colorado* (Glorieta, NM: Rio Grande Press, 1976), p. 304.

1864, the total yield of that claim, over the next sixteen years, was $500,000. Clearly, the seller realized greater profits than the buyer in this case.[25]

The simple conclusion is that mining claims in the Central City region could be sold more profitably than they could be worked during the Civil War period. The sellers, in some cases, believed that eastern capital could provide the technological cure for the ore-reduction problems. The buyers must have cherished similar hopes, but they were invariably disappointed. A local editor explained the situation as follows:

> The men who had discovered and steadily developed the country became the most inveterate speculators in the world. [Nevertheless] it is pleaded in defence of those who first sold out the mines, and of those who are keeping up the same worthy practice, that quartz mining is impossible without capital.[26]

The Gregory lode was one of the richest claims of the Colorado frontier, and it brought an exorbitant price on the eastern market. Nevertheless, the available evidence suggests that 1863–1864 had been the first period of profitable production since 1860 and that the sale of the Gregory lode in 1864 yielded greater profits than its subsequent development. In this sense, the Gregory lode represents the general situation in the Central City mining region.

Why the mines were unproductive is more important to the mining engineer than it need be for present purposes. In any case, the technical problems in milling Colorado ore are well covered elsewhere.[27] Suffice it to say that the technological problems were not conquered until Professor Nathaniel P. Hill and his Boston associates were able to adapt European technology to the Colorado problem in 1867. Until then, only the surface ores could be profitably exploited, so the placer mining industry was sustained at the expense of lode mining until 1868. Until the lodes could be harvested, gold dust continued to erode into the mountain streams and provided the basis for placer mining efforts in the gulch or creek-bed claims.

Nevertheless, during the Civil War even placer mining was in decline in the Central City region. By 1863, most of the gulch claims had been worked by a series of claimants for a number of years, so they retained insufficient dust to merit further attention. The Consolidated Ditch had been completed in July 1860, but by 1862 there was little placer mining in the districts of Gregory, Nevada, and Russell because the yield was insufficient to cover the cost of the water. There were some profitable ventures, of limited duration, but placer mining was largely abandoned until the 1870s, when Chinese laborers were used in more capital-intensive efforts. The opportunities for subsistence mining in the region, after the boom days of 1859–1860, were extremely limited in the mid-1860s.[28]

Hence, the miners of the Central City region abandoned their mining camps and either moved to the city to establish themselves as mining speculators or moved to more productive placer mines elsewhere in Colorado. During the Civil War the population of the mining camps declined. In fact, Colorado as a whole did not gain appreciable population between 1860 and 1870. Central City, however, developed from a mining supply town of less than a thousand to a municipality of more than twice that size. It was not only larger but distinctively different from the town of 1860. When officially chartered in 1864, Central City was a merchant and shopkeeper town, sustained by the declining power of the miners (relative to the power of the commercial classes) and sanctioned by the authority of Colorado Territory.[29]

The miners, in some cases, seemed to welcome territorial government and greeted the announcement with patriotic celebrations. There was, however, some lingering suspicion that the new government might represent regional business interests in opposition to the miners. A meeting was held in the Gregory Diggings in June 1861 to amend the laws of February 1860. Under the old laws, the sheriff of Arapahoe County was an ex officio sheriff for the local miners, but the amendment allowed for the election of a local sheriff and further specified that cases under the jurisdiction of the miners' court would not be removed to other courts by routine change of venue.[30] This action suggests some fear that local control might be challenged by territorial governance.

It is possible that the miners were responding not to the threat of territorial government but merely to the death of their local sheriff. Sheriff Kehler, although elected sheriff of Arapahoe County, lived in Gregory Diggings and was accepted by the miners as their local sheriff. Perhaps they feared that the next county sheriff would not be their representative. The miners did participate, however, in the election of territorial officials and even held a special primary election to support the "people's" candidate for representative to the U.S. Congress. The representative was to be chosen at a convention held in Denver, and the delegates from the Gregory Diggings were instructed to elect a candidate who would defeat H. P. Bennett (a Denver attorney).[31] In this battle the miners did not succeed, but the territorial legislature quickly declared its commitment to the local miners.

The territorial government generally attempted to preempt the claims of frontier governing authorities, including the miners' courts. As described in the history of Denver, the standard procedure was to recognize the past actions of frontier governments but to require that county and municipal officials, operating under territorial sanction, exercise local governing authority in all future actions. Of course, in Denver there were municipal and county officials who had already managed to gain concessions from the frontier authorities. In the mining camps near Central City, the miners had not yet sacrificed control to municipal or county officials. Thus territorial government faced an additional problem in the mines. In order to govern the mining camps, the territorial government had to create city and county governments, while at the same time attempting to avoid a confrontation with the miners.

As a first step, in November 1861 the legislature sanctioned the previous actions of the mining courts, while attempting to transfer authority to the newly organized Gilpin County government. Nearly one year later, however, the legislature passed another law that explicitly recognized all previous (but not future) decisions of the mining district governments. The available evidence suggests that mining districts continued to record claims and resolve disputes in 1862, although they had surrendered general governing authority to the territory. The Eureka district discontinued its miners' court as of July 1861 but maintained a "court of claims or Board of Arbitrators." In most districts, however, the miners were willing to use the Gilpin County government much as they had used their mining districts. They elected a county sheriff, who seems to have been as popular as Sheriff Kehler had been. The local Justice of the Peace, also popularly elected, governed in the same manner as the mining camp president. Overall, despite some hesitation, it seems that the miners were willing to substitute county for mining district governance, so long as local control was sustained.[32]

Beginning in December 1861, Justice of the Peace Courts were operating in both Central City and Nevada City (later named Nevadaville), and by February 1862 the territorial district court was operating in Gilpin County. In general, local residents were less than completely satisfied with the territorial court, which tended to sacrifice efficiency to achieve due process and which was staffed by federal appointees. The territorial court for District Two met in Central City in February 1862, with Justice Charles Lee Armour presiding. The criminal docket contained one murder, two assaults with intent to kill, and one embezzlement. The record is unclear as to the disposition of the assault charges, but the murder and the embezzlement cases were still on the docket in April 1863, which suggests that the territorial court was more encumbered by legal process than the miners' court had been.[33]

The district court was, in fact, overwhelmed in its efforts to maintain effective governance, which explains, in part, why the docket was filled with crimes against government. The bulk of these crimes were violations of tax or license laws, but there were a large number of contempt cases as well. Some local residents did not appreciate the undue formality and the delays associated with territorial justice, and to make matters worse, Judge Armour was attacked by Chief Justice Benjamin F. Hall as a southern sympathizer, an incompetent, and a scoundrel. Some local residents must have shared this opinion, since a jury, in a civil suit, defied Judge Armour's instructions and found in favor of the defendant, amidst allegations that the judge was in cahoots with the plaintiff. Armour, unlike the local Justice of the Peace, was a federal appointee and was not viewed as a local officer. Not only did local juries and attorneys defy the authority of Armour's court, but even territorial legislators joined in the efforts to have Armour recalled.[34]

Before Armour was replaced, additional problems arose, including an attempted lynching that was prevented only because the local sheriff defied the lynch mob and rescued the prisoner. The transition to territorial governance was not smooth, but Central City did not witness a storm of violence such as Denver experienced in 1860. In the entire decade from 1862 until 1872, only two murderers were executed and only sixteen people died in shootouts and public brawls. There were some who undoubtedly preferred the informality of the miners' courts, and there were some isolated instances of conflict between miners and the territorial authorities. In 1861, for example, a miner shot a prowling county deputy and was acquitted by the mining district on grounds of defense of property. Nevertheless, the transition to territorial authority was effected, municipal government was organized in 1864, and one resident complained that things were downright dull by 1865.[35]

It is hardly surprising that there were conflicts between miners and the representatives of the territorial government. What is simply astounding is that these conflicts were not more rancorous and protracted. Territorial government succeeded where provisional government had failed. Miners sacrified their authority to county and, later, to municipal authorities, and they eventually allowed regional authorities to control the appropriation, sale, and exploitation of mineral claims. One might be tempted to credit the diplomatic or administrative skills of the territorial governors, but abundant evidence suggests that Colorado's early governors were not distinguished by their political acumen.[36]

Territorial governance succeeded, first, because it did not challenge the control of miners who were physically laboring in the mines, and second, because physical control of the mines became increasingly unimportant during the Civil War. The territorial government did not attempt to disturb the routine exploitation of placer mining claims (gulch claims). The lode (or mountain) claims were the major territorial concern, particularly as these became the object of speculation among eastern financiers.[37] Those who physically labored on gulch claims continued to control their productive enterprise, but the significance of placer mining declined precipitously during the Civil War. Ultimately, the miners abandoned their unproductive claims. They were not forced to surrender their control, since their gulch claims were not considered valuable. Mountain claims were valuable not because they were productive but because they could be sold to speculators and eastern capitalists. Thus, even the physical possession of mountain claims was not particularly important, since productive activity was less rewarding than speculation.

The miners' control of the regional political economy declined because their economic significance declined. Their control of production was not threatened. In fact, the federal government sanctioned the authority of the mining districts in special legislation of 1864. The economic and political power of labor diminished because productive enterprise declined. Thus after the speculative frenzy of the Civil War, Central City emerged as a merchants' town, in which trade was more important than mining.

THE MERCHANTS' TOWN OF 1870

The organization of the Central City municipal government marked the transition from mining to trade as the economic basis for political organization. Few of the surviving records predate 1870, but the nature of local governance seems fairly clear. Of the seven city aldermen who served from 1864 to 1865, one was a saloon keeper, one owned a tobacco shop, and two were lawyers. One of the lawyers was Henry M. Teller, who built a deluxe hotel (called the Teller House), was active in the Colorado statehood movement, and was later elected to the U.S. Senate. The other lawyer later represented two eminent Coloradans (a Denver banker and a representative to the U.S. Congress) who were accused of fraud in the sale of a silver mine. The occupations of the other members of the first board of aldermen could not be determined, but it seems that the commercial and professional classes predominated in municipal office.[38]

Central City had existed since 1859 as a commercial adjunct to the frontier mining camps, but it developed as an independent commercial center during the Civil War. After the bubble had burst in the mining speculation market, the local gold mines suffered an even deeper depression. In 1866 and 1867, local gold production was less than half of that in 1864. During these postwar years Central City continued to supply local miners, but the market for gold and gold mines was severely depressed. After 1867, however, local mining efforts were renewed, and the regional trade received a much needed boost from the operation of the ore-reduction works at Black Hawk, just down the

Central City in the 1870s. Courtesy Denver Public Library, Western History Department

hill from Central City. Nathaniel Hill's ore-reduction works were operating in Black Hawk in 1868, and the efficiency of his mill inspired local miners to sift through previously abandoned ore specimens. The refuse ("tailings") of the abandoned lodes was brought to Hill's mill, and favorable results inspired renewed interest in the local mines. More important, ore from the newly established mining districts outside of Gilpin County was transported to Black Hawk for reduction in the local mill.[39]

By 1870, Central City had established itself as a regional trade center. Local mines were being worked, but the most important source of local wealth was the milling operations in Black Hawk. Central City became more dependent on trade, including trade in mining claims, than on miners. Mining was still a major local industry, accounting for 44 percent of the population and 27 percent of local wealth, but the trade and service industries contributed 26 percent of the population and 52 percent of local wealth.

As indicated by the data in Table 3.3, in 1870 the nonlaboring classes of Central City controlled 85 percent of local wealth, although they constituted less than 30 percent of the households. Among the local employers were a couple of publishers, several mine owners, a quartz (ore-reduction) mill,

Table 3.3 Wealth by Class Category for Central City, 1870

Class Category	Total Wealth	Percentage of Wealth	Number of Households	Percentage of Households
Nonlaboring classes	$697,000	85.13	98	29.70
Financier	10,000	1.25	1	0.00
Owner	183,400	22.99	16	4.85
Professional	214,700	26.92	24	7.27
Merchant	253,100	31.73	46	12.12
None	17,800	2.23	17	5.15
Laboring classes	118,600	14.87	232	70.30
Artisan	97,200	12.19	163	49.39
Worker	21,400	2.68	69	20.91
Total	797,600		330	

Source: U.S. Bureau of Census (1870) Population Schedules for Gilpin County, Kansas Territory.

Data come from a 33 percent systematic sample of occupied dwelling units, aggregated to household level and collapsed into class categories based on occupation. Miners and farmers are "artisans." Otherwise, "artisans" includes all craft titles, except households reporting no wealth (classified as "worker").

a foundry, and a building contractor. Some of these employed managers and engineers, who constituted the bulk of the professional classes, as well as employing wage labor. Compared to 1860, laboring households had increased from 60 percent to 70 percent of the population, but their share of local wealth had declined from 60 percent to less than 15 percent. Artisans comprised the bulk of the laboring classes and reported, on average, $596 in real and personal wealth. But these figures are deceptive, since thirty craft-title households claimed nearly two-thirds ($63,100) of the artisan wealth, reporting an average of over $2,000. Most of the households identified as "artisans" were, in fact, miners, who claimed only $256 per household.

There were still a large number of miners in Central City in 1870, but their contribution to the local economy had diminished considerably. The bulk of local mineral wealth reported in these data came from speculation rather than productive enterprise. Most (56 percent) of the mining wealth was controlled by two mining agents. Nine mine owners claimed 28 percent of the wealth, while 133 miners (92 percent of the households) claimed only 16 percent. One might conclude that the bulk of the mineral wealth was in the hands of nonresident investors, but their control was probably more apparent than real.

One wealthy mining agent named John Scudder reported over $100,000 in personal property, while the remainder of the local agents reported modest wealth. Furthermore, it seems likely that Scudder's wealth came from the sale of mining claims, not from salary or commission received as a mining agent. John Scudder had owned part of the Gunnell lode (discovered by Harry Gunnell in 1859) that was sold in the speculative frenzy of 1864. In the postwar years, Scudder controlled a number of local mining claims that were leased or worked by various mining companies during the 1870s. It is difficult to determine the source of Scudder's wealth, but in 1864 he and two partners sold 200 feet of the Gunnell claim for $80,000. Given the previous discussion of the Civil War speculation market, it seems reasonable to conclude that Scudder made most of his money selling or leasing mining claims, rather than by representing absentee owners. The number of lawsuits involving mining agents of the Central City region suggests that the absentee owners were swindled with considerable regularity.[40] Hence, it is not clear that absentee owners controlled the local mines or that mining agents were involved in mineral production.

In fact, it seems that miners and small mine owners controlled a significant proportion of local mineral production, even if they did not own the bulk of the local claims. If one ignores the $120,000 controlled by mining agents, miners controlled 36 percent of the wealth associated with the local mining industry, while mine owners controlled 64 percent. These figures seem to fit the general picture offered in analyses of the Gilpin County mines. Total production for the county was $1,552,000 in 1870, and much of this can be attributed to Clear Creek, Lake County, and other Colorado mines that shipped ore to Black Hawk for milling. Many of the local mining companies had suspended operations and were allowing miners to lease the claims. Subsequent production in the Central City region was largely financed and controlled by Coloradans.[41] In general, the Gilpin County mineral production of 1870 resulted from the efforts of small entrepreneurs. The wealth thus produced did not, however, match the wealth of local commercial and professional classes.

Thus it seems reasonable to conclude that miners no longer owned the local mines and that merchants and professionals (including mining agents) now formed the economic elite. One should not conclude, however, that Central City housed an army of penniless laborers in 1870. Although their share of local wealth was small, miners and other local workers were relatively well paid. Good mechanics earned anywhere from five to ten dollars a day, while carpenters earned from two to three. Miners, although probably paid less, did have the opportunity to lease claims and could still sustain their independence in that way. In fact, local miners were consolidating their holdings, through lease and purchase, and effectively exploiting local mines.

Thus it seems reasonable to conclude that the City of Central was organized in 1864 and sustained through the 1870s on the basis of trade. Local mineral production contributed to that trade, but the milling operations at Black Hawk were of critical importance. So long as the ore was transported to Black Hawk for milling, Central City maintained trade with the Rocky Mountain mines. Central City was, by 1864, no longer a mining supply town, providing convenience stores for the local miners. It was a commercial center for the regional mining industry and competed, in that capacity, with Denver. In short, after the Civil War, Central was no longer a miners' but a merchants' town. The distinction is evident in the operation of municipal government.

THE CHALLENGE OF NATIONAL INCORPORATION

Although Central City was chartered in 1864, the earliest available legislative records are from 1871. These proceedings evidence the operation of a fledgling municipal government. The major problem that faced the aldermen was fund raising for civic improvements. The board met thirty-two times in the calendar year and received twenty-three petitions from constituents. About half of these petitions were for tax abatement; most of the remainder were requests for sidewalks or street construction. Meanwhile, the board was trying desperately to supply the city with an adequate water supply, only to have the voters overwhelmingly defeat a bond issue that was to have financed the water works.[42]

The criminal docket of the local courts offers further insight into the concerns of municipal governance. Both the municipal court (Justice of the Peace Court) and the territorial district court were concerned primarily with crimes against government, or public order, which tended to undermine the boosters' claim that this was a safe place for investing capital and labor. The J.P. court was preoccupied with minor disturbances—24 cases of assault, 34 cases of disturbing the peace, 53 cases of public intoxication, and 25 license violations. The territorial court had 19 cases of murder or manslaughter, but most of the cases involved crimes against government. Seventy cases were for violations of the Sabbath (keeping a tippling house open), and 123 cases were for violations of licensing law (keeping a hotel, theater, etc., without a license).

As the economic significance and political strength of the local miners declined, it was no longer necessary to promote "law and order" as the defense of personal liberty or to court the interests of the laboring classes more generally. To sustain itself as a commercial center, Central City relied on taxation and licensure, typical revenue-raising strategies in merchant towns. Both the fund-raising efforts and the concern with municipal improvements distinguished merchant government from the mining camps. Mining camps did not tax property, nor did they license commerce. Mining district officials collected fees for recording claims, but preemption claims that were worked continuously did not have to be recorded. Furthermore, not only were there no license laws, but in Nevadaville license laws were specifically prohibited. Thus the interests of the merchant and the miner can be distinguished by the content of legislation.

As labor and capital abandoned the local mines, Central City merchants and shopkeepers became town boosters, attempting to attract entrepreneurial labor and capital to sustain local commerce. To some extent, their situation was not unlike that of their Denver counterparts in 1858, but one important difference deserves attention. Postwar Colorado was not a frontier. By 1865, territorial government was fairly well entrenched, and the economic basis of the Rocky Mountain region had been firmly established. Colorado was a mining region. The problem was that the mines were not sufficiently productive and that mining, in general, was not sufficiently reliable to sustain the regional economy. Central City exemplified this problem. It was the center of a mining region that was steadily declining between 1864 and 1868. Mineral production could not sustain commerce, and there were no other industries that might flourish in the rocky gorges of the Clear Creek region. Thus, it seemed that Central was destined to become a ghost town, just as it managed to gain a corporate charter.

Central City residents did not, however, merely accept their fate. Beginning in 1864, there were two distinct economic development efforts that proved at least marginally successful. The first was a concerted effort to attract capital. The second was an attempt to survive capital flight, through the efforts of entrepreneurial labor and small-scale enterprise. The former was responsible for the rail connection of 1878, while the latter established the basis for the tourist town of today. In retrospect, one might conclude that the latter proved the more successful plan for economic development, but the attempt to attract capital also deserves discussion.

Both efforts were important and are important in this analysis because they represent the class-based alliances that characterize Carnival and Caucus towns. By 1870, merchants controlled Central City. The critical question at that juncture was whether they would ally with capital or labor. In fact, both alliances were attempted, but the alliance with capital was undermined by labor's control of local production and by the failure of Golden capitalists to sustain an alliance with national actors, notably Jay Gould. Had Golden succeeded, the economic and political control of Colorado might have shifted to Golden, and Central City might have maintained its smelting operations and its position in the transportation and ore-reduction network. This was clearly the goal of the effort to attract capital.

H. M. Teller exemplifies the postwar efforts to attract capital to the Central City region. In 1864, Coloradans were offered an enabling act, virtually guaranteeing statehood if local residents would approve a constitution. The federal government was interested in increasing Republican electoral votes and was thus inspired to increase the opportunities for statehood. Coloradans saw the opportunity to establish local control of government and to reassure eastern investors that Colorado was not a fly-by-night haven for swindlers, but a respectable member of the Union. Statehood, they believed, would provide a basis for renewed investment in the Colorado mines. Teller, as a lawyer who aspired to public office, attended the constitutional convention and forged an alliance with the Denver leaders (notably Byers and Evans) who formed the "statehood faction."[45]

The statehood faction dominated the convention and was confident that the voters would accept both the constitution and the slate of officers. Evans and Teller did not include their names as candidates, since they were certain that the voters would require their services as senators once the constitution was approved. But the voters had other ideas, and various parties effectively blocked the statehood movement of 1864. Golden politicians who felt that Denverites would dominate the state government were leaders of the opposition. They were joined by owners of small businesses, who were concerned that the tax burden of statehood would be too great to bear, and by laborers, who were concerned that they would be drafted into the army. Finally, a fair number of miners and many of the residents of southern Colorado were at least sympathetic to the Confederacy and were generally opposed to the Republicans in Denver. Golden politicians, shopkeepers, and laborers and Democrats and southerners all joined in opposition to statehood, so the statehood referendum was overwhelmingly defeated.[44]

Teller then abandoned his Denver allies and joined forces with the Golden crowd, most notably W.A.H. Loveland, in efforts to shift the balance of power from Denver toward the west. Toward this end, the Colorado Central Railroad company allied with the Union Pacific and attempted to build a connection to the transcontinental rail. The goal was to bypass Denver by connecting the local mining districts to Golden and then connecting Golden to the railhead in Cheyenne, Wyoming. Golden investors convinced their parent county of Jefferson to contribute $100,000 in bonds in exchange for stock, and construction commenced in 1868. Although the railroad company was dominated by the Union Pacific, funding came entirely from Colorado, and five members of the governing board were Coloradans, including Henry M. Teller and two other Gilpin County representatives.[45]

The major responsibility of the Coloradans was to raise money, which became increasingly difficult as it appeared that Denver would win the railroad war. Nevertheless, Gilpin County offered $300,000 in bonds in 1871, contingent on the completion of the connection to Black Hawk by May 1872. The company failed to meet this condition, but Gilpin offered $250,000 if the rail reached Black Hawk by January 1873 and reached Central City by the following year. The railroad did not reach Central before 1878, but it did arrive in Black Hawk in 1872, so the county bonds were finally released.[46] Despite their railroad company, however, neither Golden nor Central City could compete with Denver as a commercial center or compete with Jay Gould for control of the Colorado railroads.

The railroad war will be discussed in detail in the history of Golden. It is sufficient to note here that the Central-Golden coalition represented an alliance of transportation and trade that had insufficient regional support and was unable to compete with national economic elites. This coalition resembled the Denver coalition of land and trade, which had promoted the Provisional

Government, and it suffered a similar fate. Even though the local mining industry was in decline after the Civil War, a coalition that excluded labor could not govern Central City, and such a coalition was not an adequate basis for regional control. This coalition did control Golden, but even Loveland came to recognize that they could not compete with the national railroad companies. After losing the railroad war, Loveland moved to Denver and Teller abandoned Central City for a career in national politics.

Teller's unsucessful attempt to attract capital was, however, only part of the postwar economic development effort. If Teller best represents the struggle to attract capital and compete with Denver for regional dominance, Peter McFarlane best represents the struggle to survive capital flight. McFarlane arrived in Central City in 1869, and after leasing a gold mine and working as a miner, he joined his cousin as a junior partner in a contracting business. Since the Boston and Colorado Smelting Company had begun operation a year earlier, and Hill's improved milling techniques were inspiring renewed interest in local mines, there was much demand for skilled labor. By 1872, Peter McFarlane had his own company, in partnership with his brother. Throughout the 1870s, McFarlane and Company did a booming business and was instrumental in developing new milling technology as an adjunct to the general contracting business. In 1874 the central business district was all but consumed by an uncontrolled fire, but the devastation brought even greater prosperity for the contractors. McFarlane's machine shop was untouched by the blaze, so the brothers could commence immediately in their efforts to build the new Central City.[47]

While Teller and his associates were playing politics in Washington and fighting a railroad war in Colorado, McFarlane and Company was hard at work. So long as the milling operations at Black Hawk were attracting the regional mineral trade, Central City was sustained as a commercial center. Also, the local mines were being worked by a new breed of miners. Immigrants from Cornwall provided the experience that had been lacking on the mining frontier, so in addition to the technological developments in milling, the local mining industry could boast a skilled labor force.[48] An army of entrepreneurial labor was leasing the mines and produced a fair amount of gold. Entrepreneurs like McFarlane benefited from both the mining and the milling operations.

McFarlane became a major local figure. He served on the Board of Aldermen for many years and was unanimously elected mayor in 1878. That same year, the Central City Opera House was opened, and this municipal enterprise was a source of both cultural enrichment and civic pride. It was, however, an additional expense that the city had to bear, just as the county was indebted for the railroad that reached Central City that year. Financing a commercial center on the basis of entrepreneurial efforts was ultimately more than the city could bear. This became evident when the Boston and Colorado Smelting Works moved to Denver, also in 1878.

Waiting for the Tourists

In June 1878, the local newspaper identified two major problems facing the Board of Aldermen. First, there was the city debt, which stood at $21,000. Second, and equally threatening in the mind of the editor, was a public nuisance in the shape of a "house of ill fame." A group of citizens appeared before the board petitioning for the removal of said nuisance, but the matter was referred to the police committee, where it was feared that little of consequence would occur. The editor offered the following suggestion:

> A little backbone, a little "sand" as it is sometimes called might do much toward this end. A license which would amount to a prohibition might bring about the desired end. The Council did not hesitate to inflict a license of $10 on traveling auctioneers, which is virtually a prohibition, and for the protection of our legitimate merchants. If the present ordinance against houses of ill-fame is nugatory and a dead letter on the books, let them try a prohibitory license, which will be some kind of protection to the virtuous and law-abiding portion of the community.[49]

City governments of the nineteenth century routinely imposed an informal licensing fee by periodically raiding the brothels and collecting a nominal fine, but the editor obviously wanted to rid the town of prostitutes rather than raise money by licensing the brothels. In any case, it seems that the citizens got what they wanted. The police court of 1880 does not include a single charge of prostitution (or "being an inmate at a house of ill fame"). In fact, only sixteen criminal cases were on the docket, and all of these were crimes against government, or public order: two charges against residents who refused to either pay three dollars or work for a day on municipal improvements (as was required by law), one case of selling liquor without a license, six drunk and disorderly cases, four cases of disturbing the peace, one unlawful discharge of a pistol, one contempt charge, and a violation of the fire code.

The district court was not much busier, although each charge generally involved multiple judicial actions (arraignment, bail, etc.). There were four assault charges, a burglary, an arson, and a case of alleged claim-jumping. The remaining cases included one charge of selling liquor without a license, another for keeping a tippling house open on the Sabbath, one for gambling, and one for indecent exposure. Clearly, the court was defending community standards of appropriate behavior, and the challenge of combating immorality must not have been unduly taxing. If these records provide any indication, it seems there was very little crime in Central City of 1880.

Nevertheless, the local editor was concerned with municipal efforts to maintain law and order, and he urged vigilance.

Our Denver exchanges come to us now-a-days with the accounts of the depredations and atrocities of footpads, evidently tramps from the eastern states, of whose arrival notice was made some time since. This appears to be the first season that Colorado has been infested to any great extent with this plague [on] social order and law. This army of vagrants, professional beggars, and thieves, which has been moving over every public highway leading from the Missouri River to the Rocky Mountains, may strike our mountain towns or may not, as the notion strikes its members. Anyhow, it would be well to prepare for such an event. In case the authorities are unable to give our citizens protection there is but one course left. That course the citizens know well and the people will not hesitate to follow it.[50]

In an adjoining editorial, the message was even more explicit:

It is hoped that our authorities will not be found napping in case of any emergency. Meet this danger halfway if necessary. Nip it in the bud. Make a striking example of the first strolling vagabond found lurking or committing any crime in our midst. Let our citizens each and every one be prepared to meet with a good sized buckshot the first attempt of any of them to violate the law. This mode of treatment is a sure cure for the complaint.[51]

By 1880, Central City was a small town of Cornish miners, artisans, shopkeepers, merchants, and owners of small businesses, an island of entrepreneurial labor and capital in a political economy that was increasingly dominated by eastern capital. Both capital and labor had abandoned Central City, so it did not face the rancorous conflicts that plagued Denver; local laboring classes were not particularly threatened by national, monopoly capital investment or political struggles to control the local economy. Nevertheless, the local editor continued to preach law and order, as the spokesperson for the shopkeepers and merchants.

As shown by the data in Table 3.4, Central City's battle against crime followed the Denver pattern. The Central City boosters, at least initially, were able to maintain public order only through defense of personal liberty, relying to a large extent on the mining district governments. Prior to the organization of municipal governance, the miners courts and the local Justice of the Peace Courts defended the rights of persons and property as well as public order (or "government"). The Territorial District Court focused its attention on crimes against government, thereby defending the merchant and shopkeeper's interest in public order. Then, gradually, the war on crime became increasingly focused on crimes against government and increasingly subject to the authority of regional (territorial and state) District courts.

Table 3.4 Criminal Cases in Gilpin County by Court by Offense for 1860–1862, 1869–1871, and 1880

	Offense against			
Court	Property	Persons	Government	Total
1860–1862				
Miners (1860).	4 (.40)	4 (.40)	2 (.20)	10
Nevada J.P. (1862)	1 (.17)	3 (.50)	2 (.33)	6
Central J.P. (1861)	13 (.26)	18 (.36)	19 (.38)	50
District (1862)	19 (.14)	10 (.07)	111 (.79)	140
Total	37 (.18)	35 (.17)	134 (.65)	206
1869 to 1871				
J.P.	4 (.02)	26 (.16)	133 (.82)	163
District	30 (.09)	29 (.09)	262 (.82)	321
Total	34 (.07)	55 (.11)	395 (.82)	484
1880				
Police	0	0	16 (1.0)	16
District	3 (.19)	4 (.25)	9 (.56)	16
Total	3 (.09)	4 (.13)	25 (.78)	32

Source: Territorial Court Records: Denver Federal Center; Miners Courts: Gilpin County Courthouse; Justice and Police Courts: State Archives, Denver.

Proportion of row total is to the right of the frequency.

After the Civil War, as Central City leaders, notably Henry Teller, attempted to attract capital and foster economic development, the District Court assumed responsibility for the bulk of crimes against property and the majority of crimes against persons, although overall crimes against government constituted the bulk of the criminal docket. By 1880, as was the case in Denver, the District Court assumed responsibility for all crimes against persons and property, while the Police Court prosecuted drunks and other threats to public order.

Central City differed from Denver mostly in the lack of criminal prosecutions. Since public order did not threaten the personal liberty of the entrepreneurial artisans and shopkeepers, there was relatively little crime. Central City did not house a large population of unskilled, alienated laborers who were incited by the racist appeals of the Democrats to vent their frustrations on Chinese laborers. Similarly, Central did not house a large population of young, unmarried, underemployed, unskilled laborers who spent their daily wages in the bars and brothels. Simply stated, Central City did not have a large number of impoverished, exploited laborers. Consequently, the police were not very busy.

The Board of Aldermen did not seem to be very busy either. They held only nineteen meetings in 1880; they generally scheduled only one meeting per month. Eight of the meetings were held in August, when the aldermen attempted to determine local tax assessments. Perhaps the board was busier than the schedule of meetings suggests, since there were reports of citizen concerns regarding civic improvements, licensing, and, of course, taxes. Nevertheless, it seems that there was little excitement in local politics. In the election of 1880, there was only one contested seat on the Board of Aldermen, and street commissioner was the only other office that attracted two candidates.

In fact, municipal politics of the period were remarkably nonpartisan, considering the three-cornered partisan struggle (between Greenbackers, Republicans, and Democrats) that typified Colorado politics in this period. In 1878, Central City residents held a "citizens convention" to nominate municipal officers. In response, the Republicans held a separate convention, and as the editor of the *Daily Register* proudly reported, "The Republican Convention at Turner Hall last evening was of that character as to dispel illusions in regard to a mixed or mongrel ticket."[52] Nevertheless, three of the Republican candidates had also been nominated by the "citizens," and Peter McFarlane ran unopposed since the Democrats did not nominate a candidate for mayor. In any case, Central City remained Republican, even if some of the Republicans were also nominated as nonpartisan candidates.

The local party of class harmony and public order did not face the difficulties that plagued the Republican Party in Denver. The Central City editor, a devout Republican, never missed an opportunity to compare the domestic tranquility of Central City to the chaos of Denver politics. In reporting on Loveland's attempt to break the Denver printers' union, the editor explained how labor and capital cooperated in Central City:

> The Register-Call, as a newspaper, a business enterprise, has never been governed by what is known as the printers' union. It has always paid liberal wages to its employees, and in return has always received the fealty and goodwill of those employed. The interests of the proprietors and the employed has always been identical, and as the Register-Call succeeded, so did every man connected with it.[53]

The employers of Central City were not plagued by trade unions and unemployed workers who were susceptible to the race-baiting efforts of the Democratic Party. Since the local economy did not attract substantial capital investment, Central City did not suffer the violent labor uprisings or partisan struggles that animated politics in Denver and Leadville. This is not to suggest that there were no laboring classes in Central City. Compared to Denver, however, the laboring class was smaller, more highly skilled, and generally less proletarianized. This was, of course, a point of local pride. During the Chinese Riot in Denver, the Central City editor reported, "Denver in the Hands of a Howling Mob," and complimented local partisans by reporting, "The processions and demonstrations of last Saturday night were a credit to the good sense and the law-abiding sentiments of the people of Gilpin."[54] In a similar vein, it was reported, "The Leadville riots will cost the state about $35,000, and the Denver riots about the same amount. Bleeding Colorado! but you are to be pitied!"[55]

Overall, it seems that local shopkeepers had eradicated the last vestiges of frontier vice and that "law and order" prevailed in 1880. Neither legislative nor judicial records indicate any particular concern with prostitution and gambling, despite the editorial concerns expressed in 1878. By 1880, municipal and county officials were routinely defending public order, supervising municipal improvements, and even adjudicating mining-claim disputes. Central had managed to establish its authority over municipal properties and, in conjunction with Gilpin County, managed to exercise general governing authority.

In this sense, the victory of 1880 fit the general pattern of municipal political struggles. Prostitutes, gamblers, miners, and capitalists left Central City as the economy declined. In all cases, municipal government won the battle when the enemy had gone. Thus Central City was established and sustained not on the tide of economic development but in the wake of economic decline. Entrepreneurial labor and capital were able to control the commercial economy because labor and capital largely abandoned the Central City region in the mid 1860s. Central suffered from the limitations imposed by its frontier legacy, but as the major economic actors withdrew from the scene, those limitations were overcome.

Central City was not bustling in 1880, but it did not die. The local mines continued to operate, and there was a small boom between 1893 and 1906. Nevertheless, it was not until 1932 that the city recovered its place in the regional economy, not as a mining town but as a tourist town. Today, the Teller House and the Opera House remain as local institutions, while "mining companies" offer train rides for the tourists, and shopkeepers sell curios. There is a saloon, which offers a blend of the old frontier, complemented with a liberal dose of country rock music, to attract clients from Denver. Central maintained itself as a sleepy mining supply town until it discovered itself as a tourist town. It was and is a shopkeepers' haven. Capital has still (thus far) ignored Central City, although Hollywood has used the town as a movie set.

From the booster's perspective, Central City was not as successful as Denver, since it failed to attract monopoly capital and did not become a major metropolitan area. A laboring class perspective, however, might suggest an altogether different conclusion. In the following chapter, these diverging perspectives on municipal growth are highlighted in the history of Greeley, where small-scale family farmers actively resisted the boosters' economic development efforts and were, in this regard, extremely successful.

CHAPTER FOUR

Greeley: Dry Farming and Utopian Capitalism

Greeley was established and sustained by small-scale family farmers who joined merchants and local businesspersons in promoting economic development within the limits of local initiative. From the outset, Greeley residents resisted outside interference, particularly speculation and eastern capital investment, which were viewed as a threat to the interests of the laboring proprietor, especially the family farmer. The early experience of political struggle in opposition to the ranchers and speculators of surrounding Weld County provided an organizational base and a tradition of class-based political struggle. The economic and political resources of the farmers essentially guaranteed that their interests would be represented in public, Carnival governance.

Their economic circumstance and political experience fostered an exclusionary consciousness, even in resistance to national monopoly capital. The farmers of Greeley thus defended their narrowly defined class-based interest as laboring proprietors, defending property as well as personal rights and distancing themselves from tenants or indebted farmers and from the laboring classes more generally. The progressive political struggles of the Greeley farmers were eventually preempted by the Republican Party.

WELD BEFORE GREELEY

Long before the gold rush of 1859, northern Colorado had been settled by trappers and fur traders. Bent and Saint Vrain, the company formed by Charles and William Bent and Ceran Saint Vrain and his brothers, was operating Fort Saint Vrain in 1835 as an adjunct to its southern Colorado enterprises. By 1858, however, the few hunters and trappers who remained were engaged in desultory trade with the local tribes.[1] As the gold rush brought the promise of renewed prosperity, trappers and traders joined the newcomers in prospecting, land speculation, trade, transportation, and even agriculture. William Byers, the Denver editor and indefatigable town booster, offered yeoman service in promoting local agricultural enterprise in Weld County and elsewhere. In his first editorial for the *Rocky Mountain News,* Byers excoriated the plowboys-turned-prospectors, claiming that agriculture offered greater opportunities for those willing to invest their labor in productive enterprise.[2]

Early Greeley. Courtesy Colorado Historical Society (F-12017)

Byers later joined with other Denver residents to establish a land claim club near the ruins of Fort Saint Vrain.

The records of the Saint Vrain Claim Club indicate that eleven men met on 6 October 1859. It is not clear where this meeting was held, but the participants were identified as "settlers and those wishing to hold claims near St. Vrain's Fort." Apparently, the interested parties included a number of Denver businesspersons.[3] In any case, the minutes record the following actions. C. P. Neal was elected chair and H. J. Graham secretary. Byers then offered two motions that were adopted apparently without discussion. First, each claimant was entitled to 160 acres that were to be staked, recorded, and improved by June 1860. Second, the club claimed jurisdiction within the bounds of Saint Vrain County, Nebraska Territory. The final act of this first meeting was the election of H. J. Graham, who, as recorder, was entitled to receive one dollar for each recorded claim.[4]

A year passed before another meeting was reported, but claims were recorded in the interim. In fact, claims were recorded in Denver beginning in July 1859—before the organizational meeting in October. H. J. Graham not only recorded claims of 160 acres (including his own), he also recorded his purchase of 80 acres (from Neal, for fifty dollars) and his preemption of an additional 80 acres. Furthermore, Ellen D. Graham claimed 160 acres and purchased Byers's claim for fifty dollars. Thus the Grahams controlled 640 acres before the claim club established laws governing the appropriation and purchase of claims.[5]

There were a number of irregularities in the records of the Saint Vrain Claim Club. First of all, the club claimed jurisdiction in Saint Vrain County, but Graham was recording claims in Denver. Second, claims were recorded before the organization of the club and were purchased before the adoption of laws regulating the sale of claims. Third, there was no mention of inspections to certify that claims had been improved, and there was no legal basis to sustain Graham's claim to more than 160 acres. These and other irregularities might well have inspired a meeting on 23 October 1860.

At that meeting, a committee was appointed to examine the club's records, and a jury was selected to adjudicate a dispute regarding Graham's claim. The jury found in his favor; the committee found the books to be in order, and a special committee was selected to drive the squatters from the Graham ranch.[6] The prime movers in these activities were a handful of claimants who collectively controlled the bulk of the local claims. George French, John Overton, S. H. Smith, J. W. Reddick, and H. J. Graham were buying and selling claims and trading in townsites, the plats for which were never recorded. These same men effectively monopolized the claim club offices, served as auditors and jurors, and generally controlled the distribution of local land until their efforts were superseded by the Weld County Commissioners in 1863.

Weld County was organized under territorial authority in 1861, but the commissioners did not meet until January 1863. Even then, they met only seven times and seemed to be preoccupied with the organization and operation of wagon road and ditch companies. The county chartered two wagon road and three irrigation ditch companies in 1863. One of the ditch companies included the county clerk (a partner in Graham's town company) among the original stockholders and retained the deputy clerk as an attorney.[7] Thus the interests of town companies, road companies, and ditch companies were well represented, as were the Weld County ranchers. The chair of the county commissioners was a large stockraiser, as was the deputy clerk, and the county commissioners' records included a registry of local brands and notices of the appraisal of stray stock "taken up" by local ranchers.[8]

When the farmers and shopkeepers arrived in Greeley in 1870, the surrounding county was dominated by ranchers, railroads, and town, road, and ditch companies. In 1870, the commissioners met eleven times and received two petitions to build new roads and a petition from citizens who requested the purchase of railroad bonds. The commissioners also received a proposition from the Denver Land Company, offering property for county offices in the city of Evans. This gracious offer was accepted, and Evans was named the county seat in 1870. There was little mention of ranchers in the minutes, but it seems that the ranchers were well represented in county government. All three of the commissioners were ranchers, and one of them had been a member of the first Colorado Stock Growers Association, organized in 1867.[9]

Thus railroads, road and ditch companies, land companies, and cattlemen were the major interests represented in the region. They controlled Weld County land and water and, as will become evident, played a crucial role in shaping the history of Greeley. It was to some extent the struggle between municipal and county actors that inspired the combination of temperance and xenophobia that united the farmers and merchants of the Union Colony at Greeley.

THE UNION COLONY

The Union Colony, which established the city of Greeley, was the inspiration of Nathan C. Meeker, the agricultural editor for the *New York Tribune*. Meeker had long been interested in the idea of an agricultural commune and had learned through painful experience the difficulties in communal living.[10] He was convinced, however, that a cooperative agricultural settlement might work, if the land were sufficiently fertile, the climate sufficiently wholesome, and the inhabitants sufficiently diligent and temperate. In any case, Meeker traveled in Colorado in 1869 and was soon convinced that this was the place where his ideal community might thrive.

When Meeker returned to New York, he approached his editor and friend, Horace Greeley, and told him of his plan for a Colorado farming community. Greeley supported his efforts wholeheartedly and offered free advertisements in the *Tribune*, as well as editorial endorsement. Thus confident in his plan, Meeker advertised for parties interested in forming an agricultural colony in Colorado. The invitation was clearly limited to "temperance men," and it was plainly stated that those without wealth were not welcome: "The persons with whom I would be willing to associate must be temperance men, and ambitious to establish good society, and among them as many as fifty, ten should have at least as much as $10,000 each, or twenty, $5,000 each, while others may have $200 to $1,000 and upward."[11] The critical concern was that the colony have adequate resources for economic development. The poor were not welcome, but representatives from all "professions and occupations [that might] enter into the formation of an intelligent, educated, and thrifty community" were urged to apply.[12]

The response was overwhelming. Within three weeks, Meeker estimated that more than 800 persons, worth more than $1 million, had responded. He noted that most of these persons were farmers, although a fair range of occupations were represented. Thus encouraged, he called a mass meeting, and the Union Colony was organized in New York City on 23 December 1869. At that meeting, Horace Greeley was called to the chair and made a brief speech before introducing Meeker, who then outlined his plan for the colony. The colonists would pay a $5 initiation fee and $150 for membership. Each member would be entitled to farmland (either 3–10 acres near town or larger tracts farther away) and could buy a town lot for $25 to $50. The sale of town lots would finance municipal improvements, and the membership fees would be used to purchase land and establish irrigation works. The Colony would be governed by an elected executive committee that would appoint a locating committee (to travel to Colorado and purchase the necessary land). It was stressed that the specific location would not be disclosed prior to settlement, since it was feared that speculators would appropriate the desired land. It was clearly stated that speculators were not welcome and that settlers would not be entitled to more than 160 acres,[13] ". . . with free homesteads as a basis, with the sale of reserved lots for the general good, the greatly increased value of real estate will be for the benefit of all the people, not for schemers and speculators."[14]

After some discussion, the meeting adjourned while a committee nominated officers and prepared resolutions. The meeting reconvened and the following officers were elected: President: N. C. Meeker; Vice-president: R. A. Cameron; Treasurer: H. Greeley; Executive Committee: R. Fiske, A. Murphy, N. Paul, C. O. Poole, and G. C. Shelton. Also, the assembly accepted the terms of the general plan that Meeker had outlined. Fifty-nine people paid $5 on the spot, and many more promised to send their initiation fee.[15] The Union Colony was underway.

From the very beginning, the corporation struggled to sustain its cooperative ideals while accomplishing its practical goals. According to the constitution and bylaws, the Colony was a joint stock corporation in which each member was entitled to one share. The Colony would finance irrigation and civic improvements, and the members would be required to pay for improvements that could not be covered by the available funds. Beyond this, members were required to improve their lands within one year, or they would not be granted title, and their membership fee would be refunded. Beyond these constraints and the stipulation that members must be temperate and "of good moral character," members were free to engage in commercial, agricultural, and industrial pursuits and to reap the profits of their individual enterprises.[16]

Among the Colorado governing authorities, discussed in previous chapters, the Union Colony was unique. Like the town companies of Denver and the Arapahoe County Claim Club, the Colony governed the distribution of land and town lots and settled disputes between claimants. Like the town companies, the Colony collected assessments (taxes) for municipal and even regional improvements. Unlike these frontier authorities, however, the Colony did not primarily defend preemption claims but was in the business of buying and selling land. In this regard, it was more like the land speculation companies, such as the Central Colorado Improvement Company, which was established as an adjunct to the Denver and Rio Grande Railroad (see Pueblo history, chapter 6). Unlike these land speculation companies, however, the Colony did not "buy low and sell dear" but did, in fact, lose money on the purchase and sale of land. The goal of the Colony was not profits but the establishment of an agricultural community. Hence the Colony attempted to control both the distribution of land and the behavior and character of the settlers.

Since the goal was to build a town for the members, the Colony suffered a distinct disadvantage in the local land market. First, the desired land had to be purchased, because preemption, as stipulated in the Homestead Act, would not allow the Colony to control distribution or collect assessment fees. Second, the land had to be purchased in contiguous sections to insure that the colonists would not have undesirable neighbors. The Colony planned to purchase land of varying quality and to distribute the land equitably among all members, retaining title until the land was improved and maintaining control over subsequent sale or development. Hence the Colony was at the mercy of land companies and private parties who had preempted adjacent properties. In order to avoid undesirable neighbors, the corporation had to pay what the market would bear for all lands in the desired area. Then, the task of equitably dividing these lands remained. The Colony faced difficulties on both fronts.

GAINING CONTROL OF LAND AND WATER

The executive committee appointed Meeker and Cameron to travel to Colorado to locate and purchase appropriate properties. They left on 3 February and were met in Omaha by H. T. West, who had asked to join the expedition and travel at his own expense. In Colorado, they met William Byers (the Denver editor), who directed their attention to the area surrounding Evans, which was at that time the last stop on the Denver Pacific Railroad. The railroad had been granted alternate quarter sections of the land adjoining the tracks, and the Denver Land Association was organized to dispose of these properties, along with whatever other property the company might acquire. Byers was an agent for this land company, so he was undoubtedly interested in the sale and was, as already noted, generally interested in promoting regional agriculture. In any case, the locating committee selected lands north of Evans, because the intemperate local population was deemed an undesirable neighbor.[17]

The Union Colony had collected close to $68,000 in initiation and membership fees, in order to purchase or preempt more than 60,000 acres of farm land. Unfortunately, the sellers of Colorado real estate demanded at least $3.00 per acre, and some tracts sold for more than $10.00. The Denver Pacific Railroad sold 9,324 acres, at between $3.00 and $5.00 per acre, for a total price of $31,058.58. The Denver Land Company originally agreed to sell an additional 120 acres for $15.00 per acre but later sold this property for $1,200.00 (or $10.00 per acre). In sum, the Colony purchased 11,916 acres for $59,040.88 and contracted for individual members to purchase additional tracts, for $3.00 to $4.00 per acre. The locating committee also filed some preemption claims in the names of various members, but records of subsequent purchases or preemptions could not be located.[18]

Aside from the unanticipated inflation in real estate prices, the Colony faced practical problems in purchasing local real estate. The New York corporation had no legal status in Colorado Territory and was thereby unable to transact business for its membership. This legal obstacle was overcome, however, by chartering a Colorado corporation, which included Meeker, Cameron, West, Byers, and Daniel Witter. Byers and Witter were named as incorporators to meet the legal requirement of five members, but it was understood that they were serving as proxies and would be replaced by actual colonists when such persons arrived on the scene. The fact that the Union Colony of New York was not a party to the original purchase was less important than it might have been, since all land was purchased for Horace Greeley, who was to hold it in trust for the Union Colony. Hence Greeley, not the corporation, held title. These legal technicalities notwithstanding, the fact that there were two Union Colonies created some confusion and led to considerable suspicion and distrust, once the actual settlers arrived.[19]

Undoubtedly, the settlers would have been disappointed in any case because the locating committee had failed to obtain land in the quantity, and at the price, that Nathan Meeker had promised. The discontent was exacerbated because the committee was less than forthright in explaining what had been accomplished in Colorado. Ralph Meeker (the founder's son, who had been appointed secretary) sent a circular to the membership, explaining that over 70,000 acres had been purchased and offering an extremely sanguine picture of the conditions that would greet the immigrants. Discount railway fares had been arranged, and detailed instructions were offered to guide the members to their new homes.[20] It is not clear why the circular exaggerated the extent of available land and failed to mention the fact that a Colorado corporation had been formed. It is likewise unclear why the colonists were not informed that the Meekers were returning to New York and would not be on hand to greet the settlers. Perhaps the colonists would have been less suspicious if they had been advised that Cameron and West would be administering the affairs of the Colony until the Meekers were able to conclude their business in New York and return to Colorado.

The estimate of available land is particularly perplexing. If one includes the property that was available for purchase (at $3 to $4 per acre) and the additional preemption claims that had been filed, the total figure might approximate 70,000 acres. The circular suggested, however, that all of this land had already been purchased and was ready for settlement, which was clearly not the case. Perhaps the secretary had only a vague impression of the total acreage and merely computed a figure that would include 160 acres per member. The secretary's records indicate that approximately 440 persons had paid their fees by April 1870.[21] If each member was to receive 160 acres, then 70,400 acres would be needed. Perhaps the secretary believed that sufficient land was available. In any case, the circular gave the impression that $155 per member had been sufficient to purchase 160 acres for each. It soon became apparent that this was not the case.

Colonists began arriving in late April, shortly after Meeker had left for New York, so Cameron and West had little time to consider the appropriate course of action. Unfortunately, the members of the executive committee were not on hand. Murphy, Poole, and Shelton did not arrive that spring, did not appear in the list of "original stockholders," and apparently never settled in Greeley. Murphy was not even listed as having paid his $155. Fiske and Paul did arrive in May, and L. Hanna, C. C. Monk, W. B. Plato, and W. C. Woodworth were added to the executive committee. At this point, Byers and Witter resigned, so that Colony governance would be in the hands of the colonists.[22] Thus the Colorado corporation had a governing committee of nine (including Meeker), which corresponded to the number of officers in the New York corporation.

It was, of course, apparent to anyone who had attended the New York meeting that the Colorado officers were not those who had been selected in New York. It soon became equally apparent that the Colony had not purchased even close to 70,000 acres, so the grumbles of discontent were soon mixed with allegations of chicanery. Understandably, the settlers wished to know where their money had gone and who was responsible for administering local affairs. David Boyd, a leading voice in the call for open disclosure of corporate actions, suggested that Cameron and West were guilty only of poor judgment, in attempting to conceal the facts, but there were others who complained much more vociferously. G. A. Hobbs published a series of allegations in the *Geneseo Republic* (an Illinois paper), claiming that the Union Colony at Greeley was "a fraud, a cheat, [and] a swindle."[23] It is not clear how many persons shared this impression, but there is no doubt that discontent was fairly widespread.

In any case, the executive committee released a circular on 16 May 1870 containing a complete statement of finances, an explanation for the Colorado corporation, and a plan for dividing the Colony lands (see Figure 4.1). According to the circular, members were entitled to purchase city lots ($50 for corner lots and $25 for others) and were granted one lot of 5 to 160 acres, depending on its distance from town. Members were also allowed to preempt 80 acres of government land (for which the Colony had presumably already filed) and to purchase adjoining railroad land (for which the Colony had a purchase agreement) for $3 per acre.

The 700 lots described in Figure 4.1 included the government land that the Colony had claimed but not the land that colonists could purchase from the railroad. Presumably, a colonist could claim one of the 80-acre lots (located four miles from town) and purchase an additional 80 acres for $240 or could choose from among the 160-acre lots (which were, apparently, farther from town). Thus the circular described what the members might expect in return

CIRCULAR.

Greeley, Colorado May 16th, 1870.

The Executive Committee of Union Colony submit the following statement for the benefit of its members, and those interested in the Colony:

LANDS PURCHASED.

Who From.	When	Acres	Cost per Acre		Amount
Denver Pacific Railway	April 11, 1870.	6,397, 66-100ths.	25 descriptions	$ 3.00	$19,192.98
"	" " "	2,766, 40-100ths.	12 "	4.00	11,065.60
"	" " "	160.	2 "	5.00	800.00
John Gates,	" 7, 1870.	320, 70-100ths.	about	10.00	3,200.00
A. J. Williams,	" 22, "	80.		9.00	720.00
W. R. Williams,	" 20, "	160.			2,000.00
David H. Williams,	" 20, "	160.			2,000.00
For obtaining the last three descriptions, we paid Dr. Tuttle for services and traveling fees, as per bill,					284.50
M. L. Smith,	April 6th, 1870.	100.			2,000.00
David Barnes,	" 11, "	126. 98-100ths.		10.00	1,269.80
E. Williams,	" 7, "	150. 18-100ths.		10.00	1,600.00
L. F. Bartels,	" 7, "	200.		8.00	1,600.00
G. W. Phelps,	" 9, "	378. 56ths.		10.00	3,788.00
D. H. Moffat, Jr.,	" 9, "	120.		10.00	1,200.00
J. Quigley,	" 7, "	160, and his homestead of 80 acres, with house,			2,800.00
"	" " "	160.			2,000.00
Bartels & Remick	" " "	320.		8.00	2,560.00
Chas. B. Farwell,	May 10, 1870.	80.		12.00	960.00

Total Number of Acres 11,916. 20-100ths.   Amount paid, $59,040.88
Preliminary Fees for Occupancy of Government Lands,   930.00

$59,970.88

TOWN LOTS.

There are in all, 1,224 lots, which are divided as follows:
Residence Lots, 50 x 190 feet, 20 ft. alleys, 144.
    "   100 x 190   "   "   408.
    "   200 x 190   "   "   108
Business Lots, 25 x 115 feet, 20 ft. alleys, 328.
    "   25 x 190   "   "   236.
Reserved for Schools, Churches, Town Hall, Court House, Seminary, and other public uses,   81 Lots.

RECAPITULATION:—Residence Lots, 660; Business Lots, 483; Reserved, 81.

PROPOSED DIVISION OF LANDS.

130	5-acre Lots,	650 acres,		70	80-acre Lots	5,600 acres,
120	10 "	1,200 "		20	100 "	2,000 "
100	20 "	2,000 "		10	120 "	1,200 "
80	30 "	2,400 "		10	140 "	1,400 "
80	40 "	3,200 "		10	160 "	1,600 "
70	60 "	4,200 "				

———Total, 708 members. ——— 25.450 acres. ———

West's circular on Union Colony operations (James F. Willard, *The Union Colony at Greeley, Colorado: 1869–1871* [Denver: W. F. Robinson Printing Co., 1918], pp. 27–29).

for the investment of $155, but it also suggested that Coloradans were especially well served by the financial policies of the Colony. First, the Union Colony paid top dollar for local lands. Those who had secured claims under the authority of the Saint Vrain Claim Club or the Weld County government were able to sell their lands for at least three times the price demanded by the railroad. A. J. Williams (a rancher and member of a local wagon road company) sold 80 acres for $9 per acre, but the rest of the Williams family, and Michael Smith (who had been active in the claim club), received $12.50 per acre.

In addition, some Coloradans were able to sell their land, pay their membership fee, and join the Union Colony. C. B. Farwell (former county commissioner) sold 80 acres for $12 per acre, moved his family to Greeley, and established a local ranch.[24] The fact that Colorado landholders such as Farwell were profiting from the Colony's land policies contributed to the distrust and suspicion, but West's circular provided all the details required for a thorough consideration of Colony affairs. Even the salaries of the officials were included, as was a rationale for the Colorado corporation. Thus armed with the relevant facts and assured that an independent audit was forthcoming, the members of the Union Colony began to consider their predicament.

After issuing the circular describing the administration of Colony affairs, the executive committee met almost daily to preempt the demands of the membership. The officials even sent a letter to the Secretary of War, requesting cavalry to protect the settlers from potentially hostile tribes. This must have been a concession to paranoia, but the committee spared no efforts in addressing the concerns of the membership.[25] The committee arranged for the construction of a public hall, the planting of trees, the provision of coal, and the survey and distribution of property. These actions were detailed in the minutes of their proceedings, and it is apparent that the officers wished to avoid any hint of impropriety.

It should also be noted that the board served without compensation, except for the officers. The demands of their unpaid offices were obviously a burden, but the committee did not consider offering salaries. When Nathan Paul reported that he could no longer serve without compensation (on 23 May 1870), his resignation was accepted. Thus for the two weeks preceding Meeker's return to Greeley, a committee of seven struggled to anticipate the demands of the infant settlement.[26] In the closing days of May, the committee faced a series of problems that required immediate attention. First, it was reported that colonists were appropriating the private property of the Colony and claiming usage (if not property) rights on the basis of membership. Also, one colonist appeared before the board, complaining that he had selected a lot before the claim register was opened and had begun improvements but was later informed that the land had been claimed by another settler. Finally, it was reported that persons were purchasing memberships and claiming lots with the intention of speculation and subsequent sale.

The committee responded to each of these problems, ordering that the private property (wagons and blankets) of the Colony be sold (not donated), recognizing prior appropriation (in good faith, by paid-up members) as the basis for property rights, and reaffirming the rule that no one might hold more than one claim, either by preemption or purchase. In fact, the committee adopted a set of resolutions, designed specifically to deal with speculators. First, the price of membership was increased to $200 (as of 6 June 1870). New members had the same rights as others, except that their fees were not refunded if they failed to improve their claims within one year.[27] Since they could hold only one claim and could not obtain refunds for additional purchases, the speculators were effectively dispossessed.

Having thus discouraged speculators and sustained the claims of the pioneer colonists, the executive committee proceeded to administer the routine affairs of the Colony. Arrangements were made to establish a school, to negotiate with the railroad for a depot, to extend the irrigation works, and to appoint a water supervisor. To finance the irrigation efforts, the Colony assessed a tax of one cent per foot on property adjoining the ditch. It was also determined that the Colony should make arrangements to organize a municipal government.

When Nathan Meeker returned to Greeley, in the second week of June, the executive committee was at wits' end. The Denver newspapers offered glowing reports of the Colony's progress and published replies to critics, but even these reports could not ignore the discontent or "dissatisfaction" that was evident in Greeley politics.[28] The executive committee attempted to deal with specific problems regarding the distribution of land but hoped that the colonists might take responsibility for general governance. Unfortunately, Colorado Territory imposed a one-year residency requirement for all public officials, so popular governance was not possible before the spring of 1871. Nevertheless the committee decided that an election should be held, if only to generate some sense of democratic due process. The initial proposal was for a special election to fill the seat vacated by Nathan Paul and replace the appointed members of the executive committee. The final decision, however, was to hold a general election for all nine members.

On Thursday, 9 June, the executive committee called for a general election to be held on Monday, 13 June. On Saturday evening, an outdoor mass meeting was held, and Nathan Meeker addressed the colonists, providing a complete statement of Colony affairs. He was followed by General Cameron, who offered a rousing speech on the future prosperity of the community. The colonists then nominated nine persons for positions on the executive committee, and these nominees were elected on Monday (13 June). Newspaper reports stressed the fact that most of the original members were reelected and suggested that the election served mostly as a statement of public confidence.[29]

The newly elected committee met every two or three days and continued with the business of land and water rights, but the people "out of doors" were routinely involved in decisionmaking. On 18 June, those attending a public meeting passed a series of resolutions, which the executive committee later recorded in its proceedings:

> Resolved, That it is the duty of the executive committee to see that proper title with the right to water be properly conveyed to each individual member; . . . Resolved, That in the true spirit of colonization, any member entering upon his lands—a part or the whole—to build, in good faith, shall be entitled, at once, to his deed for his business lot, his residence lot and his outlying land, upon respectively paying for the same.[30]

The resolutions contained explicit instructions for the governing officials and offered a reasonable profile of membership concerns. They declared that the executive committee should guarantee water rights for all Colony lands and grant title to all properties claimed by paid-up members. Also, a free public school should be opened "at the earliest practical moment," and a clause should be included in all deeds prohibiting the manufacture and sale of liquor. Until a municipal government could be elected, the executive committee should serve as a government, but the members should serve without compensation except for "actual services rendered by the president, superintendent, and secretary." Finally, an independent auditing committee should be appointed and should issue a monthly financial statement.[31]

The concerns of the membership were not ignored by the committee. Not only were these resolutions considered (and generally implemented), but the executive committee continued to encourage popular participation in governance. On 5 July, the committee called a public meeting to consider the proposed "herd law" that would prohibit members from keeping livestock "running at large." Then, on 16 July, an election was held to replace Horace Greeley with a local treasurer. Thus elections and public meetings sustained popular participation in government, despite the lack of municipal governance, while the corporation attempted to manage the affairs of the settlers.[32] In this regard, the settlers developed a tradition of popular political struggle in defense of class-based interest. The farmers, in particular, gained valuable experience in the struggle to control the land and water needed to sustain small-scale family farming.

The farmers were vitally interested in the administration of Colony affairs because the corporation held title to their land. As indicated in the popularly endorsed resolutions, title was an issue of critical importance since the farmers wanted to secure their property rights before investing in costly improvements. In sum, the basis for popular discontent was threefold. First, there was concern that the members of the New York corporation were suffering at the hands of the Coloradans, since Coloradans clearly benefited from dealing with the corporation. Second, the members desired not simply land but legal title, which the Colony was loath to grant. Finally, the Colony promised water, and there was little evidence of a satisfactory irrigation system. The protracted conflict between colonists and Colony did not stem from inefficiency or incompetence. The Colony attempted to sustain its control of land and water in order to establish the agricultural community that the founder had envisioned. To accomplish that end, the Colony needed to maintain a basis for its control and had to secure the commitment of members by tying their individual interests to the collective enterprise.

At least initially, the Colony succeeded on both fronts. The locating committee had secured its claim to most of the locally available land, and the executive committee continued to pay inflated prices for adjoining lands, which would be sold only to members and only in plots of 160 acres or less. Obviously, this was not a money-making proposition, but it secured control by the Colony. The corporation bought its way into the land market, enticing sellers and preempting purchasers. Not only were speculators driven from the market, but no one except a colonist could afford to buy. No one could compete with a company that bought land for $10 and sold it for $3. Hence settlers were induced to join the Colony. Those who desired to speculate were driven from the market, and those who wished to settle were forced to abide by the Colony's rules.

Control of water was based on the same principle. The Colony claimed riparian water rights for all its lands and guaranteed water to members in exchange for a small assessment charge. This preempted any attempts to sell water and left the colonists with no choice but to pay the assessed fees. Unfortunately, the Colony underestimated the expense and difficulty of irrigation, and its control of water became subject to increasingly bitter disputes. In the short run, however, the Colony did manage to control its land and thereby its members and to provide a limited supply of water that allowed for a modest degree of cultivation. There were continuing rumbles of discontent and ongoing problems that plagued the executive committee, but lands were distributed throughout the spring and summer of 1870, and the agricultural community was established more or less according to plan.

THE FARMING TOWN OF GREELEY

Once the city lots and the outlying lands were distributed, Greeley began to establish itself as a commercial center for local farmers. As Hall notes, "By the end of the first month the colony had three general provision stores, two bakeries, a like number of meat markets, one hotel, a boarding house, a blind, sash and paint shop, an artist's studio, a bank, a post office, a railroad depot, and a telegraph station."[33] The census of 1870 offers a similar profile of local enterprise. The only manufacturer was a hatmaker, who probably claimed more wealth than sales. The town was, however, overrun with professionals, particularly doctors and lawyers, although there was only one banker and no real estate or insurance agents.

Table 4.1. displays the distribution of wealth over class categories, which indicates the extent to which Greeley was an artisanal farming community. Generally, these data indicate a dearth of both wealthy employers and propertyless workers. Merchants and professionals constituted the bulk of the nonlaboring classes and controlled the majority of nonlaboring class wealth. The only representatives of the owner-employer class were the hatmaker and two ranchers, whose contribution to the local economy was minimal. Even some farmers employed one or two laborers, but most of the laboring class households were farmers and artisan-shopkeepers. These "artisan" households constituted 47 percent of the population and controlled 40 percent of the wealth, reporting an average of over $1,500 per household. Even the "workers," who presumably worked for wages, reported an average of $250 per household. Overall, it seems reasonable to characterize Greeley as a commercial center for local farmers, in which the laboring classes (mostly farmers who relied on family labor) controlled an unusually large proportion of local wealth, compared to other towns in 1870 Colorado. In short, Greeley was an artisanal economy, based primarily on family farming.

The distribution of wealth across agricultural occupations in 1870, as determined by the Census, indicates the prevalence of small-scale family farming. The majority (83.6 percent) of the agricultural households were laboring pro-

Table 4.1 Wealth by Class Category for Households in Greeley, 1870

Class Category	Wealth	Percentage of Wealth	Households	Percentage of Households
Nonlaboring classes	$220,250	56.71	62	29.25
Financier	6,000	1.55	1	.47
Owner	29,500	7.59	3	1.42
Professional	74,050	19.07	25	11.79
Merchant	91,450	23.55	18	8.49
None	19,250	4.96	15	7.08
Laboring classes	168,100	43.29	150	70.75
Artisan	155,830	40.13	101	47.64
Worker	12,270	3.16	49	23.11
Total	388,350		212	

Source: U.S. Bureau of the Census (1870) Population Schedules for Weld County, Colorado Territory.

Data come from population of occupied dwelling units, aggregated to household level and collapsed into class fractions based on occupational title.

prietors (farmers who relied primarily on family labor), and these farmers claimed 92.7 percent of agricultural wealth. Employment was not unknown, but it was the exception rather than the rule. Less than 10 percent of the farming households were farm laborers, and they claimed, on average, $340 in wealth (compared to $1,671 for farmers).

It is likely that the wealthiest farmers employed a few laborers and that even farmers of moderate means employed some seasonal labor. It seems reasonable to conclude that wage labor was uncommon, however, and that the laborers had the opportunity to become independent farmers. Even after the increase in membership fees, one could still join the Union Colony and claim a homestead for only $200. Given the cost of subsistence and the capital investment required for cultivation, the average laborer was, perhaps, not quite able to pay the membership fee. Nevertheless, family farmers constituted the bulk of the agricultural population, and farm laborers were at least potentially capable of joining the ranks of the landed laborer.

Generally, one may conclude that "artisans" (including family farmers and craft-title shopkeepers) controlled the essential means of production and thus sustained artisanal petty-commodity-production. One might argue that farmers were not artisans but petit bourgeois property owners, but this term obscures more than it clarifies. Blacksmiths, bakers, and even some gold miners might own property, but they are distinguished as laboring classes because they physically labored in productive enterprise (unlike the merchant, who appropriated profits based on the productive labor of others, including transportation workers as well as commodity producers). In any case, Greeley farmers were able to exert considerable influence within the Union Colony corporation. The officials elected in New York or appointed in Colorado were all members of nonlaboring classes, but after the initial controversy between colonists and the Colony, the laboring classes were able to elect their own representatives. The executive committee of April 1870 (including those persons appointed by Cameron and West) was composed of one banker (West), two professionals, and five merchants, but the committee elected in June 1870 contained three farmers and only two merchants. Thus even before the organization of the Greeley municipal government, the farmers were well represented on the Union Colony governing board.

Union Colony officials spared no efforts in attempting to serve the expressed interests of the farmers, but they were caught between the boosters, the farmers, and the stated purpose of the corporation. The boosters wanted to attract labor and capital in the interest of economic development, thus ensuring that their investment in local real estate would yield dividends and that local trade would increase. The farmers wanted to secure their control of land and water to guarantee that they would reap the benefits of their invested capital and labor. Despite the interests of boosters and farmers, the corporation had to control immigration as well as land and water in order to establish a temperate farming community, in keeping with Meeker's vision.

The Union Colony had to control not only the character of the settlers but the resources required for economic development. The initial fees were not adequate for the irrigation project, and problems with wandering livestock created additional expenses for the corporation. Unless the Colony retained legal title to land and water it could not tax the members to finance economic development. Attempting to induce voluntary contributions was problematic, at best, since the farmers were still suspicious of the intentions of the Colony officials. It was extremely difficult to convince them that the corporation was serving a collective interest in financing economic development efforts. This became increasingly difficult as the boosters gradually gained control of the Union Colony.

The Colony had relied on tax assessments to raise additional revenues for the irrigation project, but it still faced financial difficulties in 1871. Given the lingering suspicions of the local farmers, it was determined that the Colony should sell not only membership but shares of stock to those settlers most committed to economic development. This would allow the merchants and businesspersons of Greeley to bear additional financial burdens that would yield an appropriate return when the value of Greeley real estate increased. In addition, those most interested in economic development would gain control of the corporation by virtue of their stock ownership. Allowing these individuals to purchase large shares of stock would solve two pressing problems. First, it would raise revenues. Second, it would ensure that the interest in economic development was the dominant interest among the shareholders. Those who invested in additional shares would control the corporation and thus ensure its commitment to economic development, which might increase the value of their shares.

The sale of stock and the voting privileges of the large shareholders exacerbated the conflict between the Colony and the colonists. The election of 1871 was thus animated by the partisan struggle between corporate and democratic interests, which was further complicated by a struggle within the corporation. This intracorporate struggle was based on a disagreement between Cameron, who wanted to encourage immigration and eastern capital investment, and Meeker, who was concerned that outsiders might destroy his ideal community. Initially, the Meeker-Cameron dispute was not discussed publicly in the interest of Colony unity, but it proved to be a bitter controversy, as became increasingly apparent in later years. Meanwhile, the partisan struggle of 1871 produced a confusing set of issues and interests that divided the colonists from the Colony and likewise divided Colony officials.[34]

A critical issue in this struggle was the debate on corporate versus democratic governance. The Union Colony was more than willing to relinquish general governing authority but did not want to abandon its corporate enterprises.

In 1871, the Colony still held purchase options on railroad land and retained title to a considerable amount of additional property. The corporation was still attempting to establish an adequate irrigation system and was routinely assessing not only farmlands but city lots in order to finance irrigation works. The Colony had also assumed responsibility for the construction and operation of a flour mill that was to be powered by an irrigation ditch that ran through the city. In addition, the Colony had taken steps to deal with the problem of stray livestock. As a first step, a resolution was passed to prohibit colonists from allowing livestock to run at large, but the Colony soon decided to construct a fence to protect farmers from neighboring ranchers.[35]

There were some colonists who felt that these enterprises might be more efficiently administered by the municipal government, since the Colony was less than totally successful in its irrigation efforts. It had been estimated that irrigation works would cost approximately $20,000, but the actual cost was over $400,000. Also, the flour mill was a fiasco, and the ditch that was to power the mill not only was inadequate but was a potential health hazard. Aside from problems with flooding, and the resulting property damages, the ditch provided a steady supply of stagnant water.[36] Furthermore, as already noted, the fiscal crisis of the corporation had inspired the executive committee to sell not only memberships but shares in the corporation in April 1871. The Colony still limited membership to "morally approved" persons and allowed no one to claim more than 160 acres. Within these limits, however, one could purchase shares in the corporation. Fifty dollars entitled the member to one residence lot (in town) plus two shares of stock. The sum of $155 entitled the member to water rights for 80 acres and the option to buy 80 acres of railroad land or else the right to select a residence lot. In either case, the member received seven shares of Colony stock.[37]

Aside from voting privileges, the major benefit derived from owning shares of stock was the opportunity to buy land in Greeley. The Colony was definitely not in a position to pay dividends, but a number of colonists purchased more than seven shares of stock, and one individual held more than sixty. These members were not allowed to hold more than 160 acres of agricultural land, but they were able to buy multiple town lots. E. T. Nichols, for example, held forty-eight shares of stock but was not listed as holding a "water deed."[38] The 1870 census lists Nichols as a retail grocer, reporting $18,000 in real wealth and $8,000 in personal wealth. He was, in short, a wealthy merchant who owned no farm land but did own valuable municipal properties and was in a position to influence the economic development efforts of the Union Colony.

This situation provided the foundation for one of the complaints against the corporation (and in favor of civil administration): the assertion that an oligarchy controlled a majority of the shares, elected its chosen officers, and set policy for the corporation.[39] The debate regarding corporate control and control of the corporation became more rancorous as the colonists began to consider municipal organization, and increasingly the debate divided merchants and farmers. Within the Union Colony, a reform party was organized in opposition to the Colony administration. Meeker reported the controversy as follows:

> In the first place, a meeting was held last Saturday night to consider the proper policy to be pursued in Colony matters, when it appeared that a party had already been formed, called a reform party, one object of which was to transfer all matters now regulated by a Board of Trustees, to what was called civil authority. . . . They also objected to the provision of the law which entitled a man to vote for every share he possessed, . . . They also objected to the sessions of the Board of Trustees being secret.[40]

The proceedings of that meeting were not published in Meeker's newspaper, which offered limited space for the concerns of the reformers. Nevertheless, on 19 April 1871, a letter appeared in the *Greeley Tribune* recommending that local residents take steps toward municipal organization.[41] The correspondent explained that a petition (containing signatures from two-thirds of the eligible voters) had to be presented to the county commissioners, who would then appoint trustees to serve until the next general election (in May). Had the letter offered nothing beyond this proposal, it might not have inspired the rancorous conflict that ensued. The correspondent noted, however, that colonists would be ill advised to accept an appointed municipal legislature, "for reasons too obvious to mention here," and should therefore proceed to elect (or nominate) five persons whom the Weld County Commissioners might then appoint.[42] The plan was to hold a popular election on the first Tuesday in May—the date scheduled for the election of Union Colony officers. In the Colony election, it was noted, "stock votes, not men," but the municipal electors should be men rather than shares of stock.[43] Having thus articulated the "democratic" critique of the corporation, the correspondent concluded by proposing that the newly elected government should exercise general governing authority and allow the Colony to administer the irrigation works.

This modest proposal inspired a series of meetings intended to nominate both Colony and municipal officers, but it soon became apparent that there were serious differences of opinion within the Colony. At the first "nominations" meeting, N. C. Meeker spoke on behalf of the Colony, stating that he saw no reason to change the policies then in force or to surrender corporate control to the municipality. He did, apparently, favor a municipal government that would not interfere with Colony affairs. Next, Cameron addressed the crowd, beginning with the announcement that he would not seek reelection to the executive committee. Having thus disassociated himself from Colony affairs, he went on to recommend that the Colony do all within its power to encourage immigration and to thereby expand its operations. His speech was followed by a discussion of corporate versus civil control, which inspired arguments about shareholder versus popular sovereignty. Even the temperance issue was raised.[44]

The second such meeting was held two days later, and it rapidly degenerated into a shouting match. The focus of attention appeared to be the character of General R. A. Cameron, and it was even suggested that he was an opponent of temperance. This seems particularly odd, since Cameron had first proposed that Colony deeds contain the antiliquor clause, stipulating forfeiture of title if liquor were sold or manufactured on the premises.[45] Nevertheless, Cameron's commitment to increased immigration and capital investment provoked fear of outsiders who might gain control of local enterprise. Since membership had been limited to morally approved, temperate persons, temperance became a symbolic issue that represented the interests of farmers and small-scale artisan-shopkeepers, who resisted the intrusion of national capital. The large shareholders and the wealthier merchants and businesspersons favored immigration and eastern capital investment that would increase the value of local enterprise and real estate. In any case, the partisans finally agreed to disagree and arranged to hold three separate nominations meetings.

Thus three separate parties offered a slate of officers for both Colony and municipal elections. The "administration" slate was headed by Meeker (for Colony trustee) and Cameron (for municipal trustee). The "reform" slate included Meeker but not Cameron. The "independent" slate included West and some mixture of the nominees of the opposing parties. As reported in the local papers, the "administration" slate was overwhelmingly successful, although there was considerable overlap in the opposing slates and much "ticket-splitting" among the electors.[46] None of the "reform" members who were not also included on the administration slate were elected. The only administration candidate who was defeated was E. T. Nichols, who lost in the municipal election to H. T. West (of the independent party). Meeker and his "administration" party continued to control the Colony, while Cameron and West left the Colony board to join the municipal government.

To some extent, the elections of 1871 showed that the balance of power was shifting toward the farmers in opposition to the merchants. Farmers claimed three of the five Colony Trustees positions, while two farmers and three artisan-shopkeepers were elected to the Executive Committee. The elected Town Trustees included one banker, one professional (surveyor), two merchant-shopkeepers, and one farmer. The struggle between corporate and democratic government tended to divide the merchants and the farmers, since the proponents of corporate government defended the merchants' interest in economic development at the expense of the farmers' interest in controlling land and water.

In addition, however, voters took sides in the Meeker-Cameron debate regarding the appropriate strategy for economic development. Cameron proposed that the Colony should sell more shares and encourage newcomers (including eastern and foreign capitalists) to invest in economic development. Meeker was more concerned with maintaining the local community and insulating the Colony from outside influences that might promote greed and intemperance. Cameron's position was associated with the "administration" party, while Meeker's concerns were shared by the "reform" party. The "independent" party represented a compromise position of sorts, which attempted to minimize the differences within the corporation.

Candidates who held a large number (22–61) of shares of Union Colony stock were most likely to be affiliated with the administration party. Only 20 percent of these large shareholders were identified with the reform party, although the reformers claimed 46 percent of the small shareholder (seven or fewer shares) candidates. To a large extent, the conflict was between large and small shareholders, the latter clearly desiring greater influence in local affairs.

This conflict was complicated by other disputes that created additional lines of alliance and cleavage. First of all, as noted in the letter to the editor that sparked the initial controversy, colonists were united in their distrust of the Weld County government and did not want Weld County to interfere with local affairs. As noted earlier, the Weld County Commissioners were all cattlemen, and their legislative efforts suggest that they were servants of railroad, land, and water companies. In short, Weld was a Caucus county, but Greeley was a Carnival town. Both the Colony and the colonists, including the "democratic" reform party, were suspicious of ranchers, speculators, and other intemperate persons, who seemed to dominate county politics.

Meeker, in his post mortem on the partisan struggle, described it as follows:

> Before Tuesday arrived several caucuses were held by each party and when they came together, each with a well prepared slate, which, as the event proved, was broken, they could not agree on any method, when a committee of conference was appointed. After being out more than an hour they returned, reporting that each party should hold its own convention, on Thursday evening, from which time the two parties had separate existence, one being named the Regular [administration] and the other the Reform party. During these sessions there were many sharp speeches, and the excitement at times ran high; in short, politics and office-seekers were in the ascendency, and there were the same scenes as are enacted among politicians elsewhere. There were two subjects, however, on which both sides agreed; these were in regard to temperance and education.[47]

These issues distinguished the frugal family farmer from the speculators and the cattle barons. Hence temperance became a symbolic issue, and allegations of intemperance masked attempts to disassociate persons from the common interest of the community, as defended by both the Colony and the municipal government.

Cameron came under attack as an intemperate person, because he proposed that the Colony spare no efforts in promoting immigration. The Colony still had land and needed funds for irrigation and fences, so Cameron saw immigration as the obvious solution. Meeker was more cautious in promoting immigration and more concerned with the quality of local residents. Meeker wanted to maintain Colony control of membership, which required that the Colony continue to control land and water. Cameron also wanted to sustain Colony control but wanted to expand the membership base. Thus Cameron's plan for a bigger corporation elicited fears of outsiders and inspired opponents (and "reformers") to wave the flag of temperance.

The two competing parties developed in the debate over control of the Union Colony, and they generally represented the interests of large and small shareholders. Although the administration triumphed, the small shareholders fared better in the municipal elections, where one independent candidate (West) defeated the administration's nominee (Nichols). In this case, the people elected a former Colony trustee (who held only fourteen shares of stock) and defeated a relative newcomer (who held forty-eight shares of stock). In the same contest, Cameron (who was obviously an old-timer but who held no stock in the corporation) gained municipal office on the administration ticket. Clearly, the struggle within the corporation became confounded with the struggle between old-timers and newcomers and the general distrust of outsiders.

Within the Union Colony the debate focused on tactics for extending or sustaining corporate control. Within the population, however, the debate encompassed both corporate versus democratic and insider versus outsider issues. Meeker (who owned twenty-one shares of stock) made it clear, in his analysis of the 1871 election, that the people "out of doors" were less rational and efficient than a governing committee, and his paternalistic concern for the membership was apparent.[48] His paternalism was probably a source of irritation to Cameron and to some of the "democrats" in the "reform" party. Meeker appealed to the latter, however, in his distrust for outsiders. This, combined with his paternalistic concern for the people, allowed him to run on the reform ticket. On the other hand, a commitment to corporate control united Meeker and Cameron, allowing both of them to run on the administration ticket. Thus Greeley politics continued to accommodate populist and corporate interests that were united by xenophobia.

The colonists were not really paranoid, however. They were surrounded by hostile actors, so they continued to defend themselves in the region by fencing their lands, defending their corporation, and fighting intemperance. If they were to succeed, they would have to transfer authority from the Colony to the municipal, then county, then state government. The opening move in this direction indicated the path for the future. The Colony would surrender authority to civil government, so long as civil authorities continued to protect the colonists from outsiders. The newly elected town government seemed to be satisfied with this agreement.

THE CHALLENGE OF NATIONAL INCORPORATION

The Greeley Board of Trustees held their first meeting on 10 June 1871 and immediately established their commitment to the principles of the Union Colony.[49] After electing Cameron president and appointing a town clerk, three ordinances were passed. The first set the time for subsequent meetings, the second prohibited the manufacture or sale of liquor, and the third prohibited animals from running at large. On motion, N. D. Wright (a farmer) was appointed to select an appropriate site for a city pound. The meeting then adjourned.

For the next month, the board was preoccupied with efforts to restrain wandering livestock and to gain control of municipal properties. After obtaining a survey of the city, the board sent representatives to the Union Colony, asking for title to city lots, for water rights on all ditches running through town, for quit claims (relinquishing ownership) on all municipal improvements (such as trees), and for the donation of sufficient land for the construction of a city pound and a town hall. At their meeting of 11 July 1971, the Union Colony trustees granted all of the above, retaining only right-of-way for the construction of their flour mill and the ditch that was to power same.[50] Thus the cooperation of Colony and civil authority was apparent from the outset.

The Colony was undoubtedly happy to be free of many mundane responsibilities. In August 1871, the Colony sent the municipal board a note, suggesting that the grade on Maple Street required attention. It must have been a welcome change for the Colony to have been the petitioner in this affair. In any case, the civil authorities seemed more than willing to take charge. The board appointed a committee on streets and alleys and proceeded with its administrative responsibilities. In September, they ordered that water not be allowed to flow through the ditches until winter, since stagnant water posed a health hazard. The board then voted to pay its members two dollars per meeting and turned its attention to taxation.

There is little evidence of conflict between Colony and town authorities, although taxation might have been a controversial issue. The Greeley board called a general meeting of the interested public to inspect and discuss the tax assessment roll. The records indicate a meeting on 28 October 1871, attended by "many citizens," but there is no reference to specific disputes. Two days later, however, when the board met again, they agreed to only one revision of the assessment roll. The proposed tax of five dollars per share on Union Colony stock was, on motion, stricken from the assessment roll. Aside from this, there were potentially divisive issues, such as a petition asking the board to abate the public nuisance represented by the water power canal (that was to drive the Colony flour mill), but the board deferred action on this request. In general, it appears that the civil authorities tried to avoid conflicts with the corporation. The municipal authorities focused their attention on stray livestock and druggists who were suspected of selling liquor "for medicinal purposes," while the Colony worked on its irrigation and fence projects. Thus they cooperated in sustaining the family farmer and in protecting themselves from the outside world. But such a policy could not long endure, since the county and the territorial governments could not be ignored.

Greeley residents could not control local land or water without making claims on regional authorities. The Union Colony had bought its way into the local land market and was attempting to fence out the cattle and to appropriate the waters of the Cache La Poudre River. Ultimately, both efforts would require regional authority, but the isolationist policies of the Meeker regime posed serious problems in the search for allies. Colorado leaders (such as William Byers) were promoting immigration and expansion in attempting to attract sufficient population to justify the claim to statehood. Isolationists were not welcome.

Closer to home, Greeley was forced to rely on the authority of Weld County in order to enforce local ordinances. Evans was the seat of Weld County, and although the local Justice of the Peace was responsive to the claims of Greeley authorities, Greeley and Evans clearly faced distinctive problems in local government. In the Justice Court, twenty-one cases on the criminal docket (1871–1876) named the people of Greeley as plaintiffs. As indicated in Table 4.2, almost all of these were cases of trespass against the owner of stray livestock. If the owner claimed the stock, a fine and court costs were

Table 4.2 Criminal Cases by Court by Offense for Weld County, 1871–1876

Offense	Justice of the Peace Court, 1871–1876		Territorial District Courts, 1871–1872
	Cases Naming Greeley as Plaintiff	Cases Not Naming Greeley as Plaintiff	
Trespass (stray stock)	18	—	—
Nonpayment of taxes	3	—	—
Persons		10	8
Property		12	8
Government		2	14
Total	21	24	30

Source: Justice of the Peace Court: Greeley Municipal Museum; District Court: Weld County Courthouse, Greeley.

collected. If not, the animal was sold at auction. This obviously proved to be a source of revenue for the city and a source of livestock for local residents.

The other cases that appear on the docket suggest the types of cases prosecuted in Evans and elsewhere in Weld County. In the J.P. court, the standard set of assault and larceny charges was complemented by violations of liquor licensing laws, an abduction/rape, fraud, and murder. The territorial district court docket contained more crimes against government, including adultery, gambling, operating a tippling house on the Sabbath, riot, and contempt. Other charges included murder, assault, larceny, and altering cattle brands.

The riot charge is particularly interesting, because one of the defendants was Nathan Meeker's son. In October 1870, after church one Sunday morning, a group of Greeley citizens went to visit a German man who was operating a saloon outside of town. While they were negotiating with the proprietor on the terms for purchasing his lease, the building somehow caught fire. Ultimately, the building burned to the ground, and the Colony paid $200 in damages, but criminal charges were brought against a number of the participants.[51] Apparently, no charge (other than contempt of court) was ever sustained.

Also noteworthy are two charges of altering cattle brands. These and at least two larceny charges were associated with efforts to defend ranchers who allowed their cattle to run at large. Local ranchers had vast herds wandering the plains of Weld County. In fact, by 1871 they had organized a roundup in the area so that they might collectively recover their wandering herds, brand the calves, drive some portion of the herd to market, and release the remainder to graze without supervision.[52] Ironically, the territorial courts were defending the rights of the open range while the Justice of the Peace prosecuted the owners of trespassing cattle.

In this regard, one can distinguish the interests of the Greeley farmers from the interests of the Weld County ranchers by the content of the criminal dockets in the Justice and District courts. Greeley was the plaintiff in roughly half of the Justice Court cases, and virtually all of these cases were efforts to control wandering livestock. Elsewhere in Weld County, the court was struggling to contain the excesses associated with saloons and gambling halls and to protect the ranchers from livestock thieves. The Justice Court was defending the interests of the Greeley farmers, but the fine for trespass was less than $10, while those suspected of altering brands were held on $2,000 bail. This suggests the relative importance of protecting crops from wandering livestock versus protecting the livestock owners from theft.

There were few ranchers in Greeley and their contribution to local wealth was insignificant. This was not the case, however, in Weld County, more generally, or in Evans in particular. Some of the largest Colorado ranchers were located between Greeley and the northeast corner of Colorado. Among them was John Iliff, who in 1868 had purchased $45,000 worth of southern Colorado cattle to supply beef to the railroad workers and federal troops along the Union Pacific line. Iliff's herd grazed in the immense open plains between Greeley and Julesburg.[53] Only seven households listed in the Greeley area (with a Greeley postal address) were identified as ranchers in the 1870 census, and these actors controlled only 7 percent of the local wealth. Two of these families, the Farwells and the Lemmons, lived in Greeley and belonged to the Union Colony. Other cattlemen, including J. L. Brush, later settled in Greeley, but the local economy continued to be dominated by farmers. In Evans, five rancher families lived within the city limits, and six more had a local postal address. These eleven families controlled 21 percent of local wealth. In fact, ranchers residing in Evans claimed 22 percent of municipal wealth (versus 5 percent in Greeley).[54] Evans also housed railroad workers and cowboys, who were not particularly welcome in Greeley.

It is then understandable that Greeley might find it necessary to build a fence. The region was dominated by cattlemen, and the county government offered limited assistance to the farmers. In fact a herd law had been passed by the territorial government in 1864. According to this law, ranchers were required to herd their stock and were liable for damages to crops. The law was in force in Weld County, and it probably provided the legal basis for Greeley's impoundment policy, but it seems that it was not generally enforced. Cattlemen established, by legal precedent, that they were not liable for damages unless the crops were enclosed by a "prescribed" fence, sufficient to prevent the ravages of livestock. Thus, it was impossible for the ranchers to be liable, since damages were sufficient evidence to indicate that the fence was not of "prescribed" strength. Cattlemen also received generous settlements from the railroad when stray stock were killed by trains. In practice, territorial and county law sustained the claims of the rancher.[55]

Even after the Colony completed its fence (spanning some fifty miles at a cost of approximately $20,000), the county would not grant the right to put gates across roads leading to and from the town. Overall, the county consistently frustrated efforts to control the range cattle industry in the early 1870s, and the same types of frustrations plagued efforts to control water. In fact, even after Greeley gained a foothold in county government, the control of water proved, at best, difficult.

As noted above, the Union Colony was overwhelmed in its initial efforts to establish an adequate irrigation system. To make matters worse, a group of colonists (including Cameron) established an irrigation company in Fort Collins, upstream on the Cache La Poudre, and began appropriating water from the source of Greeley's supply. The company was formed in 1873, and the following year was exceedingly dry, thereby provoking a conflict between the Colony and the irrigation company that its members had established.[56] Cameron, as already noted, had disassociated himself from the

Union Colony and was investing in other localities. Among other things, he was a major investor in the town of Colorado Springs. In any case, a convention for local ditchowners was held in 1873, but nothing was resolved and the struggle for water continued.

Meanwhile, an irrigation convention was held in Denver in September 1873 as part of the efforts to encourage economic development and attract immigrants. Since 1866, Denver had hosted an annual agricultural fair to celebrate the fruits of local efforts. Then, in 1872, the territorial legislature organized a Board of Immigration charged with promoting Colorado, in the true spirit of boosterism. Thus the irrigation convention was organized not to provide information for practical concerns but to celebrate the bounty of Colorado resources. William Byers was one of the movers and shakers behind the scenes, and he was a major actor at the irrigation convention, where he attempted to advertise the unlimited possibilities for irrigated farming in the region.[57]

Relations between Byers and Greeley had cooled considerably since Byers had greeted the locating committee in 1870. Part of the problem was Meeker's isolationism. Meeker was opposed to the efforts of the Board of Immigration, and this certainly inspired some of the vitrolic editorials that appeared in the columns of the *Rocky Mountain News*.[58] To further aggravate the Denver editor, Greeley residents generally opposed the optimistic assessments offered by the Denver irrigation experts. In fact, one Greeley resident was crucified in the editorial pages of the *News* for his statements on the limited potential for extensive irrigation in Colorado.

At the opening session of the irrigation convention, Byers and F. M. Stanton addressed the assembly, extolling the prospects for extensive irrigation works and encouraging capital and labor to commence operations. Then J. Max Clark, a farmer from Greeley, addressed the convention, indicating both his class-based interest in water and his perception of the farmer's friends and foes.

> ... when I read in the report of the proceedings of the Farmers Convention of last June, what all the ex-governors, judges, lawyers and politicians had to say on the subject of irrigation, it occurred to me that if, at this meeting, there should mingle in with all that hopeful, enthusiastic, profound, professional thought ... a little more of the practical, plodding, calculating element of the farm, it might not be inappropriate in a farmers' movement. ... Theoretical enthusiasm and persistent pluck and energy, has worked wonders; it has spanned the great plains with railroads, ... it has burdened the country with bonds; it might, Mr. Chairman, we fear, dig too many ditches.[59]

Clark then produced facts and figures and detailed the limited possibilities for extending irrigation efforts. The advocates of irrigation were dumbfounded

Downtown Greeley. Courtesy Colorado Historical Society (F-5508)

but soon found an expert of their own (a farmer from the foothills), who with the editorial support of Byers managed to dispute Clark's charges. Boyd, a pioneer of Greeley, takes some small pleasure in reporting that even though nothing was accomplished in the conference and irrigation companies later wasted much capital with little result, history proved that Clark was correct.

The expertise of Greeley residents with regard to irrigation should not be surprising. They had, after all, learned by trial and error through the course of four long years. Also, the local farmers had been gathering regularly to share their experience and educate themselves in the science of irrigated agriculture. By 1874, Greeley had developed the foundation for a viable agricultural community. It needed only to overcome the barriers imposed by regional authorities in order to sustain its claim to local land and water and to achieve a dominant position in county governance.

Greeley Takes Charge

In the mid-1870s, Greeley did overcome the barriers to economic and political control of local resources. Increasingly, the farmers of Greeley were making claims on regional, territorial, and national parties, and although the farmers did not challenge the dominance of the Republican Party, they were able to gain major concessions in partisan struggle. Neither the municipal government nor the Union Colony was a major actor in the farmers' political struggle. Municipal authorities continued to deal with the problems of stray stock and intemperance, while the Colony gradually reduced the scope of its authority. The Colony began selling its lands in 1871, by which time the pioneer settlers had been granted title, subject only to the temperance clause that stipulated that title would be forfeit if alcoholic beverages were manufactured or sold on the premises. In 1872, the Colony sold the remainder of its unclaimed lands. Then, after the fence was completed, the Colony began to sell its irrigation works to the colonists and remained primarily as a symbolic defender of the principles of temperance and small-scale enterprise. Meanwhile, the farmers began to develop their own political organization.[60]

The Greeley Farmers' Club provided the organizational infrastructure for the farmers' party, although the club was not overtly political, at least initially. In 1872, when Greeley made its first unsuccessful bid to become the county seat, the farmers' club meetings were largely devoid of political discussion. The proceedings of 20 November 1872 suggest that practical agrarian concerns predominated in these meetings:

> Judge Hanna—I recently brought a few of my cows from a mountain ranch, and have some milk on the table which I invite all members to taste. It is wholly derived from the dry grass of the plains, which at first sight looks so worthless.
> The milk being tasted was pronounced remarkably rich.[61]

But even though their interests were not particularly political, the farmers were in the process of forming a regional organization.

> A letter from Mr. Perrin was read, concerning a meeting that was to be held in Denver of all the Clubs in Colorado, to take place on Friday, December 13th. Three delegates are expected from each club, and in districts where there are no clubs, farmers may select delegates. Among the objects to consider are: A closer union, and possibly a united organization, which shall amount to a Territorial Agricultural Society; the beet sugar interest; farm insurance, and like matters. Ex-Gov. Gilpin will give an address, and F. R. Elliot Esq. will read a paper on tree planting.[62]

Although the meeting was to be concerned primarily with practical problems, it soon became apparent that the farmers would have to form a political party to achieve their collective interest. Meetings such as these provided the foundation for that party.

As merchants and businesspersons in Denver and elsewhere attempted to attract national and international capital investment in Colorado irrigation, farmers became increasingly embroiled in political struggle. Reporting on the importance of the Greeley Farmers' Club in January of 1873, Meeker offered the following political prophecy:

> From what we can gather of the drift of the popular mind through the country, important changes are about to take place, regarding the rights of farmers, and their powers; in fact, with regard to all who are engaged in productive industries, and as the farmer is more independent than any other, he is expected to lead the way. It will not be long before the farmers of Colorado will meet in council to consult upon common interests, and as the Greeley Farmers' Club is an acknowledged pioneer and leader, much will be expected from them.[63]

The farmers felt, at least initially, that they might cooperate with the merchants and businesspersons of Colorado who were interested in the development of regional agriculture, but it became increasingly apparent that the interest of Colorado boosters in attracting capital investment was in conflict with the farmers' interest in sustaining their control of land and water. In Greeley, the Farmers' Club established preferred trade agreements with local merchants in the spirit of cooperation, but this soon proved untenable. By June 1873, the local farmers had decided that their club could no longer be open to the public and that their trade agreements would henceforth be limited to merchants who were members of the club. Thus the Greeley Trading Club was organized as an intermediate step toward the organization of a local Grange.

> It cannot be said too often that this is not an act of hostility to the merchants, but is designed to bring them and the producing class into more harmonious relations; to establish confidence and fair dealings on both sides, and to make their interests identical. Those who are not trustworthy in their business transactions ought not to be connected with this movement in any manner. I think the traders with whom we do business should be members of our organization; that all additions should be admitted by ballot, and all should be pledged to secrecy in our business affairs.[64]

It soon became apparent that such cooperation would not be found in the Territory, especially in Denver, and that the farmers would have to fight the efforts to attract capital-intensive irrigation companies.

The first such battle was fought between Meeker and Cameron, in 1871, but their disagreement had been muted in the popular press, since Meeker wanted to promote the image of unity. By 1873, however, Meeker was prepared to publicly attack Cameron for collusion in defeating Greeley's bid for the county seat. Meeker reported as follows, in his call to arms:

> When Mr. Greeley was here, almost three years ago, he advised us to vote for outsiders for all county offices, for we were strangers and could be interested in nothing so much as in building new homes and in getting established, it would have a damaging effect to engage in political discussions. The first political agitation was as follows: Last year, the question of removing the county seat to Greeley was put to a vote when a singular state of affairs was presented. Most of the leading candidates for county and Territorial office lived in Greeley, and these candidates declared that the people of the southern part of the county would not only vote for them, but also vote to make Greeley the county seat. It was at once suspected that a bargain had been made, that they should be elected, and that the county seat should remain at Evans, and after the election was over the people of Evans laughingly confessed that this was substantially the case. I, however, denounced the scheme in the *Greeley Tribune,* and the result was the defeat of the candidates, while, of course, the vote on the county seat was against us. . . .
>
> My opinion on the county seat question is this: There is but little chance of our getting it, unless Greeley and the north part of the county shall grow faster than Evans and the south part, because the number of votes is slightly against us.[65]

Meeker then went on to detail the political treachery of Cameron, who had conspired against Greeley in alliance with "outsiders":

> . . . he had begun to form a sort of alliance with those we call "outsiders," and, picking out some passages of my letters to the New York *Tribune,* they combined to distort their meaning, and presently, stories "made out of whole cloth" were in circulation through the county. Instead of defending me he was against me. When the liquor business broke out again, he leaned to the side of the liquor sellers, . . .[66]

Thus Meeker exploited both the fear of outsiders and the temperance issue in rallying the Greeley residents to prepare for battle, in Weld County and in the territory. Ultimately, Meeker's efforts were successful in uniting Greeley residents in the struggle to control county and territorial government.

As Greeley voters continued to cooperate, they were able to make claims on Weld County authorities. In 1873, the county granted the right to close the gates and effectively enclose the Colony during the six-month growing season. Later, the county authorized the organization of fence districts that administered the enclosure of farming and grazing lands.[67] Greeley's influence within Weld County was clearly growing. In 1874 (after an unsuccessful attempt two years earlier), Greeley was chosen by the voters as the new county seat. The election was disputed, however, and Evans regained the title in 1875. Nevertheless, Greeley prevailed in 1877, although this election was also disputed, but this time Greeley retained its position as seat of Weld County as it does to this day.[68]

Greeley also prevailed in efforts to regulate irrigation. After J. Max Clark was attacked by William Byers and the Denver boosters for Clark's efforts at the irrigation conference of 1873, he became a leading figure in the organization of the Colorado Grange. In January 1874, he explained the purpose of the Grange and urged his fellow Greeley residents to join:

> A State Grange will soon be organized. When in full communion with the National Grange and the Executive Committee, we shall possess every advantage afforded by the order, in common with the Granges of the Eastern States.
>
> This order is founded upon the principles of economy in production and consumption, which have been taught by all great political economists in all ages in the world. It realizes the truth of the famous axioms of Frounde, that there are three ways of living: by working, begging, or by stealing. It believes with Wendell Philips, who in his address before the recent New England tea party said that the great question for reformers of this age is how to prevent men from accumulating $50,000,000 of money, well knowing that fortunes of ordinary magnitude can only be amassed at the expense of the laboring classes.[69]

The farmers of Greeley, and elsewhere, were developing class consciousness. Like the frontier miners of the Central City region, they claimed to represent the interests of the laboring classes in opposition to nonlaboring merchants and capitalists.

This newly discovered class consciousness, together with political organization, provided a basis for gaining control of Colorado land and water. Another irrigation convention was held in Denver in 1879, but this time the participants were concerned with practical matters and recognized the wisdom of the Greeley delegates. A number of problems faced the interested parties, such as diverging interests separating those who owned water rights (as in Greeley) and those who rented water from ditch companies, but the convention managed to agree upon a draft irrigation bill. Territorial authorities were less than helpful, but the legislature finally passed a law establishing irrigation districts with the authority to determine appropriation and usage rights. The constitutionality of this law was questioned, but Greeley residents appealed to the Supreme Court and the law was sustained.[70]

Thus armed with state regulations, Greeley organized the Poudre River District in 1879, and the governor appointed a water referee to determine local water rights. Water was divided on the principle of priority in usage, with the greatest shares being allocated to those who had pioneered in the irrigation business. There were some outrageous estimates of the carrying capacity of the pioneer ditches, but the distribution was more rational and less subject to dispute than was the case in other areas (such as Saint Vrain), where referees were not appointed in 1879. Some districts had to petition the governor to appoint referees in 1880 in order to avoid bloodshed.[71]

Greeley was not able to withdraw from regional politics but was forced to make claims on regional governance and ultimately to gain control of Weld County. Since ranchers and irrigation ditch companies appeared to dominate Weld County in 1870, how did a band of family farmers, led by a utopian dreamer, manage to gain the upper hand? By 1880, the family farmers of Greeley outnumbered the ranchers and speculators and were thereby able to control county elections. The question, however, is why family farming took root and how the farmers managed to gain control of sufficient economic and political resources to become the dominant county interest. The answer can be found in the economic and political organization of agriculture, both in Colorado and nationally.

Locally, the lesson of the first agricultural convention became increasingly apparent to all. There were limits on the scale of irrigation that was practical in Colorado, particularly in the 1870s. The English Irrigation Ditch Company soon learned that it could not provide an adequate supply of water to sustain local agriculture and could not, therefore, collect sufficient rent to justify the expense of operation.[72] Greeley residents learned the same lesson regarding economies of scale. The greatest opportunity for such economies was in the construction of irrigation works, but the rate of return on investment was exceedingly low. This limited the possibilities for additional investment in labor or capital improvements.

Since the Colony collectivized the irrigation works and even subsidized farmers by collecting money on city lots, Greeley farmers were in a favorable position so long as they did not overextend themselves (or fall into debt). The Colony's land policies inflated local real estate prices, which made credit available for local farmers. As twentieth-century American farmers have learned, however, it is dangerous to borrow on inflated property values, when the land cannot produce a fraction of that value in crops. Thus speculators and those who desired vast tracts of land were effectively driven from the market because they could not compete with small family farmers who owned their land and water and relied on family labor. This continued to be true in the Greeley area for most of the nineteenth century.[73]

Aside from their economic advantages, Greeley farmers had a number of advantages in both regional and national politics. First of all, they were a relatively small, fairly homogeneous group, concentrated in a single location. Most of them maintained a residence in town and met regularly to discuss their collective interest. A Farmers Club was established almost immediately, and this provided the basis for organizing the Grange (in 1874).[74] Thus the Greeley farmers were a cohesive and well-organized group, and they established ties with national political organizations that defended the rights of small farmers like themselves.

The cattlemen were also organized, but they were less homogeneous, less cohesive, and ultimately less successful in both regional and national politics. Despite their growing influence in the late 1860s, cattlemen were unsuccessful in their first attempt to organize. In 1867, the Colorado Stockgrowers Association (later the Cattlemen's Association) was organized in Denver to represent those engaged in the livestock industry. A number of problems were immediately apparent. Aside from the fact that these persons were dispersed geographically across the vast eastern plains, it seems that cattle and sheep raisers, beef and dairy producers, breeders and herders all had distinctive concerns. Even among the herders of cattle, it has been suggested that the critical problem was honor among thieves.[75]

The early cattle ranchers of Colorado, as in Texas, began with fairly small herds of Texas longhorns, which were more or less available for the taking. The practice of "taking up" calves of unknown parentage (called "estrays") was common throughout the cattle country. There was always some question about who owned what, and one of the purposes of association was to facilitate cooperation in returning estrays and respecting each others' brands. The first association, after limiting their membership to the owners of horned cattle, proceeded to hire a detective to locate and identify cattle thieves. Apparently, the detective found that the officers of the association were, in fact, the leaders of the cattle thieving ring.[76] That marked the end of the first attempt to cooperate on a formal basis.

When the association finally took shape in 1872, the nature of the cattle industry was already changing dramatically. The era of the cattle baron was in full swing, but the mid-1870s were really the beginning of the end. Cattle prices declined rapidly after 1873, and European and American capitalists began developing large breeding ranches that soon displaced the herders of the open range. The invention of barbed wire in 1874 marked the dawning of a new age. Expensive breeding stock was fenced in to protect it from the wandering herds of inferior beasts, so the dominant ranching interests soon joined the farmers in their opposition to the open range. A scenario that had been played out in the cattle towns of Kansas was repeated on the eastern plains of Colorado.[77]

The cattlemen of the open plains were also losing their battle in the national political arena, just as the farmers were becoming more successful. The Grange, the National Farmers Alliance, the Greenbackers, and the Populists were potent forces in national politics, and the concerns of farmers could not be dismissed by federal authorities.[78] Perhaps the most dangerous possibility was that the increasingly militant labor movement might ally with the farmers. With the benefit of historical hindsight, this might seem an unlikely possibility, but it was a clear and present danger in 1876. In the partisan rhetoric of the *Greeley Tribune* and the Grange, one finds ample evidence to suggest the possibility of a laboring-class coalition, but such a coalition failed to emerge because of divisions within the laboring classes that were effectively exploited by national and local political parties.

The economic circumstance and political experience of the Greeley farmers fostered a distinctive class consciousness. On the one hand, the Grangers viewed their interests as compatible with the interests of the laboring classes or at least with the interests of other commodity producers. On the other hand, the Greeley Grangers (as represented by their leading spokesman, J. Max Clark) distinguished themselves from the renter or wage worker who could not subsist as an independent commodity producer. In this regard, the more proletarianized segments of the laboring classes, including poor farmers, were scorned by the landed proprietors of Greeley. Thus the Greenbackers received limited support in Greeley, at best, even though they were able to exploit the tradition of class-based political action in defense of the working farmer and enjoyed the opportunity to participate in public, Carnival government.

Nevertheless, the political experience of the Greeley farmer had reinforced the salience of property rights as the farmers struggled, from the outset, to gain control of land and water. Early on, the farmers learned that not only merchants and speculators but cattle ranchers and even other farmers were making competing claims on the land and water that provided the basis for the farmers' survival. In this regard, it might be reasonable to argue that the Greeley farmers were not really a laboring class but were, in fact, entrepreneurial capitalists. They were not, however, particularly interested in employing wage labor, and they actively opposed immigration, which might have provided a cheap source of labor.

It should be noted that Greeley farmers were not incapable of cooperating with less privileged segments of the agricultural population. In the second irrigation conference, Greeley farmers, when attempting to develop some equitable basis for adjudicating competing claims, were able to cooperate with those who rented water. The diverging interests of family farmers and less fortunate segments of the laboring classes were not inevitable. Neither was their cooperation, however. The political struggles of the 1870s created considerable tension between the boosters who supported economic development and the farmers who opposed monopoly capital investment. Consequently, the Republicans and the Democrats attempted to preempt the more progressive elements of the farmers' movement. In the course of exaggerating the ideological and policy differences between the two major parties, the distinction between the "wealthy" farmers of Greeley and the "poor" farmers who were immigrating from the east was exaggerated in partisan rhetoric.

Republican efforts to divide the farmers focused on the interests of the small proprietor and offered little sympathy for wage laborers and others who did not own their means of production. Greeley residents were particularly susceptible to such partisan appeals, since they had established their agricultural community on the principle of landed proprietorship. The investors were not, in general, poor laborers, and they hoped to establish a community of economically independent, frugal family farmers. Horace Greeley expressed his distaste for wage labor in his initial address to the prospective colonists who had gathered in New York in December 1869. On that occasion, Greeley confided, "I dislike to see men in advanced years working for salaries in places where perhaps they are ordered about by boys."[79] Meeker expressed similar sentiments and consistently advised that men without wealth not consider immigration. In January 1874, he reiterated this advice in his newspaper:

> This country is especially not recommended for men with families who are without means, for there are no particular inducements, and probably they would do full as well in Nebraska, or perhaps where they were born and brought up. Nor are there any inducements for single men without wealth, though, if industrious and willing to work for fair wages, there is room, and in time they will be sure to make headway; but this they can do anywhere else and with full as much certainty as here.... Now there is just the same chance of getting employment here as in other places, and we know of no place where the prospect is brilliant for him who expects other people to hire him, unless that he may thereby get a start and in time become his own employer.[80]

The same lack of sympathy for wage workers is apparent in the advice offered by J. Max Clark, Greeley's leading spokesman for the Grange. He was a defender of the family farmer, so long as the farmer was an experienced and independent proprietor, as he was.

> I am frequently asked my opinion of Colorado as a farming country, compared with the Eastern States, and I answer without hesitation, that I consider it incomparably superior to any of them. When I say this, I mean for the intelligent, systematic farmer, for I know of no country in the world offering fewer inducements, for what I call numb skull agriculturists, than this one.... Not every man who grows corn in Iowa and Nebraska for ten cents a bushel, can succeed in producing wheat in Colorado for a dollar and a half, and all that class of men of migratory habits, emigrating originally from extreme Eastern or Southern States, notably from North Carolina, poor white by name, rentors by habit, who have rented land in every State from the original roost westward, and never succeeded in owning a foot of their own, may as well pass us by on the other side. This is no country for them.[81]

Clark's criticism of renters brought sharp response from a local renter, and the strain of conservative reaction that characterized the Greeley Grange was a continuing source of irritation for wage laborers and renters, who were better served by the platform of the Greenbackers. In 1878, when a Greeley chapter of the Greenbackers was organized, a correspondent explained the importance of the Greenbackers as the representatives of labor:

> I see by the TRIBUNE that you have organized a greenback club in Greeley. Let me say for your encouragement that, notwithstanding the opposition of the "hardware" press, controlled by the money interests of the cities, greenback men are multiplying rapidly, and if they keep growing as fast as present, our next President will be a greenbacker. The old parties are alarmed, and their organs talk seriously of trying to affect a union of both into one large "hardware" party.
>
> As the financial question is *the* question before the people, such a union is not improbable, and should it occur and insure the defeat of the greenbackers, still the agitation will be productive of lasting good; for it involves the question of the rights of labor, of class legislation, of a mounted aristocracy on the one hand, and slave labor on the other.[82]

The rhetoric of the Greenbackers distinguished them as the party of the poor renter, indebted proprietor, or wage laborer. To these unfortunate souls, the Greeley Grangers would recommend thrift and saving toward the purchase of an independent proprietorship. From the Granger perspective, the Greenbacker was a "numb skull farmer" or a wage worker without ambition. Thus in Greeley, as in Denver and elsewhere in Colorado, the laboring classes were divided by partisan appeals. The unskilled laborers were more susceptible to the race-baiting rhetoric of the Democrats, while the poor farmer, particularly the indebted owner or renter, was more susceptible to the rhetoric of the Greenbackers. These, together with the silver mining interests, sustained the Silver Democrat alliance with the Populists that unseated the state's Republicans in 1892 by electing the governor and controlling the State Senate.

Generally, however, the Republicans were more successful in controlling the various class-based interests in Colorado. In Greeley, in particular, the more conservative and wealthier farmers of the Grange continued to predominate and continued to support the Republican Party. Meeker reported as follows on the state election of 1878:

> The returns so far received indicate that Colorado is republican by at least 1,800 majority, or nearly double the majority of 1876. This is particularly gratifying when we consider the means adopted by the Democracy to blacken the character of the leading candidates on the Republican ticket. The Greenback element, too, is not nearly as formidable as many

imagined; two weeks ago one of their speakers claimed Weld, Boulder, and Arapahoe counties for that party, but the votes do not show it. The only towns, so far heard from, in which they have a majority, are Erie in this county, and Sunshine in Boulder county. In not one county have they a majority. Thus Colorado declares in favor of sound currency.[83]

The town of Erie was not a farming community but a coal-mining town, as were many of the Boulder County towns. Apparently, the coal miners were stronger in their support of the Greenbackers than were the farmers. It is clear that the Grangers were more powerful than the Greenbackers in Greeley.

The Greeley farmers had sustained their control of land and water and were not directly threatened by monopoly capital investment in Colorado agriculture. They were fighting against the railroads and the wholesale merchants but were in this regard allied with Denver boosters, who also were concerned with the cost of transportation and were promoting federal efforts to regulate transportation rates (see Golden history, chapter 4). Consequently, the Greeley farmers did not directly challenge the Republican Party but were accommodated by the Party of Order, just as the Greenbackers were accommodated by the Silver Democrats.

These wealthy farmers of Greeley continued to dominate Greeley politics and used local and county authority to defend their interests. As shown by the data in Table 4.3, the Weld County courts were primarily concerned with protecting property, although they had a fairly balanced docket. Before 1877, when Greeley became county seat, the Greeley Justice of the Peace Court was primarily concerned with stray livestock, whereas the courts in Evans were preoccupied with assault and larceny charges. After 1877, the fence district took care of strays, the water district took care of water, and larceny was the most prevalent case on the criminal docket. There were also cases of murder, violations of the territorial antigambling law, and cases of selling

Table 4.3 Criminal Cases in Weld County Courts, by Court by Offense for 1871–1876 and 1877–1880

Court	Offense against			Total
	Persons	Property	Government	
1871–1876				
Justice of the Peace	10 (.22)	30 (.67)	5 (.11)	45
District	9 (.18)	17 (.33)	25 (.49)	51
Total	19 (.20)	47 (.50)	30 (.31)	96
1877–1880				
District	15 (.25)	24 (.41)	20 (.34)	59

Source: Justice Court: Greeley Municipal Museum; District Court: Weld County Courthouse, Greeley.

liquor without a license. Nevertheless, in contrast to Denver and Central City, where crimes against government constituted more than 75 percent of the 1880 docket, crimes against property continued to predominate in Greeley.

This indicates the extent to which the interests of farmers continued to outweigh the interests of merchants and shopkeepers. Greeley residents had gained control of Weld County, but that control was contingent upon faithful service to the farmers. Even after statehood, the farmers remained the predominant political force in Weld County politics and continued to defend their interests as laboring proprietors, through defense of their personal and property rights. The boosters' defense of public order was limited to the defense of temperance. There was no resident industrial labor force (aside from the working farmer) and no saloons or gambling halls, so the threat to public order was minimal. As was the case in Central City, there was little crime in Greeley, largely because there was no substantial lower class. In Greeley, the family farmers used temperance as a shield against the excesses associated with monopoly capital investment and proletarian industry. Thus they joined the booster in defending public order, but in this case it was at the expense of attracting eastern capital and labor. The farmers placed definite limits on the boosters' economic development efforts.

Greeley was still temperate, and the Colony retained the authority to defend temperance, bolstered by the efforts of the Law and Order League.[84] In any case, threats to public order and labor discipline problems did not plague the farmers of Greeley, largely because they did not house a substantial population of wage-laborers. In partnership with the state, the farmers developed irrigation systems, established the sugar beet industry, and ultimately found Hispanic farm workers to provide the necessary labor when the local economy was capitalized.[85] These workers, who had not taken the temperance pledge, could not live in Greeley, which remained dry until 1969, but they could work in the fields and spend their unproductive seasons in Denver.

Thus the Union Colony, with its strange combination of corporate and cooperative structure, proved effective in sustaining the efforts of the family farmers. At least, it provided experience that must have proved useful in the Grange. Additionally, the banner of temperance and the distrust of outsiders placed Greeley residents in a favorable position to form national and regional alliances. Like the National Farmers Alliance, the farmers of Greeley eventually joined government and capital in early twentieth century efforts to effect labor discipline.[86] The local farmers were advocates of temperance, frugality, and discipline.

Greeley represents a most unusual version of Carnival town governance. Established by an eastern corporation and led by a utopian communalist, it remained for many years a family farming community. Efforts to secure the farmers' control of land and water inspired conflict between corporate and democratic interests, but the coalition of farmer and merchant was sustained in opposition to the cattlemen and land speculators who dominated surrounding Weld County. The Carnival coalition combined the interests of land, labor, and trade but was clearly dominated by the traditional, small-town, temperate, Protestant, family farmer. This relatively homogeneous and well-organized community was able to form coalitions with national parties and regional capital. Despite the nineteenth-century conflicts with Denver boosters and the Board of Immigration, Denver ultimately rendered valuable service in accommodating the migrant workers who might have posed serious problems in the Greeley community after the local economy was capitalized.

Thus the Denver boosters were able to accommodate the interests of the Greeley farmers, preempting their most progressive political movement through reforms that could only be effected by the Republican Party and facilitating locally initiated economic development efforts, within the limits described by populism, capitalism, and xenophobia.

PART TWO

Caucus Towns of Colorado

The three local histories given in part one indicated that economically independent and politically organized laboring classes did not necessarily engage in radical protest in opposition to monopoly capital penetration. Such radical protest was contingent upon the experience of proletarianization and the clear and present threat of national monopoly capital investment, which reduced the possibility of sustaining even relative autonomy.[1] Thus one might expect the most radical labor organizing in the coal mines and the industrial towns, particularly in southern Colorado, where national monopoly capital established large-scale coal mining, ore-reduction, and manufacturing enterprises employing an army of largely immigrant laborers.

But the towns in southern Colorado did not have significant labor uprisings. Pueblo never faced the problem of organized laboring classes and generally ignored the interest of labor in both economic and political organization. The same was true in Cañon City and in Golden in northern Colorado. As will be indicated in the following chapters, the laboring classes in these communities were essentially excluded from frontier government because they lacked the economic independence and political organization of their Carnival town counterparts. In these Caucus towns, frontier political struggles were limited to conflicts and competition between nonlaboring classes.

In 1859, the mining industry was controlled by the miners, but transportation was dominated by nonlaboring classes. The teamsters were initially independent operators, but Colorado businesspersons controlled transportation by organizing road and ditch companies that charged tolls for overland travel and rented water for placer mining operations. In the transportation centers, labor did not have the economic resources and political organization required to successfully defend its interest in local government. Consequently, these towns were controlled both economically and politically by coalitions among the nonlaboring classes. In southern Colorado, farmers and ranchers employed Hispanic labor and controlled the local economy on the basis of claim clubs or Spanish land grants. Generally, claim clubs and town companies, with periodic vigilante assistance, governed the southern Colorado frontier, and labor was essentially excluded from political participation.

The laboring classes of these Caucus towns were in general the most proletarianized. By the turn of the century, they were generally employed by national monopoly capital and were in general the lowest paid and least autonomous segment of the Colorado labor force. Nevertheless, the coal miners in the Golden (Jefferson County) and Cañon City (Fremont County) regions were relatively docile, as were the industrial workers of the Pueblo region (in South Pueblo and Bessemer). The experience of proletarianization and the threat of monopoly capital investment were not sufficient to elicit radical labor protest. It was only when the laboring classes had the tradition of political struggle in defense of class-based interest and the opportunity to defend their interest through public, Carnival government that they were capable of offering such resistance.[2]

There was substantial opposition to the intrusion of monopoly capital investment in the Caucus towns of Colorado. It was, however, local capital rather than labor that responded to the threat of eastern capital investment, exploiting the tradition of private, business-class government, refusing to recognize federal authority, and defending local control, at times through violent struggle. Thus local capitalists resisted national monopoly capital investment to the extent that their control of local industry was threatened and to the extent that they had a tradition of class-based political action, institutionalized in private Caucus government.[3]

The nature of local governance and the struggle to expand economic and political control in these communities will be the focal concern in the next three chapters. Golden will represent the transportation centers of the gold mining frontier. It was for nearly a decade the railroad center that connected the mining and milling operations in the mountains west of Denver. After losing the railroad war, Golden suffered capital flight but later became the home of Adolph Coors, whose brewery continues to dominate the local economy. Pueblo and Cañon City will represent the southern Colorado towns. Pueblo was the center of farming and ranching enterprises of the 1870s and later developed as a major industrial center. Cañon City was the center for farming, ranching, coal mining, and oil fields. By 1870, it was essentially a farming town, but unlike farmers in Greeley, Cañon City farmers were relying primarily on hired labor. These were capitalist farmers, but like the farmers of Greeley they resisted monopoly capital investment, particularly railroad and land speculation companies.[4] Consequently Cañon City did not attract the population and industry that local boosters actively pursued, but Cañon was sustained as a farming town and was also the home of the Colorado State Penitentiary.

CHAPTER FIVE

Golden: Denver's Western Rival

Golden never approached Denver in population or regional importance, but the two communities were jealous rivals until 1880, and Colorado historians have devoted considerable energy to the explanation of Denver's relative success.[1] Generally, these explanations have failed to recognize that Golden was not a commercial center but a business center in which transportation and irrigation were predominant concerns. Golden's relation to the mining and farming community was distinctive, and this provides the key to understanding the diverging paths of the two cities. Unlike Denver, Golden businesspersons and merchants were not challenged by an economically independent and politically organized laboring class. Instead, the challenge was to accommodate the interests of regional and national capital, as owners of Golden businesses attempted to extend their control of the Colorado transportation industry. Golden's competition with Denver was less important than the resistance of Golden businesspersons to monopoly capital and federal government when these national actors threatened the tradition of local, business-class control. In this regard, Golden was a classic Caucus town.

THE BOSTON COMPANY TOWN

In March 1859, a group of Boston businessmen organized the Mechanics Mining and Trading Company for the purpose of locating and managing a western city. Initially, each shareholder invested just over $100 and served on at least one of the committees that adminstered the details of purchase, finance, legislation, and transportation to the West.[2] This company arrived in Denver in the spring of 1859 and traveled west on the road to the gold mines surrounding Central City. Some fifteen miles from Denver, on the banks of Clear Creek, they established the city of Golden.

The Boston group was not the first to establish a settlement in the foothills above Denver. In 1858, Samuel S. Curtis had established the town of Arapahoe not far from the Golden townsite, but Curtis and his associates had all but abandoned that settlement by the summer of 1859, and the land was claimed by local farmers, or "gardeners," as they were identified in the 1860 census. One of these gardeners was D. K. Wall, a former California rancher and miner

Golden in the 1860s. Courtesy Colorado Historical Society (F-25557)

who had grubstaked John H. Gregory's prospecting venture in the spring and was one of the wealthy "oldtimers" in the Gregory Diggings.[3]

Wall and other interested parties were invited to join the Boston stockholders in establishing the Golden City Association in June 1859. Wall was granted 224 city lots and 56 shares in the corporation. His brother (J. C. Wall) claimed 96 lots for himself and an additional 208 in partnership with an attorney named J. F. Kirby. Other members of the association included W.A.H. Loveland and E. L. Berthoud, who became important actors in the local transportation industry, and Eli Carter, a lawyer who became prominent in local politics. The available evidence does not indicate how shares in the Association were divided, but the distribution was clearly not equitable. It appears that the Association sold shares and that each share entitled the purchaser to four city lots.[4]

As an administrative body, it appears that the Golden City Association was not unlike the town companies in Denver. In both towns, these organizations donated lots to prospective business owners and demanded that improvements be made within a certain length of time. Also, periodic assessments were collected to finance civic improvements, and lots were forfeited if assessments were not paid. In Denver, however, the original distribution of lots was more or less equitable. The Saint Charles Association stated explicitly in its charter that lots were to be divided equally among shareholders, unless an exception be approved by a two-thirds majority vote. The Auraria Association voted to donate one share per resident and prohibited anyone from holding more than sixty shares. In Denver, the largest original shareholder had fifteen city lots, while most owned only two or four. In Golden, on the other hand, the major shareholders cornered the market in city lots.[5]

In any case, the Golden City Association was the prime mover in local affairs. The partnership between local and eastern investors precluded the possibility of competing town companies, and the resources of the Association were sufficient to promote local enterprise. In this regard, Golden differed from the three communities discussed in the preceding chapters. Unlike Denver, there were no competing town companies. Unlike Central City, regional actors did not block efforts to control city lots. Unlike the Union Colony at Greeley, the Association was able to finance local improvements and sustain control of municipal enterprise. In June, the Association purchased the toll bridge that had been erected by a local pioneer and abolished the toll. Free passage to and from Golden was offered as an incentive to attract local trade. Buildings were hauled from the abandoned Arapahoe townsite, and lumber mills were established to provide additional building materials.[6]

In August 1859, Thomas Gibson, who was then publishing the *Rocky Mountain Gold Reporter* in Mountain City, described the rapid progress of the settlement at Golden:

> Golden City—surrounded on three sides by mountains, is pleasantly located on Clear Creek about a mile from the entrance of the gulch to Gregory, Russell, and the Spanish Diggings. It is at the "head of navigation" for loaded wagons. Hardly a month has passed since this flourishing little town was surveyed; it is a mile square, has about fifty houses completed, and as many more under way, contains in the vicinity about two thousand inhabitants, seventy of whom are ladies.[7]

Gibson certainly overestimated the local population, since the 1860 census listed less than a thousand residents, but exaggeration notwithstanding, Golden was a flourishing transportation center by the summer of 1859.

Local businesspersons invested in a variety of enterprises, but transportation was the predominant industry. In the summer of 1859, members of the original Boston corporation, in partnership with a few locals, formed the Boston Company, which operated a mercantile house, an express company, and a blacksmith shop. In addition, one of the partners (George West) began publishing the *Western Mountaineer* in December. The first edition included among its advertisers only two local merchants (including the Boston Company), but there were two local express companies, which were soon joined by a third, and the editor reported that local businesspersons had just organized a wagon road company.[8]

Golden was strategically located on the road to the gold mines, and it was established and sustained as a transportation center. In the fall of 1859, after the Denver merchants had failed to control the price of locally produced gold (see chapter 3), a correspondent for the *Mountaineer* asked why Golden merchants could not sell goods as cheaply as in Denver and thereby capture the mountain trade.

> All your merchants have to do to supply this extensive country will be to pursue a liberal policy, and although you have a large advantage in geographical position it will not do to take advantage of it by even charging the actual cost to purchasers of transporting their goods to this place, why cannot Golden City sell goods as cheap as Denver? you do not have to transport (in coming from the Missouri) as far by some twenty-five miles.[9]

But local merchants and business owners were heavily invested in transportation and found it more profitable to collect tolls on the goods transported from the mines than to engage in retail trade. Nearly every edition of the local paper reported the organization or operation of a new road company or a new ditch that was to bring water to the mines.[10]

Golden in 1860 was a town of small-business proprietors on the make. J. McIntyre, for example, was a member of the Boston Company and thereby had an interest in the mercantile, express, and blacksmith business. Aside from this, McIntyre, in partnership with other members of the Golden City Association, organized the Saint Vrain, Golden City, and Colorado Wagon Road Company and the Cibola Hydraulic Company, each of which employed large numbers of would-be miners and profited from the tolls or rents that the miners paid for transportation and water. One of the partners in these enterprises was B. F. Chase, who also invested in mining claims, was a member of the Consolidated Ditch Company, and was interested in a variety of related enterprises.[11]

The extent to which local businesspersons controlled the Golden economy was apparent from the 1860 Census data in Table 5.1, which displays the distribution of wealth over class categories. Nonlaboring households represented less than 20 percent of the households but claimed more than 60 percent of local wealth, which was pretty much divided between the business and commercial classes. In Denver and elsewhere in Colorado, merchants, shopkeepers, and professionals often invested in a variety of business enterprises, but most claimed a particular occupation as their predominant concern. In Golden, however, the distinction between commercial, professional,

Table 5.1 Wealth by Class Category for Households in Golden, 1860

Class Category	Total Wealth	Percentage of Wealth	Number of Households	Percentage of Households
Nonlaboring classes	$147,210	61.96	79	19.55
Business	58,550	24.64	24	5.94
Owner	2,050	.86	6	1.48
Professional	14,550	6.12	11	2.72
Merchant	65,650	27.63	25	6.19
None	6,410	2.70	13	3.21
Laboring classes	90,380	38.04	325	80.45
Artisan	86,345	36.34	279	69.06
Worker	4,035	1.70	46	11.39
Total	237,590		404	

Source: U.S. Bureau of the Census (1860) Population Schedules for Arapahoe County, Kansas Territory.

Data come from a 50 percent systematic sample (with random start) of occupied dwelling units, aggregated to household level and collapsed into class fractions on the basis of occupational title.

and business interests was difficult to establish. Nearly 6 percent of the households were identified only as "traders," compared to 2.4 percent of the Denver households. These traders (or businesspersons) generally reported less per capita wealth than the merchants, invested in a wide variety of enterprises, and did not operate a commercial establishment.

These businesspersons controlled nearly one-fourth of the wealth in Golden, and their corporate enterprises united them with most of the commercial and professional households. Davidson and Breath operated a clothing store but also owned a ditch company. Eli Carter was a lawyer but also invested in wagon roads, as did J. M. Ferrel, the proprietor of the Miner's Hotel. All of these actors were multiply connected in business, and they were all united as members of the Golden City Association.[12] They were not especially wealthy individuals, claiming less than $2,500 in average household wealth, but collectively they claimed sufficient wealth to finance their road and ditch companies.

Golden also contained an adequate population of "workers" to meet the demands for road and ditch construction, and it is likely that many of the "artisans" were also available for wage labor. Overall, the laboring classes of Golden were decidedly less wealthy than their counterparts in Denver and Central City. Average laboring class wealth was $278 in Golden, $509 in Denver, and over $1,200 in Central City. Similarly, average wealth for "artisans" (mostly "miners") was $309 in Golden, $569 in Denver, and $1,369 in Central City; for "workers," $88 in Golden, $299 in Denver, and $668 in

Central City. Golden workers were, by Colorado standards, relatively poor. Few of the "workers" had clerical or craft-title occupations; nearly two-thirds were common laborers. In addition, the "artisans" of Golden reported considerably less wealth than the Central City "workers."

Although Golden did not have a large population of wealthy employers, the combined assets of the businesspersons, merchants, and professionals were invested in corporations that employed wage labor. Undoubtedly, transient miners and other segments of the Golden laboring classes provided much of this labor. In any case, the laboring classes of frontier Golden were neither economically independent nor politically organized. The local newspaper contained no references to a printers' union or to price-fixing agreements by local commodity producers. The expressed interests of the laboring classes were not apparent in local politics. Instead, Golden businesspersons were the major actors, both as Association members and government officials. Golden was a Caucus town, governed by a united business class.

The Government of Property and Order

Until the Provisional Government of Jefferson Territory was organized in January 1860, the Golden City Association was the effective municipal government. Throughout the summer of 1859, however, the Association was preoccupied with municipal improvements and was not concerned with general governance. In fact, there appeared to be no government except for the routine administration of Association business. Lots were donated, shares were assessed, improvements recorded, and title granted. There is no evidence of competing authorities, crime, or even civil disputes. The Association controlled the distribution of city lots and established the standards for municipal enterprise.

In the fall of 1859, however, Golden got its first taste of vigilante justice. After a dispute in a card game, Edgar Vanover went into a rage, shot up the barroom, robbed a few shopkeepers, and threatened to kill anyone who stood in his way. Although he was disarmed before anyone was hurt, a group of citizens determined that Vanover should be hanged for attempted murder. A correspondent to the *Rocky Mountain News* described proceedings as follows.

> A meeting of the citizens was held, at which all the evidence for and against the prisoner was calmly considered. After cool deliberation it was deemed necessary for the safety of the inhabitants that he be executed: not a dissenting vote was given when the proposition was laid before the meeting. A committee was appointed to carry out the will of the people, and the sad duty was performed. We refrain from extending

our remarks, believing that all good citizens, when circumstances are known, will uphold the people of Golden City in performing an act that they believed to be a duty they owed to themselves and the community at large.

Yours,
Truth[13]

The city fathers did not condone the execution, however. One week later, in a letter to the *Rocky Mountain News,* the president of the Association and other local leaders described the "lynching" as follows.

Editor News,
   Dear Sir—An article appeared in your issue of last week, signed "Truth," which did not, in scarcely a single particular, contain the truth in regard to the late lynching case at Golden City. The Citizens, it is believed nine-tenths of them, repudiate the entire act of the mob that hanged Edgar Vanover, on Monday Sept 5th.[14]

The citizens of Golden had not yet established a popular tribunal, as in Denver, so local law and order efforts were at least initially beyond the control of the "people." By December 1859, however, lawyers and politicians had established a local "citizens' court." "Judge" Eli Carter organized a citizens trial on 17 December, which served as a showcase for local attorneys. Kirby (J. C. Wall's partner in the Association) prevailed in defending a local resident charged with stealing supplies from a local ranch, and West extolled the virtues of due process in his newspaper report. In that same edition of the *Western Mountaineer,* Carter announced that he had been appointed acting county recorder and was a candidate for that office in the upcoming Provisional Government election.[15]

In that election, held 2 January 1860, no municipal officials were elected. The Golden City Association continued to control the trade in city lots, and other municipal affairs were administered by committees selected in public meetings. "The people" met in late January to select a site for the city cemetery, and "property owners" met early in February to determine the assessment rate for municipal property. Then, in March, the decision of the assessment committee was overturned, when a "citizen's meeting" determined that real estate, but not improvements, would be taxed. The "citizens" then proceeded to elect an assessor and a treasurer, both of whom were members of the Golden City Association.[16]

After dispensing with the issue of taxation, the citizens reconvened to consider the propriety of organizing a municipal government. This endeavor received strong editorial support, and a series of meetings ultimately produced both a city charter and a slate of officers. Then, on 10 April 1860, a full slate of municipal officers was elected. Of course, Association members were well represented in municipal government. S. M. Breath (clothier and ditch owner) was recorder; Loveland was treasurer, and two of his business partners (Davis and Smith) served on the board of aldermen. All of the board members were members of the Association, including the enterprising attorney, J. F. Kirby.[17]

Despite the support of local businesspersons, the municipal authorities did not exercise general governing authority, although the council apparently held meetings. In any case, a special election was held on 16 June to fill vacant offices, and three long-time Association members were unanimously elected. These officials were somewhat more active than their predecessors, but municipal affairs continued for the most part to be administered by the combined efforts of the Association and the concerned citizenry. A People's Court was organized in September 1860, and local governance was sustained by the combined efforts of civil and popular authorities. The J.P. courts were exclusively concerned with civil suits, while the popular tribunal handled criminal cases.[18]

Frontier government in Golden, and in Jefferson County, was dominated by local businesspersons who routinely defended their property rights. In Jefferson County, the Golden City Association was competing with the town companies of Mount Vernon and Golden Gate, while wagon road and ditch companies struggled to control access to the mines. Local claim clubs were competing with the Provisional Jefferson County government to control the distribution of land, and there were feeble attempts to sustain municipal government. These efforts notwithstanding, "concerned citizens" seemed to control municipal affairs through public meetings, popular tribunals, and vigilante actions, and in fact during 1859 and 1860, 30 percent of political actions reported in the Golden and Denver newspapers were those of the people's government. Other major actors were the town companies (18 percent) and the county government (26 percent). Road and ditch companies were only somewhat more active (in government) than were municipal authorities, while actions by the claim clubs and the vigilantes were rarely reported in either Denver or Golden newspapers.

It is certainly true that these findings reflect editorial bias in the determination of what was newsworthy, but this explains neither the prevalence of claims by corporate actors nor the limited number of municipal government actions. Generally, actions by "the people," especially vigilante actions, were reported in depth. Local editors usually dwelled on the actions by "concerned citizens," while vigilantism was reported by editors from other towns who wished to suggest the lawlessness and violence in the neighboring community. The Golden paper was quick to report vigilante actions in Denver (and vice versa), so local editors were hard pressed to ignore these events.

On the other hand, the routine administration of town company, ditch company, and claim club affairs was generally less than exciting and rarely worthy of coverage. Only when these actors made claims to governing authority were their activities included as political actions. Much of the routine business of these actors would have qualified as political but was not reported in the local press. Also, some of the meetings in which these affairs were administered were announced but were not included as political events because no claim to governing authority was explicitly reported. Hence, these data probably underestimate the importance of claim clubs, town companies, and other corporate actors.

Since the town companies routinely demanded assessments on local property, while road and ditch companies routinely claimed right-of-way, these actors appear to have been more active than the claim clubs. The records of local claim clubs do not suggest that the clubs were routinely adjudicating disputes. There were a few reports of legislative actions (organizing or reorganizing the club), but only one trial transcript was uncovered. It seems that neither the clubs nor the town companies were especially active in adjudication, although the Association records also contained references to trials. Both claim clubs and town companies were predominantly involved in recording claims, and while these actions were reported in the official records of the organizations, they were not usually reported in the local press. In newspaper reports, the Association was distinguished by the power of taxation, since assessment notices contained the warning that claims would be forfeit if fees were not paid.[19]

Clearly, all of the frontier governing authorities might have been more active than these data indicate, since routine, bureaucratic activities were often ignored by the local editors. This might explain why the popular government seems to have been so active, but it does not explain the inactivity of municipal, compared to county, authorities. There were scattered references to the legislative actions of the municipal government, but the City Marshall who was elected in April 1860 was not referenced subsequently. There was one reference to the local Justice of the Peace Court, but the order was signed by the County Sheriff rather than the City Marshall. Since a People's Court was organized in September 1860, it seems reasonable to assume that the municipal government was not the prime mover in local law and order efforts.[20]

As indicated by the data in Table 5.2, municipal government was preoccupied with efforts to establish general governing authority. Elections were held, and a few laws were drafted, but municipal authorities were not conspicuous in efforts to adjudicate property disputes or alleged crimes against persons. Even within the realm of general governing authority, it seems that the county and "the people" (acting as "concerned citizens") were at least equally active. In the defense of property, which was the primary concern for local authorities, "the people" and the county, along with the town companies, clearly overshadowed the municipal government's efforts.

Table 5.2 Political Actions in Golden by Issue by Governing Authority

Authorities	Issues				
	Property	Persons	Government	Unknown	Total
Town company	14 (1.0)	0	0	0	14
Road/Ditch company	8 (1.0)	0	0	0	8
Claim club	3 (1.0)	0	0	0	3
County government	13 (.65)	0	6 (.30)	1 (.05)	20
City government	1 (.17)	0	5 (.83)	0	6
People's government	13 (.57)	5 (.22)	5 (.22)	0	23
Vigilantes	1 (.50)	0	1 (.50)	0	2
Total	53 (.70)	5 (.07)	17 (.22)	1 (.01)	N=76

Source: *Rocky Mountain News,* April 1859–March 1860; *Western Mountaineer,* December 1859–November 1860.

Proportion of row total is to the right of the frequency.

Property rights were by far the predominant concern in local governance. Thus one finds evidence of Caucus government, in which nonlaboring classes unite in the defense of property and public order, virtually ignoring the interests of the laboring classes. Fully 70 percent of all actions concerned the issue of property, and all authorities except the city government were primarily (if not solely) concerned with property rights. The county government was concerned with general government, such as holding elections and establishing legislative and administrative procedures, but probate was the primary concern of the county courts, and land claims were the predominant concern of the county recorder. The people were also active in the defense of property rights, both as "concerned citizens" who determined local property assessments and as the People's Court, which claimed jurisdiction in criminal cases. Vigilantes hanged an alleged horse thief and also hanged the enraged gambler (Edgar Vanover) who was deemed a threat to property and persons as well as public order.[21] The people were also concerned with crimes against persons and were in fact distinguished as the only authority defending personal rights.

"The people" were similarly distinguished as the only authority reported to use the coercive power of government, according to 1859 and 1860 newspaper reports. Certainly, the claims of other actors were implicitly couched in the threat of coercion, but only the people, acting as the People's Court or vigilantes, explicitly used the power of arrest and execution to physically seize, harm, or destroy either persons or property. In fact, there is no evidence to suggest that anyone ever destroyed property, although property rights were adjudicated and disputed in a variety of ways. There were, however, two executions (or lynchings), one public whipping, one person encumbered with a ball and chain and condemned to forced labor, and a handful of arrests (or seizures). The lynchings were the work of vigilantes, but the People's (or citizen's) Court was responsible for all other acts of official violence.

Since the popular tribunal was distinguished both by its concern with crimes against people and by its use of coercive violence, it might seem reasonable to conclude that the people of Golden, as in Denver, used the coercive power of government to punish crimes against persons, most especially to hang alleged murderers. As indicated by the data in Table 5.3, however, the coercive power of government in the hands of the Golden people was used primarily to protect property. In general, property was protected by the routine, bureaucratic operation of county or corporate officials. Violence was used in only 11 percent of all actions in defense of property rights, but this constituted 67 percent of all violent actions. In response to crimes against persons, violence was used 40 percent of the time, but this constituted only 22 percent of all violent actions.

Table 5.3 Political Actions in Golden by Issue by Authority's Use of Violence

Issues	No Violence Employed	Violence Employed	Total
Property	47 (.89)	6 (.11)	53
Persons	3 (.60)	2 (.40)	5
Government	16 (.94)	1 (.06)	17
Unknown	1 (1.0)	0	1
Total	67 (.88)	9 (.12)	N=76

Source: *Rocky Mountain News*, April 1859–March 1860; *Western Mountaineer*, December 1859–November 1860.

Proportion of row total is to the right of the frequency.

Of the six violent responses to crimes against property, three were arrests. Two of those arrested were charged with horse theft, but neither was convicted or punished (one defendant escaped, and the other was acquitted). In the third arrest, the suspect was charged with the theft of supplies from Loveland and Company's wagons. The defendant pleaded guilty, explaining that he had been drunk, but he received twenty-one lashes and the promise of forty-two more if he did not leave the region within twenty-four hours. In another case (where no arrest was reported) the defendant was accused of stealing clothing from a toll booth on the Saint Vrain, Golden City, and Colorado Wagon Road. He pleaded not guilty but was convicted and sentenced to ten days of hard labor, shackled with a ball and chain, and was ordered to leave town after serving his sentence.[22]

Given the apparent problems in convicting horse thieves, it is not surprising that vigilantes did not rely of the People's Court but simply hanged those suspected of horse thieving. In fact, given the conviction record of the popular tribunal, it seems hardly surprising that the first case of drunk and disorderly conduct (confounded with armed robbery) was swiftly settled at the end of a rope.[23] Aside from punishing those who stole from the city fathers, it seems that the People's Court did little more than imitate due process.

The popular tribunal never convicted anyone in its war on crimes against people. An alleged murderer was arrested on a warrant from Kansas Territory, but he was promptly acquitted and the warrant was ignored. The only other alleged crimes against persons involved Daniel McCleery (a partner in McIntyre's road and ditch companies) and his son. They were charged with assault in two separate incidents but were never convicted, despite the fact that a hung jury, in one case, was divided between eight jurors finding them guilty of assault and four guilty of assault with intent to kill. The details of that case are somewhat obscured by the lack of official records, but it is evident that the people of Golden generally supported McCleery in his various legal battles. In October 1860, McCleery was fighting the Probate Court of Kansas Territory in defense of his wagon road company charter. In this case, the citizens of Golden defended McCleery against the distant power of Kansas.[24]

The fact that Golden citizens were able to bend the law in McCleery's favor is hardly surprising, because the citizens generally supported the local businesspersons. In the alleged toll booth robbery, for example, Kirby was supposed to represent the defendant, but his remarks to the jury suggest that he was less than committed to the defense:

> Before proceeding to try the prisoner, Mr. Kirby made the following statement: that he did not appear there for the purpose of defending the guilty or of preventing a just punishment from being inflicted on the perpetrator of a crime as grave as the one charged against the prisoner; but he hoped that whatever was done would be the result of sober, conscientious judgement and not of heated and excited passion. That the evidence would be undoubted, strong and perhaps overwhelming. But with the hope that the prisoner would receive nothing but Justice at the hands of an impartial Jury, he would enter upon his defense.[25]

One can thereby appreciate why the man who stole from Loveland was willing to plead guilty.

Local affairs were controlled by the local business community. The Golden City Association was the corporate creature of the business class, and local government was dominated by the property interest. Golden was a Caucus town, in which local political struggles were muted, as the business class seemed to speak with one voice that never faltered. Regional control was problematic, however, and competing authorities were not always cooperative prior to the organization of territorial governance in 1861.

REGIONAL STRUGGLES AND TERRITORIAL RESOLUTION

Overall, regional politics were more important than municipal affairs. The *Mountaineer* reported in detail the chaos of municipal governance in Denver (see Chapter 2) but offered little evidence of political turmoil in Golden. Even the Denver editors had little to say about Golden politics. Lacking any official records of preterritorial governance, it is difficult to determine the extent to which the Golden editor ignored local political struggles, but it is clear that the attention of the readership was directed to the struggle for regional governance.

Members of the Golden City Association were active in efforts to establish state or territorial government, despite the fact that Denver elites were the prime movers. Eli Carter was a member of the statehood convention, held in Denver in August 1859, and it was he who offered the resolution calling for a popular election to decide the statehood issue. Prior to that election, a convention was held in Golden on 20 September 1859 to nominate candidates for territorial or state office, and Golden was well represented at the subsequent meetings in Denver. Then, after the voters defeated the statehood proposition, Golden leaders joined in the organization and administration of the Provisional Government of Jefferson Territory.[26]

Among the Golden representatives were Eli Carter and D. K. Wall, both of whom were interested in regional governing authority, if only to sanction the operation of their road and ditch companies. In December 1859, the provisional government granted charters to the various road and ditch companies that were organized by local businesspersons, and the *Western Mountaineer* published the corporate charters, along with the details of other legislation. The provisional government passed laws to regulate irrigation and sanctioned the operation of ditch companies. It also sanctioned town companies but attempted to supersede the authority of land claim clubs.[27] These efforts created some problems for the Jefferson County government.

As already noted, county elections were held under the authority of the Provisional Government in January 1860. In the Jefferson County election, members of the Golden City Association made a clean sweep of county offices, and Golden was chosen as the seat of Jefferson County. Carter was elected County Recorder, and Kirby was chosen as Treasurer. It is worth noting, however, that the Golden victory was based primarily on the unity of Golden voters and that Golden was the most populous of the Jefferson County communities. In general, there were two opposing blocks of votes. The precincts of Golden, Arapahoe, and Henderson's Ranch generally voted together, while the voters of Golden Gate, Mount Vernon, and Bergen's Ranch generally supported the opposing candidates. As shown by the vote tallies reported in Table 5.4, this pattern was fairly pronounced.

Table 5.4 Votes Cast by Candidate by Precinct for Jefferson County Election of 1860

Office	Candidate	Precinct						Total
		1	2	3	4	5	6	
Judge	McWhirt	248	193	60	82	47	11	641
	others	72						72
Associate judge (choose two)	Smith	116	61	60	59	33	14	343
	Boyd	261	160	60	4	10	2	446
	Hawley	44	33		21	39	9	210
	Anderson	122	75			6		303
Sheriff	Pollard	70	53	60		2	2	187
	Whittemore	103				14	6	128
	Belcher	63			69	33	9	174
	Smith		143		1			144
Recorder	Carter	214	114	60	4	7		399
	Golden	41	85		79	39	11	255
Clerk	Gunnel	209	172	60	13	7	2	463
	Hollman	24	34		70	39	9	176
Assessor	McCleery	199	182	60	13	5	1	460
	Carter	20			60	32	9	127
Treasurer	Kirby	166	57	35	4	6	2	277
	Smith	51		25	76	36	9	200
	Gilmore		2					2
	McKay	28						28
Attorney	Rhodes	200	119		13	6	2	340
	Kirby	41	1		70	35	2	149
County Seat	Golden	285	40	60	4	9	3	401
	Arapahoe	2	166		79	35	6	288
	Baden	22						22

Source: *Western Mountaineer,* (Golden, weekly) 11 January 1860:2.

Precincts: 1: Golden; 2: Arapahoe City; 3: Henderson's Ranch; 4: Golden Gate; 5: Mount Vernon; 6: Bergen's Ranch.

Golden Gate was located some two miles north of Golden and was established in September 1859 as the gateway to the goldfields. Mount Vernon, located about halfway between Golden Gate and Denver, was established in December of 1859. Each community had a town company that was prepared to donate lots on the most liberal terms to those who were interested in establishing business in Jefferson County on the road to the Gregory Diggings. In January 1860, the Denver, Mount Vernon, and Gregory Diggings Wagon Road Company was organized to construct and operate a road from Denver to the mines. This road was to pass from Denver to Mount Vernon, go through Bergen's Ranch, and enter the mountains at Golden Gate, thereby bypassing the city of Golden. Aside from the local investors, members of this road company included Joseph Casto, who had been secretary of the original Gregory mining district, and William Byers and R. B. Bradford, two of the Denver men who had been members of the Saint Vrain Land Claim Club.[28]

Simply stated, the electoral cleavage in Jefferson County politics was a direct reflection of the competition between the Denver and Golden wagon road companies. This was apparent in the controversy that filled the pages of the *Western Mountaineer* with competing claims regarding the shortest route to the mines. Since many Golden businesspersons were shareholders in the Saint Vrain, Golden City, and Colorado Company, the issue was hotly contested. Casto, of course, promoted the Denver road, but local correspondents were prompt to point out that the road that bypassed Golden was longer because it made unnecessary detours to Denver and Mount Vernon. The Golden road bypassed Denver and saved the traveler many miles of needless hardship. The *Western Mountaineer* seemed to support this position, since a map of the Golden road was published in each edition, beginning in February 1860.[29]

It was apparent, however, that many immigrants did not choose to bypass Denver, so the Golden road company was forced to accommodate the Denver traffic. In March 1860, Golden citizens met to discuss the possibility of establishing a free wagon road, but they were not successful. The Saint Vrain, Golden City, and Colorado Company did decide, however, to remove the toll booth that was near the Mount Vernon turnoff and thereby provide free passage to Golden. In this way, the Golden road could capture some of the Denver traffic and still maintain its preferred route to the mines. As the competition mounted, this move was countered by the Mount Vernon company, which erected a toll booth on the entrance to the Golden road. Through the summer of 1860, this "illegal" toll booth was the subject of considerable debate.[30]

Meanwhile, Eli Carter was embroiled in a debate with Thomas Golden, a shareholder in the Golden Gate Town Company. Golden had been Carter's opponent for Jefferson County recorder, but their personal vendetta was far more serious than electoral rhetoric might suggest. Golden accused Carter of using his office for personal enrichment, by charging outrageous fees and preempting claims for his own benefit, even after registering these claims for others. Aside from a slanderous exchange in the local papers, Carter and Golden were parties to a civil suit, and ultimately they attempted to sustain competing claims to governing authority. In April, Golden organized the Golden Gate Land Claim Club, in defiance of the county recorder, and Carter replied, in August, by warning settlers not to accept claims sanctioned by this club.[31] The conflict between Carter and Golden continued until Carter's authority was superseded by the territorial government in 1862.

The authority of the Provisional Government rested on an inadequate governing coalition. The competition between Denver and Golden created problems for provisional authorities, but the critical problem was that miners in particular, and the laboring classes in general, did not support the provisional government. In Golden, the interests of miners were not a major concern, except as these impinged on either the operation of ditch companies or the competition with Denver. Golden governors did, however, have problems with local farmers and ranchers like Thomas Golden, who refused to recognize the authority of Jefferson County. The provisional government was supposed to supersede the local claim clubs, but even in Denver it was not successful in this regard. In Jefferson County, claim clubs were organized after the regional authority was established, in response to the claims of the Jefferson County government.

The Junction District Land Claim Club was organized in August 1860, just as Carter was issuing his ultimatum to the Golden Gate Club. On paper, it was a typical claim club, in which claims of 160 acres were recorded and held as real estate so long as they were improved within three months. The original charter also stated that a claimant was entitled to purchase an additional 160 acres but could hold no more than a total of 320 acres.[32] At least initially, the letter of this law was obeyed, and there was a lively trade in 160-acre lots. Then, through partnerships and intricate webs of familial and business relations, a few large ranching and lumber mill claims were established, and the laws were modified in 1861 to allow for larger purchases and preemptions. By the spring of 1861, ranches and lumber mills predominated, and a handful of investors, who formed partnerships among themselves, were busy buying and selling large tracts of land.

The Junction District land owners were united in multiple partnerships that provided the basis for large-scale speculative ventures. The scope of these ventures can be illustrated by tracing the affairs of John and James Bell through the claim club records of 1861. John B. Bell, in partnership with C. E. Carter and John Ruby, claimed 320 acres in February 1861. In March, James Bell sold 320 acres and bought 160. Then John Bell, Ruby, and William Lanham claimed 640 acres, and Lanham sold his share to James Bell. James Bell and Simon Cort then claimed 640 acres, and Bell sold his share to Cort. Next, John Bell and Ruby sold 960 acres to Cort, James bought another 90 acres, and John began again by preempting 160 acres. Before the year was out, Bell, Ruby, and Lanham sold an additional 160 acres to Cort. Then Bell, Ruby, and "others" claimed 480 acres to erect a sawmill. Meanwhile, James Bell bought an additional 640 acres, so that Bell, Bell, and Ruby could close out the year by selling 1,200 acres (with sawmill).[33]

Jefferson County, like Golden City, was filled with businesspersons on the make. They formed multiple partnerships and invested in ranching, farming, gardening, sawmills, and most of all land. Of course, the road and ditch companies were anxious to cross these lands, so they sought the authority of provisional government to sanction their right-of-way claims. They also attempted to supersede the authority of the claim clubs with the Jefferson County government, but the local land speculators would have none of this. Thus both municipal and regional politics were animated by the claims of concerned citizens and corporate actors, who struggled to protect the rights of property.

The businesspersons of Golden and the landholders of Jefferson County shared an interest in property and a commitment to local autonomy in governance by executive committee. The property interest provided the basis for a business-class Caucus alliance that might have sustained regional governance. The interest in local autonomy was a barrier to regional alliance, however, and undermined efforts to establish regional government. The claim clubs refused to recognize the authority of the Provisional Government of Jefferson Territory or its administrative creature, the County of Jefferson. Thus preterritorial politics were plagued by the struggle within the propertied classes to retain and expand economic and political control.

Golden businesspersons were able to have their way in municipal affairs, but claim clubs and competing town and wagon road companies were a barrier to regional governance. Nevertheless, the McCleery case indicates that by October 1860 there was at least a limited basis for a regional alliance. When McCleery was attempting to defend his wagon road charter against the government of Kansas Territory, residents of Golden Gate, including Thomas Golden, stood by the Golden City residents in their defense of the local road. Businesspersons, ranchers, mill operators, and land speculators were allied in their opposition to the government of Kansas Territory. Provisional government was not an adequate umbrella for a regional alliance, so local actors continued to operate their distinct forms of governance and allied only in opposition to the distant power of Kansas. Nevertheless, the desire for local control united the land owners and businesspersons of Jefferson County and provided a basis for their support of Colorado territorial governance.

The Territory of Colorado was established by federal decree in February 1861, but the territorial government did not commence operations until August. Even then, frontier authorities were slow to surrender control to the newly constituted government. In Jefferson County, as already noted, land claim clubs were active throughout 1861, and the territorial version of the Jefferson County Commissioners did not begin its deliberations before 1862.[34] Ultimately, however, local authorities supported territorial government for three reasons. First, it offered an adequate regional authority to arbitrate between the diverging interests of municipal and regional actors. Since its authority was accepted by the miners as well as the nonlaboring classes, it could arbitrate in regional disputes. Second, it offered a county government that could serve as both a land office and an administrative center for the developing transportation industry. Territorial government made concessions to miners, claim clubs, and other provisional authorities by recognizing their previous actions while requiring that they surrender control to the county. This might explain the flurry of activity in the Junction Claim Club in the closing days of 1861. The local landowners wanted to consolidate their claims and conclude their transactions before the county took charge.[35]

The third and most important reason why Jefferson County residents supported territorial governance was that it provided a basis for expanding local control. In 1862, Golden was named Territorial Capital, which must have been good news for local businesspersons who stood to benefit from increased demand for local services and increased traffic on local roads.[36] Golden was the political center of Colorado Territory and was at the same time establishing itself as the transportation center. The Civil War and the accompanying decline in Colorado mineral production might have deflated the market for road and ditch companies, so the trade in politicians might have been most welcome. In any case, the war did not seem to interfere with the construction and operation of local toll roads.

In fact, the Jefferson County Commissioners seemed to be interested in little else. In their first year of office, the commissioners received five different road petitions. Two of these simply requested that the county sanction the operation of existing roads, but three requested permission to construct new roads. The county denied none of these requests and approved the construction of a road from Bergen's Ranch to the Western County Line (toward the mining region) as well as the Golden City, Clear Creek, and Guy Gulch Wagon Road, which passed through Golden on the road to the mines.[37] Thus wagon roads that followed the general paths of the Denver and Golden roads (which had been bitter rivals under provisional authority) were chartered under county authority in 1862.

The same spirit of compromise was reflected in the election of county commissioners. D. K. Wall and T. P. Boyd represented the interests of the Golden City businesspersons, but T. C. Bergen (for whom Bergen's Ranch was named) also served on the board. There is little evidence to suggest that the conflict between Golden and regional business interests continued to plague county officials, although there might have been some conflicts not far beneath the surface of tranquility that official records suggest. First of all, the election precinct at Golden Gate was abolished in June 1862, although it was reestablished in August. There was also a hint of impropriety when the county treasurer was indicted for election fraud in May, but there is no record of his conviction. Finally, two petitions before the board requested charters for roads to Guy Gulch. The record suggests that Loveland, Smith, and Smith presented their petition on the same day as another company, but the latter petition was withdrawn, and the Loveland road was incorporated.[38]

Aside from efforts to sanction the organization and operation of road companies, the county was concerned with general governing activities, notably taxation and the administration of elections. Beyond this, the commissioners granted eight liquor licenses at twenty-five dollars per annum and issued one auctioneer license (for five dollars). The auctioneer was "Judge" William Train Muir, who had achieved some notoriety as the gun-toting judge of Gilpin County and the judge of the Nevada mining district. His activities had generated considerable controversy in 1861 in the conflict that divided mill men and miners and also involved some members of the Golden business community.[39] Nevertheless, the petty squabbles that had animated provisional government were not apparent in 1862. It seems that frontier authorities were willing to sacrifice their control to the Jefferson County government.

If, in fact, municipal government was sustained through the 1860s, it left few traces of its existence. The Justice of the Peace gradually came to claim jurisdiction in both civil and criminal cases, but this court was not specifically municipal. There are no official records of city government prior to 1871, and there are no references to city officials in the local paper. The *Western Mountaineer* ceased publication during the Civil War while its editor served in the Union forces, but upon his return in December 1866 the *Colorado Transcript* was established. Prior to 1871 the paper was filled with news of the Territorial government; there were references to county government but no mention of municipal authorities. In fact, a city directory (published in the *Transcript*) listed both county and territorial officials and even public school teachers, but made no mention of municipal officers.[40]

Under territorial authority, there was, if anything, even less concern with municipal governance. In 1862, despite territorial organization, the Association remained the prime mover in municipal affairs. In fact, Association records contain a list of jurors selected in February 1862, although there is no record of subsequent trials. Apparently the Association did not surrender its authority until December 1863, when W.A.H. Loveland purchased title to all unclaimed city lots in a transaction authorized by the Jefferson County Probate Court. In sharp contrast to the "Lot Question" in Denver, there is no evidence of controversy surrounding Loveland's purchase.[41] Instead, Loveland proceeded to take control of Golden as part of a more general attempt to establish the Loveland empire, which rested on the authority of both county and territorial charters. That empire sustained Golden as the hub of regional transportation for approximately twenty years.

THE CHALLENGE OF NATIONAL INCORPORATION

As noted in discussing the pioneering efforts of Golden businesspersons, transportation was a major if not primary basis for local enterprise. Aside from the Saint Vrain, Golden City, and Colorado Wagon Road Company, which served the local mines, there was a concerted effort to build a road that would connect Golden to the transcontinental traffic. In 1861 E. L. Berthoud surveyed a route to Salt Lake City to entice the overland stage company to follow this shorter path across the Rockies. That same year, Loveland initiated the survey of a railroad route from Denver to Central City by way of Golden, but neither Loveland nor Berthoud was able to move beyond the survey. In 1863 Loveland and his partners were granted a territorial charter to build a road along the line that Berthoud had surveyed, and construction efforts finally commenced. By 1864, however, Loveland and company had their charter amended so they could construct a railroad connecting Golden to Central City, Boulder, and Denver.[42]

In 1865 the company was rechartered as the Colorado Central and Pacific Railroad, with plans to build to the western border of the territory and to connect with the Union Pacific or Kansas Pacific somewhere on the eastern plains. Loveland attracted investors from New York and Chicago and attempted to incorporate the Colorado Central into the transcontinental railway. By the winter of 1866-1867, the Union Pacific decided to cross the Rockies in Wyoming, so Loveland offered the U.P. a substantial interest in the Colorado Central and commenced construction of the rail that was to link Colorado mining and milling operations with the transcontinental railroad. Technical and financial difficulties limited construction in the late 1860s, but the Cheyenne connection was effected in 1870, and most of the local lines were completed in the early 1870s.[43]

Meanwhile Golden was becoming something of an industrial center. When George West returned to Golden and established the *Colorado Transcript* in December 1866, he proudly recounted the story of industrial growth. West asserted that Golden then housed two of the finest flour mills in Colorado as well as a large brick factory, and he predicted that Golden would soon be "*the* manufacturing town of Colorado."[44] Advertisements in that edition included not only flour and brick companies but also a brewery, a sash and blind manufacturer, coal and lime pits, sheet metal and copper manufacturers, and a variety of crafts such as shoemaking and dressmaking. In short, during the 1860s the industrial base of the Golden economy shifted to a large extent from trade to manufactures. At the same time, the local business community, which had invested widely in wagon roads, irrigation ditches, and gold mines, began to concentrate on transportation and manufactures.

This transformation was evident by 1870 in the distribution of wealth across industrial sectors. The Golden economy by that time was based primarily on the development of four sectors—finance, manufactures, transportation, and service. A small group of financiers, including banking, insurance, and real estate interests, controlled a substantial share (18 percent) of local wealth. Manufactures included a larger proportion (14 percent) of the population and a slightly larger share (20 percent) of local wealth. Relatively little money was invested in construction, since Golden did not grow appreciably during this period, but a fair number of persons were employed in the construction industry. Transportation accounted for 12 percent of the households and 13 percent of the wealth, and the service sector represented the largest proportion of both population (20 percent) and wealth (23 percent).

Since the territorial capital had moved to Denver in 1867, few government officials were in Golden. Few households reported no occupation, and relatively little wealth was not invested in some form of local enterprise. The households that were classified in the "unknown" industrial sector were primarily laboring households. Service industry workers generally reported occupational titles other than "laborer," so the laborers were probably employed in transportation, construction, and manufactures, but it is difficult to determine how their labor was divided among these industries.

Golden's class structure in 1870 is illustrated in Table 5.5. The nonlaboring classes claimed 42 percent of the households and 86 percent of local wealth. The "owner-employer" class had expanded to encompass 10 percent of the households and 28 percent of local wealth, claiming on average $8,108 per household. The laboring classes constituted 58 percent of the households but claimed only 14 percent of local wealth. Artisan-shopkeepers claimed the bulk of laboring class wealth, but "workers" (presumably wage workers) were the most numerous segment of the laboring classes. They constituted 41 percent of the households but claimed only 2 percent of local wealth. Overall, these data indicate both a wealthy employer class and abundant wage labor.

To some extent, the general picture is not unlike Denver in 1870, except for the relative wealth of owner-employers versus merchants. In Denver, there were a few wealthy members of the owner-employer class, but merchants

Table 5.5 Wealth by Class Category for Households in Golden, 1870

Class Category	Total Wealth	Percentage of Wealth	Number of Households	Percentage of Households
Nonlaboring classes	$622,800	86.26	103	42.21
Financier	127,000	17.59	2	0.82
Owner	202,700	28.07	25	10.25
Professional	136,200	18.86	26	10.66
Merchant	136,800	18.95	31	12.70
None	20,100	2.78	19	7.79
Laboring classes	99,200	13.74	141	57.78
Artisan	83,500	11.57	42	17.21
Worker	15,700	2.17	99	40.57
Total	722,000		244	

Source: U.S. Bureau of the Census (1870) Population Schedules for Jefferson County, Colorado Territory.

controlled 42 percent of local wealth and trade was the leading sector. In Golden, the merchants and shopkeepers claimed proportionately less wealth, and the service sector (including restaurants and hotels for the traveling public) was more important than trade. In addition, the owner-employer class controlled a larger share of local wealth, as did manufacturing and transportation. Golden was a manufacturing and transportation center; Denver was a commercial center.

The laboring classes of Golden in 1870 claimed greater per capita wealth than they had in 1860. They were still less wealthy than their Denver counterparts, but the gap had narrowed considerably. On the other hand, 62 percent of the laboring households were "workers," and the disparity between "worker" and "artisan" wealth had increased dramatically. Golden artisan-shopkeepers claimed $1,988 per household; workers, $159. On balance, the laboring class was wealthier and somewhat smaller than in 1860, but relatively few laborers were independent artisans. This change was due largely to the departure of "miners," who in 1860 claimed little wealth but were, to the extent that they were engaged in mineral production, economically independent. In any case, Golden continued to house an adequate supply of labor.

Thus Golden maintained the tradition of business-class control, particularly in the transportation industry. By 1870, the laboring classes of Colorado, particularly the miners, had generally lost their economic independence and were reduced to working for wages, but this did not produce labor discipline problems in Golden. The miners had not been particularly involved in the Golden political economy. For the most part, the frontier miners had worked in the Central City region and had traded in Denver. Those enumerated in the 1860 Golden census were either passing through town or, perhaps, spending the winter. There never was much mining in Golden, although it is likely that "miners" had been used as wage labor in road and ditch construction and other Golden enterprises. In any case the struggle to control the Colorado mining industry did not significantly affect Golden City investors, who were willing to collect tolls or rent water to whoever might be engaged in mineral production.

The businesspersons of Golden became increasingly involved in transportation and manufacturing, and the local laboring classes, which had never enjoyed economic independence or political organization, were docile in the face of capital accumulation. They had neither the memory of economic independence nor the experience of class-based struggle. Hence, unlike the miners of Leadville, the farmers of Greeley, and the skilled trades of Denver, the workers of Golden were not united in opposition to local or national capital. For Loveland and his Golden associates, the challenge of the 1870s was to sustain local control while cooperating with national capital. This proved at best difficult, as national capitalists struggled to control the Colorado railroads.

In Golden, the attempt to control regional transportation was the predominant concern for local economic and political elites of 1870. This is apparent in the proceedings of the Jefferson County Commissioners, who met eighteen times during 1870 and received twenty-six petitions: six to build new roads, five to change the location of roads, one to raise toll rates, one protesting against the location of a road, five asking the county to locate roads, and only eight on matters other than roads.[45]

The presentation of road petitions occupied much of the commissioners' time, but that was merely one component of the county's involvement in transportation. The business of the transportation industry also inspired various reports by committees appointed to oversee the construction or location of roads, as well as orders and appropriations for construction and administration efforts. Other county business included the decision to grant right-of-way to the Colorado Central railroad and to redeem the railroad bonds issued in July 1868. It seems reasonable to conclude that the county was routinely engaged in efforts to facilitate the growing transportation industry. Not only were the county commissioners granting charters and overseeing the construction and operation of wagon roads, they were also raising funds for the construction of the Colorado Central and Pacific Railway. Thus the county was a critical actor in facilitating the development of regional transportation and in securing Golden's position as the railroad center of Colorado.

By 1871, however, Golden had managed to establish municipal government and was finally subject to the authority of a republican civil authority. Municipal authorities took responsibility for the purely local concerns that in Mount Vernon and elsewhere were still subject to the authority of the county commissioners. Thus Golden City took responsibility for maintaining the grade on its city streets, regulating the flow of local water, and restraining livestock from running at large. The council considered the possibility of building sidewalks but decided to defer action on that issue. They did, however, pass a series of laws regarding public nuisance and licensure and did, in this regard, represent the interests of local merchants and shopkeepers.[46]

Thus in 1871 municipal government administered the affairs of local actors, while county government continued to serve the interests of regional actors involved primarily in the transportation industry. The establishment of municipal authority relieved the territorial court of some of its judicial responsibilities, but municipal organization did not markedly affect the criminal dockets of either Justice or District Courts. The Justice and County courts of the provisional government (1860–1861) had been concerned solely with civil suits, according to newspaper accounts. By 1862, however, both the Justice Court and the Territorial District Court had limited criminal dockets, as shown by the data in Table 5.6. The first six years of court dockets contained only sixteen criminal cases in the J.P. Court and forty-four in the District Court.

Table 5.6 Criminal Cases in Jefferson County by Offense by Court, 1862–1867 and 1869–1872

Court	Offense against			Total
	Persons	Property	Government	
1862–1867				
J.P.	2 (.29)	4 (.57)	1 (.14)	7[a]
District	6 (.14)	17 (.39)	21 (.48)	44
Total	8 (.16)	21 (.41)	22 (.43)	51
1869–1872				
J.P.	11 (.48)	7 (.30)	5 (.22)	23
District	3 (.05)	15 (.26)	39 (.68)	57
Total	14 (.18)	22 (.28)	44 (.55)	80

[a]Sixteen cases were on the criminal docket, but no charge was recorded in nine of these cases.
Source: State Archives, Denver. Territorial District Court Records are also at Denver Federal Center. Proportion of row total is to the right of the frequency.

Prior to 1870 neither court heard many cases alleging crimes against persons. As was suggested in the analysis of frontier newspaper reports, local government in Golden was dedicated to the defense of property and public order. In the classic Caucus town tradition, the rights of persons were largely ignored, even in the local Justice Court. The J.P. Court heard two assault cases between 1862 and 1867, and the District Court heard three assault and three murder cases. The major crime against property was larceny, although the Territory also prosecuted cases of counterfeit gold dust, killing livestock, and violating estray laws (which stipulated the procedures for advertising the discovery of unbranded calves). The District Court was distinguished by its concern for crimes against government, which in the early years were primarily violations of licensing law.

In this regard, the Golden court records indicate the same judicial division of labor that was evidenced in the Carnival towns. At least initially, local courts defended the interests of persons and property, while the federal (territorial) District Court concentrated on crimes against government. The only difference in this general pattern is that in Golden the local J.P. was more concerned with crimes against property, rather than persons, particularly in comparison with Central City and Denver. Yet more striking, however, is the relative stability of this pattern after 1870. By that time the local courts of Denver and Central City had all but surrendered jurisdiction for crimes against persons or property and were essentially rousting drunks and prostitutes, leaving the more serious crimes to the territorial authorities.

Unfortunately there are no Jefferson County court records available for 1880, so it is difficult to determine a pattern. It appears, however, that Golden, like Greeley, did not witness a substantial change in the business of local and regional courts. There is no apparent trend toward the increasing centralization of judicial authority (as witnessed in Denver) or the increasing concern with crimes against public order (or government) that is apparent in both Central City and Denver court records. In Golden, the interest of the merchants and shopkeepers (the traditional booster interest in public order) was not nearly so overwhelming as it was in Denver and Central City. The Justice Court in Golden continued to prosecute assaults and larcenies, although more serious crimes (particularly crimes against property) were adjudicated in District Court. It appears that there was no municipal police court defending public order in Golden.

Once municipal government was established in 1871, the J.P. Court became somewhat more involved in prosecuting crimes against persons and government. Most of the assault charges were adjudicated by the J.P., but the bulk of the "morals" charges were still heard in District Court. These District Court cases included charges of fornication and adultery but mostly charges of gambling and keeping a tippling house open on the Sabbath. The territory was no longer prosecuting violations of licensing law, but the District Court did prosecute charges of selling liquor to intoxicated persons.

Thus public morals in Golden were defended by the regional District Court of Colorado Territory. The concern for morality was not as great in Golden as was the case in Denver, Greeley, or Central City, but these concerns were expressed at the county level and defended in District Court. In the J.P. Court, between June 1871 and April 1872, there were no prosecutions on moral charges and only one prosecution for selling goods without a license. In this case, the unknown defendant was not found and the case was dismissed.

Overall, it seems that crime was not particularly threatening in Golden or in Jefferson County. The courts were not particularly burdened and there is no evidence of a special police court that routinely processed drunks and prostitutes (as was the case in both Denver and Central City). The marriage of manufactures and transportation seemed quite capable of exercising local control. The *Colorado Transcript*, in 1871, was dutifully reporting the ordinances passed by the municipal legislature, the cases before local magistrates, and the civility and order that characterized the elections of that year.

In describing the municipal elections of 1871, West distinguished Golden politics from the chaos and acrimony witnessed in Denver. As the editor noted, municipal elections in Denver were plagued by controversy regarding the final settlement of the "Lot Question." Fortunately, the Golden polity was immune to such disputations. West explained this good fortune as follows:

> We here at Golden have reason to felicitate ourselves upon our titles having been made perfect by the foresight of one of our prominent citizens—Hon. W.A.H. Loveland, who was the original claimant of the land upon which Golden is located, and who procured the passage of the

law . . . through our Legislative Assembly in 1864, for the purpose of making assurance doubly sure."[47]

West had been one of the original members of the Boston corporation that had established the Golden City Association. Surely he knew that Loveland was not the original claimant but had purchased all unclaimed lots within the city and in March 1864 had sponsored the territorial law that would sanction his ownership of Golden. One can certainly appreciate why Loveland wished his title to be "doubly sure." By 1871, Loveland was in control of local enterprise and no challenges to his control of the local economy were apparent.

In fact, local control was never a very pressing problem in Golden. As has been noted above, it was the struggle for regional control that proved problematic in Jefferson County. By 1871, county governance and even municipal governance were effectively established, but Golden faced still greater difficulties. By then, local elites, most notably W.A.H. Loveland, were struggling to establish their control of the territory, and that struggle involved not only Coloradans but national actors as well. This struggle and its implications for the future of Golden City are best captured in analysis of the railroad war of the 1870s.

The Golden Rail

The broad outlines of the Colorado railroad war have been offered in the analysis of Denver and Central City, but it is appropriate here to focus on the actors and actions that had a direct bearing on the Colorado Central Railway and on Golden's rise and fall as a railroad center.

The first act of this drama has already been presented. Loveland and his Associates agreed to grant a substantial share of stock in the Colorado Central to the shareholders of the Union Pacific in 1867. The Colorado Central then commenced construction of the rail system that was to connect Golden to the mining and milling operations of the region and eventually to the Union Pacific. The Union Pacific attempted to establish a cooperative venture, in which Denver would build a rail to Cheyenne while Golden would build to Denver and to the regional mines and mills. This project proved impossible, however, because the Colorado Central seemed to be intent on building a line from Golden to the Union Pacific (in Cheyenne), with a spur line to Denver. Arapahoe County voters refused to support this scheme, and the plan for cooperation fell through.[48]

This marked the opening of the battle between Denver and Golden, on the local front, and between the Union Pacific and Kansas Pacific, within the national arena. Initially, Denver was nonaligned, because local voters refused to pay either of the national roads the price they demanded for a rail connection. Instead, Denver organized the Denver Pacific railroad and built a connection to Cheyenne. Meanwhile, the Kansas Pacific, aided by federal monies, completed its route to Denver, so the Queen City had two rail connections in 1870.[49]

According to federal legislation of 1866, the Union Pacific and the Kansas Pacific were to meet somewhere in the eastern plains and to operate as a single company according to a prorating agreement. When the Kansas Pacific was linked to the U.P. via the Denver Pacific road to Cheyenne, the directors of the Kansas rail approached the Union Pacific and requested a prorating agreement. The U.P. declined, however, stating that the roads did not meet, since the Denver Pacific was an independent company. The K.P. directors petitioned Congress in 1870, but the petition was lost in the rush to adjournment, so the Kansas and Denver roads continued to suffer from the intransigence of the Union Pacific directors.[50]

The alliance of the Union Pacific and Colorado Central effectively monopolized the transcontinental traffic and sustained Golden as the transportation center of Colorado. The Kansas Pacific could not capture the through traffic and could not be sustained by the regional trade. Hence, in 1872, the K.P. directors decided to build a separate connection to the West that would connect Denver with the western mining and milling operations and would cross the Rocky Mountains, eventually reaching Salt Lake City. This road was to follow the route of the old Mount Vernon wagon road, thereby avoiding Golden and recapitulating the wagon road dispute of 1860. The fact that Loveland controlled the right-of-way across the Rockies, while the U.P. controlled traffic to and from Salt Lake, ultimately convinced the Kansas directors to abandon this plan.[51]

In September 1872 the Kansas Pacific was negotiating with the Denver and Rio Grande to construct a rail from Denver to Pueblo. At the same time, the Denver and South Park Railroad was established as Denverites struggled to gain a foothold in local and regional trade. The financial panic of 1873 closed these options and left the Kansas Pacific in dire straits, more than willing to negotiate. The condition of the Kansas line had deteriorated markedly since 1870, as revenues were insufficient for maintenance and repair. When money became yet more scarce, the company went into receivership and, in desperation, agreed to cooperate with the Union Pacific in 1875.[52]

The Union Pacific agreed to merge the Colorado Central with the Kansas Pacific in exchange for $10,000 in consolidated stock (representing shares in the new company), so long as the Kansas company agreed to drop its claim for a prorating agreement. The K.P. directors had no alternative and agreed to merge with the Colorado Central, much to the chagrin of the Colorado investors. Under this agreement, Colorado was denied direct access to the Pacific coast and had to pay exorbitant rates for transportation via the

Union and Denver Pacific. In addition, Loveland and company were to be dispossessed, as the Colorado Central was absorbed by the Kansas Pacific.[53]

In December 1875, Loveland attended a meeting of the directors of the Colorado Central in which the following proposals were approved. First, Coloradans were to sell all of their Colorado Central shares at 20 percent of par value in exchange for Boulder and Gilpin county bonds to be accepted at par. Second, the agreement between the Kansas and Union Pacific was ratified. Thus the Colorado investors were to relinquish their shares in exchange for bonds issued by their county governments. These would become worthless as soon as the Colorado Central became a subsidiary of the Kansas road. Needless to say, the Coloradans rebelled.[54]

First, the Boulder shareholders refused to relinquish their shares. Then, at a stockholder's meeting held in Golden in May 1876, Loveland and his associates refused to recognize the proxies sent by the Union Pacific shareholders. Instead, they proceeded to elect their own board of directors and refused to comply with the resolutions passed at the December board meeting. After the U.P. obtained a restraining order, Loveland and associates physically seized the rolling stock and replaced employees who were not faithful to the local directors. Then, as the company was about to be placed in the hands of David Moffatt (a Denver capitalist), Judge Wilbur F. Stone was kidnapped to delay the court-ordered receivership. Suits and countersuits continued for years and were readjudicated after Colorado became a state in 1876. Finally, in 1877, Loveland was able to negotiate a settlement with the Union Pacific that ended the law suits and sustained his control of the Colorado Central.[55]

By then, the war between the Union Pacific and Kansas Pacific had been rekindled. The Denver Pacific was in receivership, and the completion of the Colorado Central route to the U.P. marked the end of Denver Pacific traffic. The Central then operated a line that ran from Golden to Boulder, to Greeley, and along the Platte River to the northeast corner of the state, where it joined the Union Pacific in Julesburg. Thus the Golden rail connected the mining and milling operations and the farming communities of the Platte to the transcontinental rail. Loveland and company had clearly won the battle, having weathered the U.P. alliance with the Kansas rail and having established an independent connection to the East.[56]

The war, however, was far from over, and Denver politicians managed to convince the federal government to intervene. In December 1877, Congress declared an end to the price war, and the restoration of the Kansas Pacific commenced. Jay Gould was elected as one of the new K.P. directors, and a court-appointed receiver supervised the renovation of the Kansas rail. By 1879, Jay Gould and other shareholders in the Union Pacific had purchased a controlling interest in the Kansas road, and under Gould's direction they were to have finally consolidated the competing roads. Gould's associates, however, were not willing to follow his lead. They therefore suffered his vengeance in the final act of this drama.[57]

Gould, in partnership with Russell Sage, purchased a controlling interest in various eastern railroads and announced the intention to extend the Kansas Pacific through Loveland Pass to Salt Lake City. Gould and Sage had sufficient capital to finance the construction, and the railroads that Gould and Sage controlled would have then formed a continuous line from Saint Louis to Salt Lake. Gould also controlled both the Kansas Pacific and the Denver Pacific and could easily provide an attractive alternative to the Union Pacific route to Cheyenne. In these terms, Gould offered the U.P. directors an offer that they were too frightened to refuse. They bought their way into Gould's consolidation scheme in 1879.[58]

THE END OF A GOLDEN EMPIRE

In November 1879, the Colorado Central was leased for fifty years to the Union Pacific, and the local roads were consolidated under U.P. control. This marked the end of the Loveland railroad empire and the end of Golden's reign as the railroad center of Colorado. Loveland moved to Denver in 1880, purchased the *Rocky Mountain News*, and became the local champion for the Democratic Party in opposition to monopoly capital, labor unions, and Republican protectionist policies. Gould and Sage unloaded their shares in the various companies that had been used as leverage against the Union Pacific directors and left the U.P. teetering on the edge of bankruptcy in 1883.[59] Needless to say, Gould made a tremendous profit, which allowed him to purchase a controlling interest in the railroads of southwest Colorado. Gould will reappear in the histories of Pueblo and Cañon City.

Within the context of this history of Golden City, the railroad war was the final act in the struggle for regional control. In the opening scene, in the spring of 1859, Golden businesspersons attempted to control the mining industry by controlling regional transportation and water. This inspired competition from Denver and from regional businesspersons who had established local land claim clubs. Under the umbrella of territorial governance, this competition was institutionalized and regulated, but the struggle for regional control continued. Loveland and his associates were able to control Golden City and to a large extent Jefferson County. They could not, however, control Colorado, not because of competition with Denver but because of competition with national actors. The railroads represented the cutting edge of capital penetration on a scale previously unknown to Colorado. Gould and his associates could buy and sell enterprises that would dwarf the productive capacity of the entire territory. Capital penetration and established relations with these national actors meant that Coloradans were to assume the status

Golden in the 1880s. Courtesy Colorado Historical Society (F-23771)

of junior partners in both economy and government. Loveland and associates would not be coopted, so they were crushed.

Golden represents a classic example of the Caucus town path to the national polity. The business class dominated the local economy and government but resisted national capital and attempted to sustain local control. The challenge of national incorporation was not control of labor but cooperation between local and national capital. In the short run, Loveland and his associates were able to physically control their railroad through vigilante tactics, but they could not defeat national capital or ignore the authority of the federal courts. Clearly, efforts to resist national capital and federal government were likely to fail in the long run.

Golden City did survive the loss of its most enterprising citizen. Today, Golden is the home of the Coors brewery, and the city is most accommodating in facilitating the expansion of the Adolph Coors empire. Golden did not succeed, however, in displacing Denver as the Queen City of the Rocky Mountain West. By 1880, that contest was over, but Pueblo was a new contender for the crown.

CHAPTER SIX

Pueblo: Skins, Steers, and Steel Center

Frontier Pueblo was a classic Caucus town, sustained by the interests of land and trade in an economy based on the exploitation of Mexican-American labor. Pueblo elites had limited difficulties in controlling local labor, and unlike their counterparts in Golden they were successful in accommodating national capital. The merchants and businesspersons of frontier Pueblo were able to cooperate with regional landowners and ranchers in sustaining economic and political institutions controlled by the nonlaboring classes. Pueblo residents were also able to accommodate the Denver boosters, and they supported the Provisional Government of Jefferson Territory.

By 1870, however, as Pueblo boosters promoted economic development by courting monopoly capital investment, conflicts between local and national capital erupted, first in disputes over railroads and later in disputes over land. The federal land office at Pueblo became the focus of a protracted struggle over conflicting land claims and illegal appropriations of the public domain. In fact, these disputes, particularly as they relate to Mexican land-grant titles, continue to occupy an army of federal attorneys. Ultimately, the major challenge for the landowners and merchants of Pueblo was to accommodate the intrusion of national capital and federal authority in a political economy traditionally controlled by a Caucus of land and trade interests. In the course of this struggle, conflicts between the merchant-boosters of the city and the speculators and ranchers of the county were institutionalized in the struggle between Pueblo County Republicans and Democrats, who offered competing partisan solutions in the battle for control of the Pueblo political economy.

TRADING ON THE ARKANSAS RIVER:
THE EARLY YEARS

Pueblo is located on the Old Santa Fe Trail, near the junction of Fountain Creek and the Arkansas River approximately fifty miles east of the Royal Gorge and one hundred miles north of Raton Pass. This is an ideal location for a commercial settlement, with convenient access to the southern Rockies, Kansas, and New Mexico. Consequently, the Bent and Saint Vrain fur-trading company had established a trading post near this site in 1830, and after they moved their operation farther east, another set of traders established Fort Pueblo in

1842, not far from the present site of Pueblo City. The traders had commercial contacts in Taos, Mexico (in what became the Territory of New Mexico in 1850), and were engaged primarily in exchanging the products of Taos labor (most notably, whiskey) for the buffalo robes produced by the southern Colorado tribes. In addition, however, they exploited Mexican labor in irrigated farming and ranching enterprises, which ultimately inspired the Utes to drive the traders out of the region in 1854.[1]

Nevertheless, Ceran Saint Vrain sustained his claim to a substantial section of the Arkansas Valley, and Charles Autobees maintained a ranch near the present site of Huerfano, about twenty miles east of Pueblo. Furthermore, a number of the old fur traders (notably, Joseph Doyle, R. L. ("Uncle Dick") Wooten, William Kroenig, and Ceran Saint Vrain) returned to Colorado from New Mexico in 1858, after Denver and Auraria were established. These traders were prepared to capitalize on the gold rush of 1859.

When the somewhat exaggerated news of the Pike's Peak gold deposits reached Saint Louis in the summer of 1858, a group of would-be prospectors set out along the Santa Fe trail and followed the Arkansas River to Fountain Creek, near the abandoned Fort Pueblo. Apparently this party never intended to settle on the Arkansas but merely to make camp in the fall and move to the gold mines in the spring. Meanwhile, they were met by Kroenig and a representative from Autobees's ranch, who told the immigrants of the successful settlements that had preceded them. The Missouri folks decided to stay, and thus was Fountain City established. A substantial territory was surveyed and platted by two engineers from Missouri, and the settlers survived, initially, by trading with the Arapaho Indians who had camped nearby for the winter. In the spring, the old Fort Pueblo irrigation ditch was reopened, and locals began growing vegetables for the Denver market.[2]

Fountain City was an agricultural and commercial center sustained by cattle ranching and irrigated vegetable gardening. Kroenig and other pioneers of the fur trade maintained their commercial contacts in Taos and established retail outlets in Denver, where both Doyle and Saint Vrain established stores. Would-be prospectors were willing to pay exorbitant prices for vegetables as well as whiskey, hence many Fountain City merchants claimed regional farmlands and employed Mexican-American laborers, producing vegetables for the regional trade. In this regard, there was no substantial conflict between merchants and farmers, at least initially.[3]

Fountain City, like Denver and Auraria, was part of Arapahoe County, Kansas Territory, although the land was still occupied by the Arapaho, Shoshone, Cheyenne, and Ute tribes. Furthermore, since the Arkansas River was the boundary betweeen Kansas and New Mexico, there was some confusion regarding jurisdiction over settlements that spanned the river. Fountain City was in Kansas, but many local ranchers lived in New Mexico. In any case, local residents rejected the authority of these distant governments and joined the Denver leaders who attempted to establish the Territory (or State) of Jefferson in the fall of 1859. Fountain City residents numbered approximately two dozen adult males who were legally entitled to the franchise, but through ingenuity that might have impressed a Cook County precinct captain, Fountain City polled 1,500 votes, all for the same slate of candidates.[4]

Clearly, the merchants, ranchers, and farmers of Fountain City were able to present a united political front, defending their collective interest as nonlaboring employers. The Provisional Government of Jefferson Territory was the government of property and trade, representing the interests of the nonlaboring classes. Thus the Fountain City merchant-farmers were defending their class interest in supporting the provisional government. The fact that they were able to produce 1,500 identical votes suggests that the interests of land and trade faced no organized opposition in Pueblo. Thus local nonlaboring classes were able to control (if not pervert) frontier political institutions.

The Denver boosters must have been impressed, because a Denver delegation appeared that winter with the surveying team of Buell and Boyd to plat a competing town, which they named Pueblo. Within a year, Pueblo overshadowed its neighbor, and most of the original Fountain City residents soon moved to the new metropolis (or to the new town of Cañon City, located farther west at the entrance to the Royal Gorge). Colonel Albert G. Boone, of Denver, opened a general store that was managed by Dr. W. A. Catterson, and Colonel John M. Francisco transported goods from New Mexico. Whiskey was a staple of the local trade, and horse racing was a favorite local pastime, offering an opportunity for speculation that appealed to the gambling spirit of the pioneers. The Fountain City settlers were more than willing to accommodate the Denver businesspersons, so long as the local land owners might continue to enjoy the benefits of regional trade.

In July 1861, the Cañon City editor described the Pueblo settlement as follows:

> The town, consisting of one store and a dozen houses, is prettily situated on the Arkansas, and with the luxuriance of verdure that surround it, would make a delightful sojourn for the ruralist. Fountaine City, just across the Fountaine qui Bouille, is a Mexican town, which looks very characteristic with its adobe homes, and dark inhabitants in the negligent and loose costumes. Leaving the station, the road winds along the serpentine Arkansas, which looks beautiful—its banks heavily fringed with trees. Along its borders are improved farms, their crops looking very promising, and the amount of land under cultivation indicating a strong faith in the richness and fertility of the soil of the extensive bottom lands of Colorado. We were surprised at the goodly character of the improvements, the number of houses, the many men employed in field labor, and the amount of stock grazing in the verdant valleys.[5]

As the Cañon City editor noted, farming and ranching absorbed most of the available capital and labor, including the labor of the Mexican-American residents of Fountain City. Aside from Colonel Boone's store there was no evidence of active trade in city lots. No records of town companies have survived from either Fountain or Pueblo. There was a reference to a "City Company" in the Cañon City paper in January 1861, indicating that Catterson was managing the company's affairs. R. M. Stevenson (who wrote the section on Pueblo's history in O. L. Baskin's *History of the Arkansas Valley, Colorado*) also refers to a town company in reference to a lot-jumping incident, but there were no advertisements or published assessment notices, as was the case in Cañon City and elsewhere. In 1860, Catterson operated the only commercial establishment in town, except for saloons. He must have sold everything, including city lots, but again, there are no records of such sales.[6]

Local residents were not terribly concerned with the trade in city lots but were more anxious to secure their claims to agricultural lands and water. Hall reports that "Judge" W. R. Fowler was the effective government in pre-territorial Pueblo, and Stevenson refers to "Judge" Howard, in Fountain City, as the representative of "law and order." Both Fowler and Howard were associated with the government of Cañon City, and Fowler was appointed election judge in Pueblo in 1861. Both individuals were associated with law and order efforts in both towns, but they left no preterritorial records in Pueblo.[7]

Pueblo had no newspaper prior to 1868, so it is difficult to determine the nature of frontier government, but there was no elected authority prior to territorial organization. The Denver papers referenced a wagon road leading up the Arkansas to the southern Colorado mines, but local government was not discussed. The Cañon City paper referred to a wagon road operated by Jack Wright (of Pueblo) but was silent on the issue of formal government sanction. Quite possibly, municipal government was, as Hall claims, in the hands of the honorable "Judge" Fowler, who presided at "citizen" trials. In any case, there is little evidence to the contrary.[8]

The Fountain City residents were supporters of the Provisional Government of Jefferson Territory; therefore wagon roads and other such enterprises were in some cases sanctioned by "territorial" authority, even though neither municipal nor county government was established. The provisional government did issue a charter to the Fountain City Bridge Company, in December of 1859, and it is possible that the wagon road was also chartered. By January 1861, estray notices were routinely published in the Cañon City paper, and these included notices of stock "taken up" in the Pueblo vicinity. There was also a report of a "citizen trial" for an alleged theft of oxen in the Pueblo vicinity. Quite possibly, "Judge" Fowler presided at that trial, which might have been an informal gathering at Catterson's store. In any case, some form of due process was observed, because the accused were released for lack of evidence.[9]

Despite the influence of Denver and Fountain City investors, there is no evidence of booster "law and order" campaigns or competing claims to governing authority. Apparently, there was no attempt to establish municipal government and thus maintain public order in the interest of attracting capital and labor. Local merchants seemed content to operate under the authority of Jefferson Territory, relying on local capital and labor, including the inhabitants of Fountain City. Nevertheless, while municipal residents seemed satisfied with the law of "Judge" Fowler, the ranchers of the surrounding region were determined to control livestock theft by establishing the certainty and severity of punishment for those who might be inclined to steal cattle.

In August 1861, they organized a vigilance committee that claimed jurisdiction between Huerfano and Beaver Creek (thus including Wooten's farm) and extending south of the Arkansas to encompass the ranches claimed by Zan Hicklin, Joseph Doyle, Charles Autobees, and William Kroenig. The committee claimed the right to try and punish murder as well as crimes against property and specifically stated the intent to protect stock and to prosecute those who sold liquor to the Indians. Clearly, Uncle Dick Wooten and the other old fur traders were "law and order" advocates who had, perhaps, seen the error of their early days. It is not clear that they ever enforced the liquor law, but someone did lynch a horse thief, although the committee did not publicly claim responsibility for the hanging.[10]

While the ranchers around Pueblo were organizing their vigilance committee, territorial government was being established in the region. There is no evidence of conflict between the vigilance committee and the territorial authorities. The official District Court records do not predate 1862, but the Cañon City newspaper reported the opening session in August 1861, when Chief Justice Benjamin F. Hall organized the judicial district. That same month, a meeting was held in Pueblo to nominate candidates for territorial office. Despite some squabbles regarding the relative voting strength of the various Arkansas Valley settlements, local residents as a whole clearly supported territorial government, if only to persuade the federal government to settle the "Indian question," which continued to threaten the security of Arkansas Valley land claims. In the fall of 1860, local tribes refused to sign a new treaty, and the army had already begun a limited campaign against the Navajo in New Mexico. The bloodiest battles were yet to come.[11]

PUEBLO IN THE TERRITORY

Despite the sectional hostilities and violent confrontations associated with the Civil War in Colorado, Pueblo politics remained remarkably peaceful in the early years of territorial government. Unlike the situation in Denver, there was no apparent struggle between local frontier authorities. The town dwellers seemed content with "Judge" Fowler's law, and the ranchers had their vigilance committee. Generally, territorial government did not disturb this arrangement. The vigilance committee continued to operate through the 1860s, but "Judge" Fowler was superseded by Territorial Justice A. A. Bradford, who presided in the Third District Court at Pueblo beginning in 1864. He was reportedly well liked and viewed as a man of the people, but Bradford was not a "hanging judge." He seemed content to enact due process while allowing the vigilance committee, or "soldiers," to eradicate the criminal menace.[12]

Few of the defendants who appeared before Judge Bradford were found guilty, and almost no punishments were ordered. Lorenzo Maez was found guilty on one of three counts of grand larceny, but no punishment was recorded. Jose Rodriquez pleaded guilty to tax evasion and paid fifty dollars plus costs. Juan and Ramon Silber and Juan Jacques were charged with contempt and had to pay court costs. For some of the remaining charges, no disposition was recorded, but nearly half of all cases were definitely not prosecuted. It is not possible to determine what proportion of these cases involved innocent defendants, but local histories suggest that Albert F. Bercaw, Jose Trujillo, the Espinosa brothers, and the Reynolds Gang were all guilty of murder, robbery, and various crimes. All of these men were charged but not prosecuted in Bradford's court. Quite possibly they were never arrested.

The Espinosas and the Reynolds Gang were later killed by "soldiers" under somewhat mysterious circumstances, the Reynolds Gang having been in custody and killed while trying to escape. In general, the coercive power of government was not in the hands of Judge Bradford, but in the hands of vigilantes and army irregulars, who were organized to combat criminals, rebels, and hostile Indians without discrimination or very thorough investigation. In short, Pueblo was subject to paramilitary rule. The territorial authorities followed due process, but armed bands of "soldiers" or vigilantes dispensed justice, such as it was. This was not a major change from preterritorial governance. Local histories suggest that the "People's Court," presumably Fowler's Court, was timid and generally allowed disputants to settle their differences on their own. If one person killed another, there was no trial, so long as "the people" were satisfied.[13] The territorial authorities modified this practice only slightly. Allegations inspired criminal charges, but the accused were not usually prosecuted.

In any case, the umbrella of territorial authority did not immediately foster the development of municipal government. If anything, at least initially there was less municipal government than there had been under "Judge" Fowler. No general store operated in Pueblo from the time Catterson left for military service until John A. Thatcher arrived in 1862 and opened a new one—the only one until the post–Civil War boom. Prior to 1863 there was no regular communication with Denver, and the Santa Fe trail was all but closed to traffic until 1864, when Confederate raids diminished. In short, there was little commerce and hardly sufficient activity to justify the term municipal enterprise. Then, in 1864, efforts to renew local enterprise were dealt a nearly fatal blow by the war with the plains Indians. Stevenson reports that "little of interest occurred in Pueblo" between 1864 and 1868.[14]

The ranchers and farmers of the surrounding region continued their efforts, however, and they were well represented in county governance. Wooten was appointed county commissioner in 1862, as was O.H.P. Baxter, a local rancher. The first elected commissioners (in 1863) were Colonel Boone (owner of the first Pueblo store and also a large landowner), Baxter (the rancher), and W. H. Young, also a wealthy rancher. The commissioners held few regular meetings, but they did hold seven special sessions to deal with the pressing business of governance. Aside from building a courthouse and regulating the construction of county roads, the commissioners taxed liquor and merchants, peddlers, or anyone selling produce (including meat) raised outside the territory. Thus the local ranchers and farmers were protected from competition and Boone was protected from peddlers and hawkers. It is not clear that the competition was very fierce, however, since the available court records contain no reference to violation of license laws prior to 1868.[15]

In any case, the ranchers and farmers were concerned with their land and water rights and sought federal protection for their claims. In December 1862, J. H. Haynes wrote to the Surveyor General, informing him of the situation in Pueblo.

Dear Sir,

I live on the Arkansas River, five miles west of the Indian Reserve and twenty miles East of Pueblo in the best portion of the territory for farming, and wish to call your attention to the great inconvenience we are laboring under for want of a survey. There are now twenty-five claims between the mouth of the Fou. qui Bouille and the Ind. Reserve a distance of twenty-five miles, occupied by bona fide settlers; Some have good houses and plank fences, one in particular has a house that cost five thousand dollars and a fence two miles long, occupied by Col. A. G. Boone. V. D. Boone and Seth Hayes all wish to make more substantial improvements & cannot do so safely without a survey. Five townships, one North of, and four South a base line run from the S.E. corner of the Township Pueblo is in would cover the whole ground and would bring much more cash immediately than the expense would be of surveying, besides I would suggest the idea of asking Congress to allow you to have claims run out as now held provided the occupants would pay cash down for land or within the year and pay for surveying if necessary. I know many in this country who have had peaceable possession of 2–3 & some 500 acres that would be glad to have their claims surveyed and pay for them any time, and I believe the Government would get more for the territory that way than any other. Where I live we have a ditch nearly completed that will cost five or six thousand dollars 7 miles long. All wish to plant fruit trees this season and will undoubtedly suffer much loss unless there is something done for their relief.[16]

These settlers were concerned because they had invested so much capital in land to which they did not hold legal title.

Unlike Doyle and the other fur-trade pioneers, Haynes and his neighbors had not purchased their land and did not claim title on the basis of Mexican land grants. They did not organize a land claim club but merely claimed squatters' rights, protected by the vigilance committee. Haynes and his neighbors did not register their claims with the Arkansas Valley Claim Club, which was organized in Cañon City. They did, however, organize the Arkansas Valley Ditch Company, which recorded nine claims, in February 1864. The by-laws specified that water would be divided into nine shares and that the excess would be sold or rented. Members were charged assessments, payable in cash or in labor, and a man was hired to maintain the ditch. Water rights could be transferred, if authorized by the secretary, and excess water could be purchased at three dollars per acre. This purchase price was considerably higher than the member's fee of five dollars per share, presumably because of the capital investment that the members had made.[17]

It seems likely that the value of these water rights declined considerably during the Civil War. The territory of Colorado and southern Colorado, in particular, were hard hit by the Civil War and the accompanying battles with the tribes of the plains. Then, when the transcontinental railroad was built through Wyoming, many town boosters and speculators abandoned their claims and moved north. It was not until the railroads came to Colorado in 1870 that the economy recovered from the Civil War doldrums. Meanwhile, the territory faced serious problems. The first governor (William Gilpin) raised troops to fight alongside the Union forces in Mexico against the Confederate Texans, but the treasury could not support these efforts. The second governor (John Evans) raised troops to fight the Indians, but the Sand Creek Massacre (1864) inspired not only retaliation but a federal investigation of affairs in Colorado.[18]

As serious as these problems were in Denver, they were further complicated in the Pueblo region by political cleavages within the southern Colorado population. Many Pueblo residents had emigrated from southern states, and they also were tied commercially to the trade in Missouri and to the Texas cattle trade. Aside from that, they were to some extent in competition with Denver, which was a northern Republican town. Although some Pueblo residents, such as O.H.P. Baxter, joined the Colorado regiment of the Union army, the region also harbored a band of confederate irregulars, who trained at Mace's Hole (near Zan Hicklin's ranch). One account suggests that the local residents were divided almost equally between Union and Confederate sympathizers, who nearly came to blows on 4 July 1862 when the opposing camps disputed the choice of which flag to fly at the Independence Day picnic.[19]

Even those who joined the Colorado regiment were more concerned with Indians than with rebels. The local courts were less than effective in prosecuting the rebel raiders of the Arkansas Valley and relied on Union troops, recruited in Denver, to combat guerrilla banditry. O.H.P. Baxter joined the Third Regiment in 1864 and recruited a large number of Pueblo men for the attack on the "hostile" plains Indians. This regiment never managed to engage the "hostiles" but attacked a settlement composed primarily of women, children, and old men who had complied with Governor Evans's orders and encamped under the protective custody of a U.S. Army fort. This "battle" is more commonly known as the Sand Creek Massacre.[20] The desire to extinguish Indian claims to the eastern plains was what ultimately united the two settlements. Hence, Pueblo residents, with the support of Denver businesspersons (who financed the regiment) and territorial if not federal authority, distinguished themselves in Colorado's most spectacular Indian massacre.[21]

In any case, the Sand Creek Massacre and the subsequent struggle to subdue the "hostile" tribes of the plains eliminated what had proved to be the major barrier to the agricultural industry of the Arkansas Valley. The Colorado regiment, in its bloody raid on the Arapaho and Cheyenne of the Sand Creek settlement, managed to enflame Anglo-Indian tensions to the point where federal troops were forced to act. Thus the federal government finally did defend the land claimed by the Arkansas Valley settlers, not through the Surveyor General's Office but through a military campaign.

Despite the anti-Union sentiments of many Pueblo residents and the local-national conflict on Indian relocation policy, local residents recognized that federal authority was a critical factor in the economic development of the Pueblo region. Aside from removing the tribes of the plains and securing property rights, the government facilitated the development of Colorado railroads. Pueblo's renewed prosperity was based, to a large extent, on the railroads that arrived in the 1870s, but by 1868 Pueblo was already growing rapidly. Its population, which had dropped to less than fifty in the previous year, had tripled by 1868, and more than doubled in that year. Commercial enterprise thrived, and a local newspaper was published. In 1869, a brick factory was established, and the first Board of Trade was organized. The Pueblo boosters were thus united to spread the good news regarding economic growth. The Board estimated municipal commerce in 1869 at $390,980 and local manufactures at $36,500.[22] The products of industry for the county are displayed in Table 6.1.

Pueblo in 1868. Courtesy Pueblo Library District

Pueblo was a commercial center in 1870, but manufactures were developing slowly and local actors were also involved in the transportation industry. Nevertheless, the town thrived on trade, and the trade depended on the cattle and farming industries, which developed rapidly in the 1870s. In 1870, the assessed value of Pueblo County land was $857,811. The value of Pueblo livestock (particularly cattle and sheep) was comparable, and Pueblo was a major livestock market. It was not, however, a "trail's end" cattle town, like Dodge City or Abilene, in Kansas, where the Texas herds converged at the railhead on the prairie. Instead, Pueblo served as a commercial center for

Table 6.1 Products of Industry in Pueblo County, 1869

Source	Amount	Value
Number of acres under cultivation	18,830	$188,300
Value of ditches for irrigation		188,300
Number and value of cattle owned	26,427	774,408
Number and value of sheep owned	12,055	24,755
Number and value of hogs owned	2,325	19,118
Number of bushels of corn raised	254,640	275,740
Number of bushels of small grain raised	67,836	171,590
Pounds of vegetables	2,335,600	70,068
Bushels of corn to acre	37	
Sacks of flour manufactured	11,210	67,260
Pounds of wool produced	18,800	37,600
Pounds of butter made	17,645	8,882
Gallons of native wine made	1,092	4,368

Source: Frank Hall, *History of the State of Colorado*, 4 vols. (Chicago: Blakely, 1889–1895), 3: 456.

the ranchers and farmers of southern Colorado, who were well established by the end of the Civil War. Trade dominated the municipal economy, and cattle dominated that trade.[23]

Among the southern Colorado cattle barons was John W. Prowers, who organized the Bent-Prowers Cattle and Horse Growers Association in March 1870. Prowers grazed livestock along the Arkansas, maintained cattle and sheep breeding ranches, and was known in Pueblo for his "well bred beeves." By 1870, few of the Arkansas Valley ranchers were trailing longhorns from Texas. Charlie Goodnight (who maintained a local ranch) had established that business during the Civil War, but in the 1870s he was breeding improved stock, and his "law and order" boys enforced his law prohibiting Texas steers from crossing the Goodnight range. Since Arkansas Valley ranchers did not maintain an open range, conflicts with local farmers, which were endemic in Greeley, were far less rancorous in the Arkansas Valley. In any case, the farmers of the Pueblo region fenced their gardens and often raised cattle themselves.[24]

The extent to which the cattle trade dominated the Pueblo economy of 1870 is apparent in the census figures from that year. Trade was the predominant local industry, accounting for only 12 percent of the households but over 60 percent of local wealth. Twelve of the thirty-one merchants were engaged in the wholesale cattle trade, and they controlled $292,666 in wealth. In short, the cattle merchants of Pueblo represented 39 percent of the merchant class and controlled 59 percent of commercial wealth. This amounted to 37 percent of total municipal wealth.

Pueblo contained a substantial nonlaboring class that controlled sufficient wealth to employ the laboring classes, which constituted 62 percent of the households but controlled only 8 percent of local wealth in 1870 (see Table 6.2). The artisans were relatively wealthy, claiming $368 in average household wealth, but they represented only 21 percent of the laboring class households (or 13 percent of the local population). Wage workers comprised the bulk of the laboring classes. They constituted 49 percent of Pueblo households but controlled only 3 percent of local wealth, reporting on average only $160. Most of these workers were common laborers, working on farms, flour mills, or in the brick yard. There were also a few craft-title households (carpenters, for example) that reported no wealth and were thereby coded as wage workers.

Merchants, particularly livestock merchants, controlled the bulk of nonlaboring class wealth, but there were a sufficient number of "owner-employers" to provide wages for the laboring classes. There were freighters, flour mill operators, and brickyard owners, but the major employers in the Pueblo region were farmers and ranchers. Unlike their counterparts in Greeley, the farmers of Pueblo were not members of the laboring classes. They generally employed more labor than their families provided. Some of the wealthy farmers maintained something like a hacienda (or estate) populated with Mexican-American laborers. William Craig, for example, reported $100,000 in real wealth and

Table 6.2 Wealth by Class Category for Households in Pueblo, 1870

Class Category	Wealth	Percentage of Wealth	Households	Percentage of Households
Nonlaboring classes	$725,346	91.92	105	37.77
Owner	120,030	15.21	32	11.51
Professional	46,200	5.85	12	.32
Merchant	548,166	69.47	49	17.63
None	10,950	1.39	12	4.32
Laboring classes	63,745	8.08	173	62.23
Artisan	41,995	5.32	37	13.31
Worker	21,750	2.76	136	48.92
Total	789,091		278	

Source: U.S. Bureau of the Census (1870) Population Schedule for Pueblo County, Colorado Territory.

$26,100 in personal wealth. His live-in labor force included his wife and a nineteen-year-old female, who claimed no occupation, as well as eleven male farm laborers, ranging in age from twenty-five to forty-one. Four of the laborers had Anglo-Saxon surnames and were born in Europe or in the eastern states. Seven had Hispanic surnames and were born in New Mexico.

Craig was unusually wealthy and employed more laborers than the average Pueblo farmer. In general the farmers controlled virtually all of the agricultural wealth but constituted only one-third of the agricultural population. The distinction between laboring and nonlaboring farmers is, of course, a matter of degree, since most farmers did physically labor in productive enterprise. In Pueblo, however, the farming industry of 1870 was characterized by the employment of wage labor. This is best illustrated in comparison to Greeley. Pueblo farmers claimed 92 percent of the wealth but constituted only 33 percent of the households, whereas in Greeley that same year farmers claimed 93 percent of agricultural wealth and constituted 84 percent of the households. Pueblo farm laborers claimed 4 percent of the wealth and constituted 56 percent of the households. In Greeley in 1870 farm laborers claimed only 2 percent of the wealth and constituted only 10 percent of the agricultural population.

If anything, these data underestimate the difference between Pueblo and Greeley, since some of the wealthiest Pueblo farmers and poorest farm laborers, including Craig and his workers, did not live within the city limits. In Greeley, all of the original settlers were entitled to a residence in town, and many of the wealthier farmers were enumerated as town residents. Nevertheless, the farmers both in and around Greeley relied on family labor. In contrast, the Pueblo farmers relied on wage workers.

Pueblo, in 1870, was a town of merchants and gentlemen farmers who relied on Mexican-American labor and commercial relations with the cattle barons of southern Colorado. Pueblo was a Caucus town with a long tradition of business class control. Although no longer selling whiskey to the Indian tribes, Pueblo traders were continuing the tradition of exploiting Mexican (or Mexican-American) labor.

In this regard, it is important to understand how the laboring classes of Pueblo were divided by ethnicity. In the census reports, Anglos were much more likely to be enumerated with a particular occupation. In fact, Mexican-American farm workers were always identified as "farm laborers" or "common laborers," but some (although not all) of the Anglos were enumerated with the distinctive occupation of "works on farm." These "workers" earned more than the "laborers." In fact, average wealth for farm "workers" was $380; for farm laborers, $124. In Greeley, where there were no Mexican-American households, average wealth for farm laborers was $340, and the "farm worker" category did not exist. Thus the Pueblo farmers (who claimed average wealth of $4,800, compared to $1,671 in Greeley) employed a segmented agricultural labor force. The labor aristocracy was the "worker," and only Anglos were admitted to this favored position. The "laborers" were divided into Anglo and Hispanic fractions, the latter being denied opportunities for mobility.

In addition, although legally entitled to vote as natives of New Mexico, the Mexican-American laborers were excluded from social and political participation by virtue of language. Nearly all were enumerated as illiterate ("can not read" and "can not write"), while virtually none of the Anglos were so distinguished in the census records. It is possible that the immigrants from New Mexico could read and write in Spanish, but since there was no Spanish newspaper published in Pueblo in 1870, there was little opportunity for mobilization of the Mexican-American labor force, particularly since they were geographically isolated as a rural laboring class. In March 1870, the territorial legislature considered translating territorial laws into Spanish, but the bill was defeated and the Mexican-Americans remained, for all intents and purposes, politically disenfranchised.

THE CHALLENGE OF NATIONAL INCORPORATION

In 1870, Pueblo established a municipal government that served the interests of merchants and shopkeepers by defending public order and predictability in trade, thus facilitating booster efforts to attract labor and capital investment. At the same time, the Pueblo County government became increasingly involved in efforts to finance railroad construction and establish Pueblo as the transportation center of Southern Colorado. Although these were not incompatible enterprises, there was considerable conflict between town and county as well as conflicts between local, regional, national, and international capital.

By 1870, the Pueblo County Commissioners had secured their control of county affairs after eight years in office, but they still faced serious problems. The board still met infrequently, mostly in special session, and received few petitions or communications from constituents. They were primarily concerned with the construction and maintenance of county roads and the appropriation of sufficient revenues to sustain public enterprise. Money was the most serious problem, since a local official had absconded with the school funds, leaving his bondholder and the county without adequate resources to replace the stolen funds. Hence the commissioners reevaluated the amount and the security of the bonds required for public officials.[25]

To raise much-needed revenues, the commissioners taxed property and established licensing fees for lawyers as well as for merchants, peddlers, and shopkeepers. The commissioners also cut costs by routinely refusing to pay bills tendered for rent, materials, or services. The bills for rent on jury rooms and jail cells were cut by one-third to one-half, and the fees for county officials were similarly reduced. At the same time, the cost of housing prisoners and paupers was defrayed by their forced labor, and all bills were subject to cost-cutting scrutiny. The most novel fund-raising effort of this period was the decision to sell town lots—county property that bordered the town of Pueblo. The original town plat, as surveyed by Buell and Boyd, contained an area far beyond the reach of the commercial enterprise of 1860. Hence, as the settlement began to grow in the late 1860s, the county was able to raise revenues by selling some of the properties that were on the fringe of the original settlement.

In 1870, commissioners received a petition requesting that Pueblo be incorporated as a town. This was immediately done, and the commissioners established the legal bounds of the new Town of Pueblo on 22 March 1870. They also appointed a group of local businesspersons to act as trustees until the next election (in April). In that election, there were some complaints by local residents who discovered that they did not reside within the legal bounds of the town. The commissioners, undaunted, reaffirmed their decision regarding the town boundaries and proceeded to sell those lots that lay outside the newly established town limits. It is not clear that the county was appropriating town property illegally, but the incorporated town of Pueblo was smaller than the settlement platted in 1860. No town company records were preserved, so it is impossible to determine if there was any legal basis for disputing the commissioners' actions. They had, as requested, incorporated the town and called for municipal elections.[26]

Town trustees were elected in April 1870, but no official records of their deliberations prior to 1875 have survived. The first meeting of the appointed trustees was reported in the *Colorado Chieftain*, which also reported election returns. The election was contested by candidates of the "City" and the "People's" parties. The former swept the election, although Henry Cooper (a local manufacturer) and O.H.M. Baxter (a rancher and former county commissioner) were elected on the "People's" ticket. It is unclear which "people" they represented, however, since both had been among the appointed trustees, all of whom were elected to municipal office. It appears, however, that the "people" were local industrial classes, particularly farmers, ranchers, and manufacturers, who resisted the booster efforts of the "city," as the investment of national capital and the imposition of federal authority threatened to undermine local control of Pueblo County industry.[27]

It is clear that the municipal government represented the interests of the merchants and shopkeepers by licensing peddlers and defending public order. The city thus protected established business from transient competitors and facilitated booster efforts to attract labor and capital by assuring the reluctant easterners that their persons and property would be secure. The Board licensed not only peddlers but also auctioneers, billard halls, bowling alleys, and saloons. They also prohibited carrying weapons (including knives). There was a municipal police court, from which no records have survived, but the local paper often reported the cases that appeared before the local court. In February 1872, the local paper listed two assault and battery charges, three charges of carrying weapons (or concealed weapons); two riot charges, and three charges of drunkenness. All those charged were convicted and fined five to ten dollars.[28]

Meanwhile, the Third District Court continued to enforce the territorial law, and Judge Moses Hallet, who served from 1869 through 1871, was somewhat more involved in the war on crime than his predecessor, Bradford, had been (see Table 6.3). Hallet had a fairly balanced criminal docket, although his court seems to have been more concerned with government and property than with persons. Hallet's docket lists 11 assault cases, 3 murders, and 1 rape as well as 4 charges of illegally altering brands, 24 larcenies, and a set of other crimes against property. Crimes against government were a mixture of gambling (25), license violations (15), and keeping a tippling house open on the Sabbath (17), with a sprinkling of contempt and similar cases.[29]

Table 6.3 Criminal Cases by Offense in the Pueblo District Court, 1864–1866, 1869–1871, and 1880

	Offense against			
Date	Persons	Property	Government	Total
1864–66	20 (.30)	29 (.43)	18 (.27)	67
1869–71	15 (.12)	32 (.25)	79 (.63)	126
1880	10 (.32)	16 (.52)	7 (.23)	31

Source: Docket of Third District Court of Colorado Territory, Denver Federal Center. Records from 1880: Pueblo District Court, Colorado State Archives.

During this period (1869–1871) when Pueblo was emerging as the commercial center for the Arkansas Valley agricultural industry, the criminal docket of the Territorial District Court reflected the industrial shift from land to trade in the corresponding shift from crimes against property to crimes against government. The town boosters (particularly the merchants) gained relative advantage not only in economic resources but also in political organization after establishing the Board of Trade in 1869. Consequently, their interest in public order became the predominant concern of local government. Particularly in the years of transition, as boosters attempted to attract monopoly capital in the early 1870s, the concern with public order was overwhelming.

If one included the actions by the Police Court as reported in the newspaper, the shift would be even more dramatic. Even within the District Court, however, the concern for public order (or crimes against government) was much greater in the 1869–1871 period than either before or after. The District Court was enforcing not only the antigambling statute passed by the territorial legislature but also the licensing laws. It was defending public order in the interest of local boosterism, protecting property and even persons to some extent. In addition the court by this time was more successful in bringing the guilty to justice or, at least, in punishing those convicted.

The rapist and one man convicted of assault with intent to kill were each sentenced to one year of hard labor. Two other crimes were punished with prison labor: an assault with nine months and a larceny with eighteen months. Many cases still were not prosecuted, but the court was exercising general authority and according to Hall, "Judge Lynch fell into disrepute" after a secure jail house was constructed.[30] Most important, the court was routinely collecting fines from persons like R. L. Wooten, who continued to sell liquor without a license, and Charles Autobees, who refused to pay his property taxes and was also convicted of selling liquor to soldiers. It seems that the U.S. Army had driven the tribes from the plains, but the liquor trade continued nonetheless. In any case, unlike the vigilantes and the "soldiers" of the Civil War period, the territorial officials prosecuted even the most respected members of the nonlaboring classes. This merely aggravated the growing animosity between the new city boosters and the traditional, landed interests of the county.

By 1870, commerce thrived, government was firmly in the hands of elected local officials, and there was a concerted effort to establish "law and order." After a Republican slate of municipal officers was elected, the local police court was actively defending public order, but the Pueblo County vote in territorial and county elections of 1870 was almost evenly divided between the two parties (see Table 6.4). The business and commercial interests of the city voted for Republicans by a considerable margin, whereas the county vote favored the Democrats. For instance, the Republican candidate for district attorney garnered 136 votes out of 229 within the city, but that was not enough to offset the 208 votes out of 339 for the Democratic candidate in the county

Table 6.4 Pueblo City and County Vote in the 1870 Territorial Election

Office	Candidate	Party	City	County[a]	Total
Delegate	Chaffee	Republican	144	134	278
	Miller	Democrat	87	207	294
District attorney	Green	Republican	136	131	267
	Macon	Democrat	93	208	301
Probate judge	Smith	Republican	144	101	245
	Hepburn	Democrat	87	223	310
County commissioner	Baxter	Republican	144	149	293
	Stone	Democrat	87	195	282
Assessor	Rice	Republican	144	148	292
	Boone	Democrat	86	185	271

Source: *Colorado Transcript* (Pueblo, weekly) 15 September 1870:2 and 22 September 1870:2 (for county total).
[a] County vote excludes the votes cast in Pueblo City.

precincts. The Democrats won all but two offices, and W. F. Stone, the defeated Democratic candidate for Pueblo County Commissioner, even claimed that he lost the election due to fraud. The editor of the *Colorado Chieftain* explained the irregularity as follows.

> For reasons of informality, Precinct No. 2 (Boonville) was thrown out, which would have made the difference of eleven votes in favor of the Democrats for Delegate to Congress, and for County Commissioner a difference of seven votes in favor of Stone, which, with a miscount of five too many for Baxter in Hicklin's Precinct, would elect Stone by one majority.[31]

There might well have been fraud in the counting of ballots, but the charges were never substantiated.

Given that the Republicans in Washington were supporting efforts to open up western lands for homesteaders, large landholders of the Pueblo region remained loyal to the Democrats. Doyle's Precinct, for example, located on the Vigil and Saint Vrain grant, voted unanimously (62–0) for the Democratic slate. In Pueblo, however, support for the Republican platform was combined with local efforts to establish public order. Toward this end, the editor of the *Colorado Chieftain* frequently addressed the newly elected Board of Trustees and pointed to the challenge faced by the infant municipal government of 1872:

> *the Calaboose*—We learn that the calaboose is in a filthy and outrageous condition. The inmates are compelled to sleep on the floor with only one blanket, while the place is fairly overrun with vermin. Again, it is

not safe and any man with ordinary pluck and a good jack knife, can whittle himself out in a few hours. We hope that the board of trustees will look into the matter.[32]

The editor continued to promote law enforcement efforts while at the same time defending Pueblo against criticism in the Denver press. In 1872, an alleged murderer was seized from the Pueblo jail and hanged by impatient vigilantes. The editor did not report the lynching in any detail but did make reference to the reports in other newspapers.

We notice that the eastern papers in alluding to the recent "necktie festival" held in this place, uniformly give the name of White as Garraghty, and locate the scene of the hanging at Denver. This is unjust but we are consoled by the reflection that glory is hardly ever rendered to whom it properly belongs. Denver has acquired such a reputation for hanging, that whenever a man is stretched up, he is credited by the outside world to that place and no questions asked.[33]

Thus the editor celebrated the fact that Pueblo, unlike Denver, was safely under the control of elected officials who, with the occasional assistance of vigilantes, had succeeded in establishing public order and protecting persons and property.

Attracting Eastern Capital

The lead story in the *Colorado Chieftain* on 10 March 1870 was a response to a recent editorial (from an unnamed source) that applauded the courage of a congressman who had proposed that the United States seize Mexican land grants and divide the land into small tracts for homesteaders. The Pueblo editor's decidedly caustic reply betrayed a distaste for eastern (or northern) capitalists in suggesting that this proposal was akin to the declaration that freed other people's slaves. He went on to offer a defense of land grants and a rationalization for monopolies, noting that Daniel Boone had received a land grant for valuable services rendered and that other pioneers were similarly rewarded by the U.S. government. The editor complained that the government had granted excellent grazing lands to the remnants of the Colorado tribes and suggested that it was certainly more appropriate to offer lands to those who rendered service, such as railroad companies. Finally, the editor noted that capitalists such as Commodore Vanderbilt were free to buy "half a State." Hence the concern for monopoly seemed suspiciously misplaced.[34]

An adjoining editorial spoke more directly to the railroad question, while extolling the virtue of political dissension and the discussion of opposing views. The editor argued as follows.

Few projected railroads have been killed by opposition. . . . Many a railroad and other public enterprise has been helped along by a wholesome attempt to stop it. . . . Denver has had and is still having her attack of the railroad pox. . . . We too shall have a railroad running in our midst, and that soon. . . . We are not speaking for the Town of Pueblo, but for the Arkansas Valley; we will get roads into the country first; the towns will take care of themselves.[35]

As might be inferred from the editor's remarks, the railroad question in Pueblo inspired considerable controversy, with competition between Arkansas Valley settlements and struggles between local and national capitalists. In some ways, the southern Colorado railroad wars were simply an extension of the northern struggles. To a large extent, the same cast of characters appeared in both scenes, but there was a newcomer who played an important role in bringing the railroad to Pueblo. General William J. Palmer was an ambitious young man who had worked for the Kansas Pacific, directing the survey of the southern route in 1867. Although the K.P. decided not to build along the Arkansas Valley, Palmer was convinced that southern Colorado was the ideal location for constructing a small railroad empire. Thus inspired by his dream, Palmer quit his job with the Kansas Pacific and returned east in search of capital.[36]

On the way, he had the good fortune to meet William Proctor Mellen and the good taste to fall in love with Mellen's daughter, thus securing with this marriage an invaluable business association. Palmer was a most persuasive young man, and he soon secured the cooperation and assistance of Denver businesspersons, including John Evans, A. C. Hunt, and F. Z. Solomon (J. B. Doyle's former partner). In addition, British and American investors were attracted to the scheme, including Wilson Waddingham, who allowed Palmer to sell his share of the Maxwell (formerly the Beaubien and Miranda) grant to help finance the railroad company. Thus assured of adequate support, Palmer organized the Denver and Rio Grande Railroad (D.&R.G.) in October 1870, with capital stock of $2,500,000 and headquarters located in Denver. Thus while this company was controlled by eastern financiers, it was considered a Denver railroad.[37]

Palmer's general plan was to build a railroad from northern to southern Colorado, then south to New Mexico and Texas and west to the coal mines of southern Colorado, eventually connecting with the transcontinental traffic in Salt Lake City. To finance this ambitious effort, Palmer and his associates planned to purchase federal land and establish settlements along the chosen railroad route, selling the land at inflated prices. Since both the Denver and Kansas Pacific railroads were suffering at the hands of the Union Pacific and Colorado Central, the plan to build a southern railway system met with enthusiastic support from Denver businesspersons and from the Kansas Pacific.[38]

In fact, the southern railroad received strong support from the northern Colorado settlements that were at the mercy of the Union Pacific. R. A. Cameron, from Greeley, formed a partnership with Palmer in his plan to establish a settlement in the vicinity of Colorado City (about halfway between Denver and Pueblo). The new settlement, called Colorado Springs, was not a replica of the temperate agricultural community in Greeley. Instead, it was to a large extent a health resort and country estate for wealthy British investors who enjoyed a bit of Old World culture in the wholesome yet decidedly primitive Territory of Colorado. The efforts to attract the British gentry were so successful that Colorado Springs soon became known as "Little London."[39]

The prosperity of Colorado Springs was achieved at the cost of all but destroying the pioneer settlement of Colorado City, which was across the tracks but was denied a railroad depot. In 1871, as the first stretch of Denver and Rio Grande track was completed, the company established a pattern of service to local communities. The company would approach two settlements that might be on the path of the railroad and request municipal bonds from each town to finance construction efforts. When the bonds were secured and the rail connection completed, the company would build a depot on railroad land between the two existing towns and invite local residents to buy town lots near the depot. Thus the railroad played one town against the other, received bonds from both, and then established a new town, further profiting from the sale of town lots. In defense of Palmer, he did not play that game with Colorado City but merely established his railroad town. He did, however, run a version of this operation in Pueblo and attempt to capitalize on the rivalry between Pueblo and Cañon City. Thus one might appreciate the perspicacity of the Pueblo editor, who suggested that the railroad be attracted to the region, allowing the towns to fend for themselves.[40]

Once Palmer and his associates had established rail service between Denver and Colorado Springs (in January 1872), grading commenced on the proposed route to the Arkansas Valley. The company's charter had explicitly described a rail connection to the coal fields at Labran, not far from Cañon City. This route was to pass "near Pueblo" on the way to the "Grand Cañon of the Arkansas" (now called Royal Gorge), which is just above Cañon City. Pueblo citizens were concerned that the rail might bypass their community and make Cañon City the transportation center of the Arkansas. To allay these fears, A. C. Hunt of Denver met with the interested public in March 1871 to explain that although Pueblo was not on the route that the company had planned to build, it was possible to change plans, given an adequate expression of local interest and support.[41]

Then Cañon City residents were persuaded to offer $50,000 in bonds, thereby inspiring Pueblans, in June, to approve $100,000 to aid the construction efforts. This grant was deemed inadequate, so on 1 January 1872 the Pueblo voters approved an additional $50,000 in bonds. Apparently, these additional funds were not really necessary, because the D.&R.G. had already contracted for the construction of a road with a depot within one mile of the Pueblo courthouse. In any case, the railroad arrived in June and a gala celebration, with a host of Denver dignitaries, was held in Pueblo on 3 July.[42] Whatever good will this celebration might have engendered, relations between Pueblo and the "Denver" railroad were never particularly cordial and soon deteriorated to the point of open hostility.

Pueblans initially felt that they had been duped into approving additional bonds for a railroad that was already under construction; the mistrust of the railroad company was aggravated by the machinations that followed. It is likely that Palmer had never intended to establish a depot in Pueblo but had only constructed a temporary depot there to secure the promise of county bonds. In November 1871, two months before the railroad reached Colorado Springs, Palmer and his associates had already organized the Central Colorado Improvement Company in order to purchase the Nolan grant from Charlie Goodnight (the cattle baron) and two other claimants. After securing some 40,000 acres on the south side of the Arkansas River, the railroad company moved its Pueblo depot, thereby establishing the town of South Pueblo. This so enraged the Pueblo officials that they refused to issue the bonds that had been promised, and although Palmer sued the county, Judge Hallet concluded that the bonds were in fact forfeit.[43]

The "Denver" railroad represented the entering wedge of monopoly capital interference in the heretofore unchallenged affairs of Pueblo County capitalists. This first assault was successfully countered with the assistance of the District Court, in but the first of a number of decisions that Hallet rendered with regard to the operation of the Denver and Rio Grande. Before the end of the decade, Palmer became extremely familiar with the law of Judge Moses Hallet, and Palmer was convinced that his prospects for a favorable decision were limited in that court. Since much of this legal controversy was related to the control of the Royal Gorge, the details of those proceedings will be discussed more fully in the history of Cañon City. For present purposes, it is more appropriate to turn to the other railroad that helped to establish Pueblo as the transportation center of the Arkansas Valley.

In September 1872, representatives of the Kansas Pacific railroad came to Pueblo to discuss the possibility of building a line from eastern Colorado to Pueblo. Initially, the K.P. asked for $300,000 in bonds, but local businesspersons refused to consider this proposal or to sponsor its presentation to the county commissioners. Instead, it was agreed that the county would ask its citizens to approve a $200,000 bond issue in a special December election. The *Colorado Chieftain* published notice of this election, along with a rather confusing discussion of the corporate sponsorship for the construction of this railroad. According to the *Chieftain* and its correspondence with a Kansas Pacific official, the K.P. was attempting to form a partnership with the Atchison,

Topeka & Santa Fe (A.T.&S.F.) to construct a southern route to the Arkansas Valley. If such a plan was indeed in the works, it never did materialize.[44]

Instead, the A.T.&S.F. approached the Pueblo County Commissioners with a plan to build an independent line if Pueblo could raise an additional $200,000 in bonds. This inspired considerable controversy, as partisans defended the claims of the competing railroad companies. According to Hall, the A.T.&S.F. company was somehow able to convince the county to delay the vote on the K.P. bonds until the voters had the opportunity to approve the A.T.&S.F. proposal. In any case, the electors were treated to twin elections, and they approved both the A.T.&S.F. bonds, on 14 January, and the K.P. bonds, on 21 January. Amid allegations of corruption and favoritism the local editor was firm in his support of the A.T.&S.F. Editorial remarks warned the readers to beware of the unscrupulous efforts that the K.P. officials might make in attempts to purchase votes.[45]

> It is rumored that the Kansas Pacific proposes to colonize three or four hundred voters—imported from Kansas City—in the east end of the county, for the purpose of voting against the Kansas and Colorado bonds and in favor of their own. . . . Let the qualified voters of the county, uninfluenced by corrupt considerations, untrammeled by undue, illegal pressure of a powerful moneyed corporation, decide the issue now prominently before the people of Pueblo county.[46]

The local editor applauded the decision to accept the A.T.&S.F. offer, at the same time accepting the fact that the people were responsive to last-minute appeals that ultimately insured the success of the K.P. bonds. The overwhelming support of the A.T.&S.F. bonds seems to have been based on three factors. For one thing, negotiations with the Kansas Pacific suggested that Pueblo residents were somewhat suspicious of that company, perhaps because of its relations with both the City of Denver and the Denver and Rio Grande railroad. The original agreement stipulated that the bonds would not be released unless the depot was built on the north side of the Arkansas rather than in the railroad town of South Pueblo. A second point was that the businesspersons of Pueblo probably preferred the A.T.&S.F., at least partly because it was in competition with the Denver railroads. Finally, W. B. Strong, manager of the Atchison and Topeka road, confided that he intended to establish Pueblo as the commercial center of Colorado. Clearly, he joined the Pueblo elites in their aspirations to unseat Denver as the Queen City of the Rockies. Thus it is not surprising that the A.T.&S.F. was given the first chance to influence the electorate.[47] As the local editor explained,

> . . . the preference of this paper has been from the first, with the Atchison Topeka & Santa Fe road, believing as we do that it is the only corporation

which will give us an independent competing line to the markets of the east; . . . we look upon it as the one and only line calculated to free us from the odious discrimination and unjust tribute exacted by Denver, . . . In assuming this position we have not been activated by a selfish motive, but have been controlled by the broad principle that our leading businessmen are the best judges of the railroad enterprise best adapted to their business interests. Their expressed sympathy and their desire is unmistakably with the Atchison and Topeka road.[48]

Why did the Pueblo County voters choose to accept an additional $200,000 of debt to attract the Kansas Pacific? Perhaps this was an effort to equal the rail connections of Denver and to establish the centrality of Pueblo. Local interest in the construction of multiple railroads also undoubtedly inspired electioneering efforts. James Carlile and William Moore were prominent Pueblo businessmen who had enriched themselves through the construction of railroads. They contracted with the Denver Pacific, the Kansas Pacific, the Atchison Topeka, and even the Denver and Rio Grande. They did not operate railroads and had no particular interest in the various companies. Instead, they contracted to grade the roadbeds and lay the track for whoever might wish to build. They were, above all, well served by the railroad wars. The greater the number of railroads, the greater the business for Moore and Carlile of Pueblo.[49]

The railroad contractors and the commercial and industrial interests of Pueblo all thrived on the railroad war between the Atchison, Topeka & Santa Fe and the Denver and Rio Grande. In the machinations of railroad kings, Pueblo residents were, for the most part, spectators. Given the experience of Loveland and his Golden associates, this was probably the best position for the Pueblo businesspersons to assume. They clearly seemed to favor the Atchison Topeka road, but the local economy did not rise and fall with the future of that company. The future of Pueblo was tied not to the control of railroads but to the control of trade and, at least equally important, to the control of land and water. In the late 1870s, that trade was still predominantly based on relations with farmers and cattle barons, but that situation was changing rapidly.

PUEBLO IN THE EIGHTIES AND BEYOND

The railroads were the leading edge of capital penetration and accumulation in Colorado. The initial stage in the process of economic and political development, associated with the closing of the Colorado frontier, was marked by the coming of the railroads. This process fundamentally transformed Colorado in the 1870s. By 1876, statehood was proclaimed, and by 1880 Colorado suffered from the same types of problems that were plaguing the more established communities of the east. In the closing decades of the nineteenth century, there were race riots and skilled trades strikes in Denver, bloody battles in the mining industry, Grangers and Greenbackers at the polls, and even a Populist in the governor's chair. The frontier towns of Colorado, including Pueblo, were forced to accommodate these economic and political transformations.

The farmers and merchants of Pueblo managed to accommodate railroads and to expand the basis for local trade without endangering their relations with the cattle trade of the Arkansas Valley. In 1879, Pueblo County supported 36,000 head of cattle valued at $600,000. In addition, there were 100,000 sheep, valued at $210,000. The 219,718 acres under cultivation were valued (with improvements) at $550,728.[50] These figures might be subject to qualification, but they do suggest two conclusions. First, the assessed value of county lands had declined since 1874, and second, stockraising had become more remunerative than farming. In any case, even though agriculture continued to contribute to the local trade, Pueblo was becoming increasingly industrial. In 1878, Mather and Geist established an extensive smelting operation to process the ores from the Leadville mines and the other mining operations to the west. In 1880, the Colorado Improvement Company (land agent for the Denver and Rio Grande Railroad) joined forces with other companies and established the Colorado Coal and Iron Company. The following year, the Denver and Rio Grande completed its connection to Leadville, and Pueblo established itself as the manufacturing and refinery center for the mineral wealth of southern Colorado. Pueblo was surrounded by rich deposits of coal, copper, and limestone—all the raw materials required for industrial growth. Once the railroads connected Pueblo to the east and west, its industrial base expanded rapidly.[51]

Pueblo enjoyed a tradition of business class control and tolerance of monopoly (despite the protestations of the city editor), which facilitated the capitalization of the local economy. South Pueblo was established as an industrial center by the Central Colorado Improvement Company. It housed its own labor force, built its own factories, and maintained itself as a railroad town across the river from the commercial settlement at Pueblo. Later, when the Colorado Coal and Iron Company was established, it established its own little steel mill community at Bessemer. Thus until 1886 (when Pueblo and South Pueblo were united) Pueblo was three towns—one owned by the railroad's landholding company, one owned by the joint stock venture that united the railroad with local capitalists, and one the traditional home of the farmers and traders. This last town, Pueblo, was able to attract large wholesale mercantile houses that competed with Denver merchants in claiming a share of the regional market.[52]

Of course, corporate capital also invaded the traditional domain of the cattle barons, but some of the Arkansas Valley residents were prompt to take advantage of the influx of eastern and European capital. A case in point is

Pueblo in the 1880s. Courtesy Colorado Historical Society (F-1014)

that of Hiram S. Holly, who in 1871 had driven some 1,300 head of Texas cattle to his ranch on the Arkansas River. Holly formed a partnership with Dennis Sullivan, a Denver financier, and constructed a fenced grazing range that purportedly contained 640,000 acres, including 20–30 miles along the Arkansas River. In 1881, 15,000 head of cattle grazed on the Holly ranch, and many of these actually belonged to Holly and Sullivan.[53]

In 1882, Holly decided to sell his ranch to the Arkansas Valley Land and Cattle Company (of London), who agreed to pay $875,000 for 640,000 acres, 17,000 head of cattle, and all ranching equipment, horses, and so on. Holly's ranch was, however, decidedly smaller than had been estimated. Even after J. A. Thatcher (the merchant) agreed to throw in his 2,400 acres (for one-third of the purchase price), the total package included only 440,000 acres and fewer than 9,000 head of cattle. In fact, the Coloradans held title to only slightly more than 14,000 acres, the remainder being government land held by virtue of water rights and fencing. In any case, Holly, Sullivan, and Thatcher agreed to absorb the cost of fencing an additional 200,000 acres of the public domain, and they reimbursed the London company for the livestock shortage. The final purchase price was thereby adjusted to $707,680. This tidy return on investment in fences was then used to establish the Colombia Land and Cattle Company, in which Holly, Sullivan, and Thatcher were joined by two additional associates. This company sold 3,000 shares of stock (at $100 per share) and conducted ranching (or land speculation) operations from a Denver office that administered affairs in Pueblo and elsewhere in Colorado.[54]

Holly was only one of many actors involved in the purchase and sale of ranches on the Arkansas. Among others, the Colorado Cattle Company (owned by eastern capitalists) was reported to have controlled 80,000 acres south of Pueblo. The Prairie Cattle Company was equally prominent in the Arkansas Valley and appears to have been involved in a limited sheep war in the late 1870s. In general, however, ranchers and farmers near Pueblo were not particularly involved with the war between cattle and sheep, because their lands were mostly fenced and many of them raised both cattle and sheep.[55]

Local ranchers faced more serious problems in efforts to control the public domain. By 1880, federal courts were attempting to sort through the complex and often contradictory land claims in southern Colorado and New Mexico. One such case received extensive coverage in the Denver newspaper, which by then was under Loveland's editorial control. The editor explained that the Mexican government had issued a large grant of land to "Bobian" (Beaubien) and Miranda, who never did fulfill the terms of their grant by establishing a permanent settlement:

> In 1861, or thereabouts, settlers commenced to arrive and to occupy the rich bottom lands along the Purgatoire river. These people were mostly Mexicans, and with no knowledge of this undefined grant—this imaginary title—which was then only on paper. The settlers built their houses and commenced to cultivate the soil, lived happily and undisturbed twelve years—until 1873. At this time, C.A. Cook was made receiver at the land office at Pueblo, and immediately inaugurated the land steal in Southern Colorado.[56]

The land office had been exploited by local capitalists, who secured large parcels of what was then called the Maxwell grant. A large portion of this property had been offered to W. J. Palmer to help finance the Denver and Rio Grande railroad, and this land was sold through the Central Colorado Improvement Company, which then purchased the Nolan grant and established South Pueblo on that site. Clearly, the Denver and Rio Grande as well as the local farmers had been speculating in Mexican land grants, the validity of which remained to be established by federal courts. The heirs to the Vigil and Saint Vrain grant were somewhat more successful in defending their title, based on the dubious claim that Autobees had sustained a permanent settlement on his ranch.

Other disputes focused on control of the unclaimed land that should have been available for homesteaders. As noted above, local ranchers were claiming squatter's rights on some rather large tracts of land. In the Pueblo region, these lands were often fenced, despite the fact that claimants did not hold title. Then, as foreign investors became interested in Colorado ranching, large fenced parcels of the public domain were sold to British and other foreign investors. By 1883, it was estimated that 2,640,750 acres of government land were illegally fenced within the State of Colorado. This fencing enterprise came to an abrupt end that year, when Secretary of the Interior Henry Teller declared that all illegal fences would be cut. This opened the door for land-hungry settlers who invaded the last refuge of the Colorado cattle barons.[57]

Of course some of the Arkansas Valley ranchers, like Holly and his associates, had managed to sell their ranches to foreign investors before state and federal authorities declared an end to massive appropriations of the public domain. Thus the marriage of trade, transportation, and manufactures sustained Pueblo through the 1880s, as control of these industries became increasingly concentrated in the hands of eastern corporations. Local capitalists were accommodated only if they were willing to sell their interests and withdraw from the cutthroat competition that characterized the corporate takeover in what soon became the monopoly sector.

The Colorado Coal and Iron Company, formed in 1880 by the merger of three corporations, was capitalized at $10,000,000. In 1888, Meyer Guggenheim entered the growing Pueblo industrial economy, on a small scale, with the construction of the Philadelphia Smelter (an investment of $1,250,000). Initially, Guggenheim was less than successful, but he was able to capitalize on technological developments and was a major actor in the 1890s.[58]

In 1892, the Colorado Coal and Iron Company was reorganized as the Colorado Fuel and Iron Company. This company managed to survive the financial panic of 1893, but it could not resist the invasion of the conglomerates. While attempting to stave off an assault by E. H. Harriman, the "local" company sought assistance from George Gould and John D. Rockefeller. In 1899, Rockefeller's Standard Oil Company joined a group of like-minded corporate actors, establishing the American Smelting and Refining Company, capitalized at $65,000,000. By 1901, the Guggenheims were convinced to join the smelting trust, and they exchanged their properties for one-third of the conglomerate's stock. By then, however, they had managed to purchase sufficient additional shares to control 50 percent of the corporation. Meanwhile, George Gould (Jay's eldest son) had assumed control of the railroad empire, so that the Guggenheims, the Rockefellers, and the Goulds were firmly in control of Pueblo industry.[59]

Like Golden, Pueblo was a Caucus town, dominated by business and landed elites. In Pueblo, however, local control of land and trade was more important than control of transportation, which facilitated cooperation with national actors who promoted railroads as the leading edge of capital penetration. Ultimately, Pueblo succeeded where Golden had failed because the traders and farmers were content to allow eastern capital to control local enterprise. There was no attempt to control transportation, or even ranching, as long as productive enterprise was able to sustain local commerce for the farmers and businesspersons of the valley. Even the valley was for sale if the price was right. In any case, most of the Pueblo businesspersons were involved in a variety of enterprises. When Moore retired from the railroad construction business in 1877, he turned his attention to real estate and construction in South Pueblo. Carlile retired in 1881 and then raised horses with his brother on a local ranch. After that, Orman and Crook maintained the construction company, but they were also involved in various real estate and construction efforts that reunited them with either Moore or Carlile, or both.[60]

Thus Pueblo was sustained as a transportation center in a railroad empire controlled by the Gould family and as a manufacturing center in an empire dominated by the Guggenheims and the Rockefellers. What Pueblo never quite achieved was commercial success that would rival Denver, although the city fathers continued for many years to defend their community against the ambitions of the Denver promoters. Through the first decades of the twentieth century, Pueblo was able to veto plans for state sponsorship of the Moffatt tunnel, which would have established the basis for a northern route across the Rockies. Finally, in 1921, the Arkansas River flooded, nearly devastating the Pueblo settlement and thereby inspiring a compromise with Denver. Flood control for Pueblo was exchanged for the Moffatt tunnel, allowing Denver to extend the reach of its commercial enterprise.[61]

Hence the river, which continues to separate two distinct Pueblo settlements, was the final arbitrator and the basis for an alliance with Denver. With state assistance, Pueblo was finally able to control the waters of the Arkansas, but that control was purchased at the cost of the transportation monopoly. Even so, it is not clear that Pueblo lost much ground in this battle with Denver. Pueblo remains to this day a substantial settlement on the Arkansas River. The dark shadows of its industrial heritage are broken by the interstate highway that separates the manufactures from the still substantial central business district.

Just south of City Hall, a bridge spans the Arkansas, providing access to the old town of South Pueblo. There one is greeted by an old locomotive that stands as an appropriate monument to the enterprise that established that settlement. Beyond the tracks is a Hispanic community, reminiscent of the settlement at Fountain City as described by the Cañon City editor in 1861. One hundred years of history have not passed unnoticed, but some things still endure. Although the industrial labor force changed dramatically with the infusion of east European workers in the late nineteenth century, one still finds commerce sustained by overwhelming industry and a large population of Mexican-American (or Hispanic) laborers.

CHAPTER SEVEN

Cañon City: Gateway to the Southern Rockies

Cañon City might have become the commercial and industrial center of southern Colorado, but it lost in the competition with Pueblo. Like Pueblo, Cañon City was all but abandoned during the Civil War, although some of the county residents were able to secure their land claims under authority of the Colorado Territory. Immigration of a new set of merchants and farmers in the closing years of the war was responsible for the revitalization of the local political economy. Like their counterparts in Greeley, the local farmers were able to gain control of Fremont County government and of land and water and thereby establish limits on municipal booster efforts. Cañon City failed to attract capital and labor because the boosters were unable to mobilize local support for their economic development efforts. Consequently, eastern capital was invested in Pueblo, where the nonlaboring classes were more willing to sell their control of local industry. Hence Cañon City remained a small farming town, while Pueblo became the industrial center.

Cañon City Before the War

Cañon City was established by Denver and Fountain City residents who decided to move closer to the mines and thereby preempt the Fountain Creek boosters, after Pueblo was established in the fall of 1859. The Cañon City claimants included William Kroenig (fur-trade pioneer and rancher) and W. H. Young (another Pueblo rancher), who were able to entice regional wholesale merchants to the new metropolis, surveyed and platted by Buel and Boyd (of Denver) in March 1860. In September, the *Cañon City Times* was published and included, among its advertisers, J. B. Doyle and Company, Dold and Company (of Denver), and Saint Vrain and Easterday, all large wholesale merchants. Hall, Perkins, and Company and C. W. Kitchen were also trading in general merchandise, and other local enterprises included a shingle manufacturer, a flour mill, a sawmill, architects, and builders. During that autumn of 1860, the number of local businesses multiplied rapidly. The *Cañon City Times* reported that the foundations for twenty-five residences were built in one week of September.[1]

The construction boom fostered the development of local brickyards, sawmills, and marble quarries, but the surrounding region contained riches that were yet to be exploited, including coal and oil deposits. All of these enterprises, plus farming and ranching, enjoyed a steady flow of available labor as miners passed through the region in their seasonal migration to and from California Gulch. In addition, there were Mexican-Americans, who continued to provide the physical labor in Anglo enterprise along the Arkansas River. Kroenig had twenty-five men working on his land raising vegetables for the gold rush trade, as an adjunct to his freighting business.[2]

Frontier Cañon City housed some of the largest mercantile and freighting companies in Colorado, including many companies that also operated in Denver. In addition, the surrounding County of Fremont supported farmers and ranchers, who were among the leading actors in municipal enterprise. W. F. Stone, a local attorney who later became a Colorado judge, operated a ranch in partnership with Middleton and held two farming claims in partnership with W. M. Stewart and N. H. Hopkins. Stone was also a member of a local ditch company, in partnership with J. W. Reid, J. B. Cooper, Judge Howard, and Anson Rudd. Mat Riddlebarger, the publisher of the local newspaper, was a partner in the ditch company and advertised himself (in his paper) as a real estate dealer.[3]

In general, local commerce was dominated by corporations or partnerships representing old Indian traders like J. B. Doyle and Saint Vrain or Denver firms like the ones operated by William H. Russell, William B. Waddell, and Alexander Majors. Nevertheless, local merchants and businesspersons, as in Pueblo, maintained farms and ranches in addition to their commercial or professional enterprises, so conflict between commercial and landed interests were minimal, at least initially. William C. Catlin, who established the first local brickyard, was also a rancher and farmer and a member of the land claim company. Saint Vrain's partner, N. E. Easterday, and their local agent, W. W. Ramage, were both members of the local claim club. Cañon City was controlled by merchants, businesspersons, and local landholders, even during the boom days of the early 1860s, but the farmers and ranchers were able to cooperate with the large commercial establishments and accommodate the army of gold seekers, who were the major consumers in the market for local produce.[4]

Before the rapid expansion of Cañon City in the fall of 1860, the town was governed by the Cañon City and Arkansas Valley Land Claim Club, which registered 160-acre claims for farming, 640 acres for sawmills, and 1,280 acres for town companies. The claim club was governed by a president, vice-president, secretary, and six directors, who held legislative and judicial authority. Apparently these officers served without compensation, except for the secretary, who was paid one dollar for each claim recorded. As might be expected, the bulk of the club's business was recording claims, although there were reportedly monthly meetings, occasional trials, and even a little legislation. In principle, the club required settlers to improve their claims and allowed only one preemption claim per customer. It seems, however, that some claimants held multiple farming claims, and a number of members were involved in town companies, mill claims, or irrigation ditches. J. W. Reid, a physician who operated a local drugstore, was president of the club in 1862 and was interested in the Middle Town Company, among other enterprises. J. L. Dunn, another local physician, was also active in the property trade.[5]

Aside from the claim club, which sanctioned the regional real estate business, town companies not unlike those found elsewhere were busy distributing municipal properties. Three town companies were registered with the claim club—the East, North, and Middle companies, but no official records of these organizations have survived, and newspaper reports suggest that a single town company controlled the distribution of town lots. The *Cañon City Times* reported regular meetings, and the company donated lots to local businesspersons, taxed lot-holders for municipal improvements, and sold lots at public auction when assessments were not paid. Overall, it seems that the town company was the effective local government, at least until September 1860, but it is difficult to distinguish the town company from the claim club, just as it is difficult to distinguish local farmers from local businesspersons.[6]

In any case, the influx of miners and would-be prospectors, prepared to spend the winter in Cañon City, inspired local residents in September 1860 to organize a more suitable form of local governance, which would defend public order in the finest booster tradition. The local editor reported that the town was filled with newcomers, and he offered editorial support for the citizen meeting that organized the Law and Order Committee.

> On our first page will be found a set of rules passed by the citizens—measures that our people thought proper to take to preserve order and administer justice. Removed as we are from legal restraint, it becomes us to take "Time by the forelock,"—to take steps that insure peace and safety to the community, and to punish with promptness those who shall deserve it.[7]

The organization resembled the People's Court of Denver although it was, in many ways, more like the Denver Vigilance Committee. The Committee had officers and members, rather than relying on assembled citizens, and it claimed the power of legislation as well as enforcement and trial. Like the People's Court and the mining camp courts, however, the committee selected twenty-four potential jurors and allowed both the defendant and the prosecutor to summarily dismiss up to six jurors. Furthermore, its trials were public, although proceedings were not usually reported in the local press.

The law of Judge W. R. Fowler (president of the Law and Order Committee) was adequate for local needs, at least initially. Local histories suggest that Cañon City was a rather raucous entertainment center and Judge Fowler a benevolent if somewhat stern disciplinarian. It is probable that he tolerated some of the excesses associated with frontier vice and relied on moral suasion as much as coercion. Fowler specialized in vice and preached virtue, but he did have occasion to deal with fraudulent business practices as well. Nevertheless, the Law and Order Committee did not interfere with the business of the town company and the claim club. Instead, these three versions of local governance cooperated in providing distinct services for a common membership, and some individuals were officers in all three organizations.

In many ways, the situation was not unlike that in Denver in 1859, although there was less conflict between local actors and less cooperation between local and regional governing authorities. In fact, among the various municipal and regional actors, it seems that only the local ranchers were cooperating with the government of Jefferson Territory. The Provisional Government had established "estray" laws for Jefferson Territory, and newspaper records suggest that local ranchers were complying with the law. More generally, however, local support for provisional authorities was quite limited, particularly in comparison to Denver and Pueblo. The local editor noted that there was, at best, lukewarm support for Governor Steele's administration:

> There appears to be a general and almost unanimous indifference to the proclamation of Gov. Steele, and the probability is that there will be no election held on the Arkansas.—Much fault is found with the representation as apportioned by his honor.—Many of the citizens think that at least one-third, perhaps one-half of the actual settlers of Jefferson are included in district No. 1, and it does not meet their approbation that they are allowed so small a representation. We should be glad to see any kind of government inaugurated if it has the support and confidence of the people, but unless such is the case, it will prove of no benefit to the country.[8]

By the fall of 1860 even Denver boosters were inclined to abandon the Provisional Government, given the extent of laboring class opposition to the government of property and trade. It is possible that Cañon City boosters were able to preempt such opposition and, at the same time, avoid conflicts with Arkansas Valley Democrats by essentially ignoring the territorial government. It seems that conflicts between landowners and merchants were minimal, and there is no evidence of organized laboring class opposition to the governments of Cañon City. If anything, the nonlaboring classes were, at least formally, better organized than their Pueblo counterparts, since the Cañon City and Arkansas Valley Land Claim Club united the owners of municipal and county land.

In any case, Cañon City residents were content to maintain local governance without regional government sanction. The law of Judge Fowler was deemed inadequate, however, for adjudicating civil disputes. Fowler was something of a religious zealot, who preached morality as he administered justice. This was appropriate for dealing with the criminal menace but not for disputes within the business class. Hence, in December 1860, after months of public meetings and legislative sessions, a municipal charter and a civil code were approved, and Judge John Howard began his rather colorful career on the Cañon City bench.

Howard's opinions were often less than orthodox, but municipal government did assume a more formal appearance, with legal notices published in the paper and a definite code of local law that eventually covered both civil and criminal charges. In December 1860, the Law and Order Committee was operating alongside the municipal government, the latter claiming jurisdiction only in civil suits. Procedures for criminal prosecution were soon established, however, and Fowler's court was discontinued, although the civil docket remained the primary concern in Judge Howard's court.[9]

Through 1862, the claim club and the town company operated alongside the municipal government, each claiming limited jurisdiction, without any apparent conflict between authorities. Neither was any conflict apparent between miners and merchants. Denver's experience in 1859 seemingly guided the efforts of Cañon City merchants. The local business community did not support the Provisional Government, whose authority the miners generally repudiated. Thus Cañon City merchants and businesspersons were not plagued by the miners' opposition to the Provisional Government, and they maintained domestic tranquility without regional government sanction.

Cañon City in Colorado Territory

Canon City boosters displayed a mixed reaction to territorial authorities of 1862. They resisted the intrusions of outsiders, like Territorial Chief Justice Benjamin F. Hall, who did not seem to appreciate local custom and was viewed as a carpetbagger. As one local businessman later explained:

> The Judge's first official act was the cause of his future unpopularity, and was taken almost as an insult to the people. It was in the appointment as Clerk, of one Dr. J.C.W. Hall ("Alphabet Hall" as he was called), who was what is known as a "dead-beat." The appointment was so obnoxious to the people that they notified the Judge that, unless he reconsidered the appointment, the mandates of his court would not be obeyed. However, they compromised with the Judge, which was, that the Clerk was permitted to serve that term only, after which he must "skip." The court then proceeded to organize; but the Judge was so mortified at his reception amongst us, that he did not put in a second appearance, and soon left this broad judicial field for some small enclosure east of the Mississippi River, better suited to his tastes and talents.[10]

Nevertheless, the local paper applauded the efforts of federal soldiers at Fort Wise, who punished the Arapaho who had allegedly attacked settlers on Purgatory Creek:

> We learn from a gentleman just from the Picket-Wah [Purgatoire Creek] that there has been a fight between a band of Arapahoe Indians, and a body of U.S. troops. . . . Twelve Indians and one soldier were killed. Their lodges were all burnt, and the Indians compelled to retreat. We think they will be more careful in the future before interfering with peaceable settlers; and we imagine that there will be no more trouble, as the time is at hand for their meeting the agent at Fort Wise.[11]

In the early years of the Civil War, Cañon City maintained its frontier authorities, who sanctioned land claims, enforced business contracts, and maintained a version of public order. Territorial authority was superfluous and was not immediately embraced, but federal authority, while desperately needed, was not adequate for local needs. Thus Cañon City, like Pueblo, faced the doldrums of the war years.

In August 1861, Judge Hall organized the local district court, and Cañon City delegates went to Pueblo to nominate candidates for the territorial legislature. There was some controversy at that convention, since Cañon City seemed to have been granted most of the delegates. Nevertheless, the local editor reported, "There appears to be very little political excitement among the farmers of the Arkansas. They are doing better by attending to their own interests."[12]

Such studied indifference to larger political concerns could not long be maintained, however. Territorial government proved to be an important actor in the political struggles that closed the first phase of local economic development. The territory organized regiments to fight both Confederate raiders and "hostile" tribes of the plains. These efforts were directed largely toward maintaining Colorado's political and commercial relations to the East, but the thrust of territorial policies indicated a decidedly northern bias. As a local businessman later reported: "Cañon City, at one time bade fair to become a formidable rival of Denver, but, after Government protection was withdrawn from the Arkansas River route, and the stage line of Barlow, Sanderson & Co., from Kansas City to Fairplay via Cañon City temporarily discontinued, Cañon declined rapidly."[13] Not only were the Colorado regiments loyal to the Union cause but the military campaign against the Colorado tribes exhibited a marked tendency to protect Denver and the Platte River trade at the expense of Pueblo, Cañon City, and Arkansas Valley commerce. Consequently, Cañon City suffered a fate that was yet more extreme than that of its eastern neighbor, Pueblo. The town was abandoned in 1863, when only Anson Rudd, the village blacksmith, remained to secure his claim, as sanctioned by the town company and the claim club. One might conclude that local government was sustained, but commerce and municipal enterprise took refuge in Denver or Pueblo.

Territorial authority was fairly well established by 1863, but there was little if anything to govern. Anson Rudd, Lewis Conley (who operated a flour mill), and J. B. Cooper (a local builder) had been appointed Fremont County Commissioners in 1862, but no records of their actions have survived. The Cañon City and Arkansas Valley Claim Club, after recording over 250 claims in just under two years of operation, officially surrendered its authority in January 1862. The Fremont County Surveyor recorded twenty-five claims (including the claim of the East Cañon Town Company) between December 1861 and April 1862 but apparently closed up shop after that. Chief Justice Hall surrendered the district court to Alan Bradford, who heard four criminal cases between December 1862 and May 1863. Bradford's docket indicates that both Vincent Moore and Gabriel Bowen (the Oil Springs claimant) were held on bond for larceny, but no dispositions were recorded. Two other defendants were charged with manslaughter, but both cases were dismissed. Thus Bradford's efforts in Cañon City were not unlike his Pueblo justice, except that his Cañon City docket was extremely limited.[14] He was, however, much more popular than his predecessor, Hall, had been: "Judge Bradford's court was as popular here as Judge Hall's was unpopular. Judge Bradford stands high socially and in the legal profession. He was not a carpet-bagger from some of the older States, provided with an office as a reward for pot-house political service."[15]

Bradford did little if anything to interfere with local government, such as it was in 1863. There was, in fact, no apparent conflict between local and territorial government after Bradford replaced Hall. Those settlers who remained in Fremont County were willing to use the county government much as they had used the claim club. Many of the large landholders did not record their claims with the county surveyor, perhaps because they left the region before the county government was established. Those who remained, however, took advantage of the opportunity to secure legal title. Jesse Frazer claimed 160 acres under claim club sanction and recorded this claim with the county on 13 February 1863. That same day, Stephen Frazier (who had purchased the Costan claim) also filed with the county, as did Henry Frazier, William Ash, and W. Helm. The Ash claim, as noted in the surveyor's records, was made at the request of Jesse Frazer. The Helm claim had passed through many hands. It was preempted by Sylvester Sturgis in 1860, sold to John Shields, then to Jesse Frazer, then to Henry Frazier, and then in 1862 to William Helm.[16]

Some of these residents might have abandoned their claims in 1863, but they did manage to secure title, and, along with Rudd and Fowler, they were on hand to greet new settlers who fueled the revival of 1864. In September of that year, twenty families from various parts of the country came to Cañon City to claim the abandoned farms and revitalize the abandoned business district. They were in general people of moderate wealth who were prepared to capitalize on the opportunities for agricultural and commercial development. Hall described the settlers as "not an indiscriminant horde, but numbers of 'real folks' who saw the opportunities and seized them."[17]

Anson Rudd and William Catlin (pioneer farmer, stockraiser, and brick manufacturer), together with a few of the new immigrants, quickly seized the opportunity to secure title to the town plat. The U.S. Surveyor General had surveyed the Fremont County area, so Rudd and company were entitled to claim the townsite under federal authority. They did, however, respect previous claims and grant deeds to the original occupants who requested title to their abandoned property. Nevertheless, the general lack of interest in local real estate allowed more than enough surplus for the new arrivals.[18] With their claims secured by federal law, local residents reestablished commerce and industry, and Cañon City was, once again, a going concern.

County government was revitalized in response to renewed economic enterprise, and the Fremont County Probate Court, with G. B. Frazier presiding, began hearing cases in November 1864. Probate and other civil suits made up the bulk of this court's docket, and in fact only one criminal case was reported in the first ten years of court records. John L. Scott was accused of fraud in 1865, and a warrant for his arrest was issued, but no evidence of prosecution was recorded. There were no criminal cases on Bradford's District Court docket from 1863 until August 1868. Meanwhile, a new set of county commissioners (most of them farmers) was holding monthly meetings.[19]

The commissioners faced serious problems in maintaining an adequate supply of county officials and in raising sufficient revenues to cover operating expenses. Probate Judge Frazier resigned in February and was replaced by M. M. Craig, but in April, Craig and Johnson (J.P. for District 1) both resigned, so Richardson was appointed J.P. and Frazier was reappointed as probate judge. Throughout the year, constables, judges, and even sheriffs resigned, but Thomas Macon remained as county attorney, and Frazier remained as probate judge. Perhaps there were other judges who were active in this period, but Frazier's docket is the only surviving record of adjudication. In any case, in addition to the personnel shortage, the commissioners faced difficulties in attempting to raise revenues. The commissioners required that local businesspersons, merchants, shopkeepers, and professionals purchase county licenses, but many neglected to pay their fees. In November, the clerk was ordered to submit delinquent accounts to the county attorney for prosecution, but no prosecution records have survived. Additional revenues were collected after the commissioners levied a tax of nine mills for county improvements (mostly roads), three mills for school, and two mills for the poor.[20]

The major county enterprise was the construction of a transportation network that would serve local agrarian and commercial interests, and the major problem was raising sufficient funds and maintaining officials who might well earn more in private practice. The Frazier and Macon families provided at least some of the legal talent required, and they were rewarded for their efforts by favorable reaction to their petitions for county roads. Macon, as will become evident, was a particularly important actor in representing the interest of Cañon City in the territorial legislature. John Locke (one of the wealthier local farmers) was similarly active at the county level, where he served three successive terms as commissioner. It was he who suggested (in 1865) that the county bring suit against "non-resident stock owners of Fremont County."

The territorial legislature had passed a law in 1861 prohibiting nonresidents from importing cattle, sheep, hogs, goats, or mules into Huerfano, Pueblo, Fremont, Jefferson, Boulder, or Costillo counties. This was the first attempt by Fremont County to enforce this law, and it is not clear that any prosecution resulted.[21] Nevertheless, Fremont, like Pueblo County, was determined to protect local farmers and ranchers from "foreign" competition. It is not clear, however, that the county was equally committed to the concerns of the merchants and shopkeepers, who argued that regional economic development was the ultimate goal that united the merchants and farmers.

THE CHALLENGE OF NATIONAL INCORPORATION

The merchants and businesspersons of Cañon City attempted to attract capital and develop local manufacturing and ore-reduction works to process the regional mineral wealth. Nevertheless, in 1870 Cañon City was still dependent on local agriculture, and the farmers who controlled county government were less than cooperative in efforts to develop a more diversified industrial base. The merchants and businesspersons dominated the municipality and used local government to establish public order and facilitate industrial development. At the same time, they attempted to induce the farmers to use the authority of county government to underwrite the cost of economic expansion. In this regard, they were unsuccessful.

Cañon City had been an impressive frontier metropolis in 1861, but the exploitation of regional reources had been limited. There had been some attempts to produce coal for the local market, but most Fremont County residents were growing vegetables and raising cattle for the gold miners of the southern Rockies. Then, during the Civil War, the decline of local commerce all but destroyed efforts to develop an industrial base. The second phase of Cañon City's development, beginning in 1864, was characterized by the expansion of regional industry, most especially agriculture but also coal and petroleum. Cañon City was no longer to be an extension of the Denver commercial network but the center of local industry. This would, of course, require capital, but local boosters were prepared to cooperate with eastern capitalists.

The petroleum industry of Fremont County was to provide at least a partial basis for the anticipated industrial revolution. Oil was a new commodity on the American market, and the petroleum industry was just beginning to develop in Pennsylvania when A. A. Cassidy attempted to establish the oil fields of Florence. After purchasing Bowen's Oil Springs claim in 1862, Cassidy had produced no more than 10,000 gallons of oil prior to 1865, but he had made a tidy profit during the war when commerce with the East was all but halted. Thus in 1866 Cassidy was able to attract eastern capital, and he formed a company in Boston to develop the local oil fields. The oil fields of Florence produced more litigation than oil, however, as several claimants and various corporate actors tried unsuccessfully to tap the local oil deposits. Petroleum production was limited prior to 1880, and even the capital-intensive efforts of that period never managed to rival the productive capacity of wells in northern Colorado.[22]

The coal mines of Fremont County proved to be more valuable than the oil fields, although their development was a long and arduous process. Jesse Frazer and other local pioneers had claimed land near the mouth of Coal Creek, on the Arkansas, where the coal mining town of Labran was later established. Frazer and others had mined a little coal in the early years, but the deposits were not systematically exploited until the Central Colorado Improvement Company (C.C.I.C.) commenced operations in 1872. John Locke, long-term county commissioner and local farmer, had been grazing cattle and horses along Coal Creek, but he sold his ranch to the C.C.I.C. in 1872, so that the town of Labran could be constructed to supply the Denver and Rio Grande Railroad with coal. As will be discussed subsequently, the railroad town at Labran became a source of local agitation in the course of the regional railroad wars.[23]

In the interim, neither the coal mines nor the oil fields proved to be an adequate basis for the industrial revolution in Cañon City. Local leaders were actively promoting industrial development in the late 1860s, but their efforts were frustrated at every turn. In 1867, B. M. Adams (a local minister), B. F. Rockafellow (a wealthy merchant), and Thomas Macon (the county prosecutor) were delegated to meet with officials of the Kansas Pacific Railroad to encourage the consideration of a southern Colorado rail. Palmer and Greenwood surveyed the route and recommended that the Kansas Pacific directors redirect their efforts and build to Cañon City, rather than to Denver, as planned.[24] The directors decided to build to Denver, however, and thereby connect with the Union Pacific via the Denver Pacific route to Cheyenne.

Thus Cañon City lost the first round of its intermittent competition with Denver, but Thomas Macon, although not able to gain the rail connection, was able to secure some local advantage in the territorial legislative session

Downtown Cañon City. Courtesy Colorado Historical Society (F-33154)

of 1867–1868. As Denver and Golden representatives were marshalling their forces in the struggle for regional dominance, Macon formed an alliance with the Denver crowd, securing the Arkansas Valley vote for the resolution to move the state capital to Denver. In exchange, Cañon City was granted the Territorial Penitentiary, thereby securing a captive population that might remain at the Fremont County seat and sustain at least modest industrial enterprise. The legislature approved this location in January 1868, and the penitentiary was open for business in June 1871.[25]

By 1870 Cañon City businesspersons thus had managed only limited success in establishing local industry. The town remained for the most part a commercial and service center for the regional farming and ranching industry. The federal census of 1870 enumerated only eighty-one households in Cañon City, and residents reported wealth that totalled just over $150,000. The bulk of this wealth (69 percent) was concentrated in the trade and service industries, with the latter absorbing more wealth and considerably more households. A few wealthy merchants controlled considerable wealth—Benjamin and George Rockafellow, for example, reported $18,000 in real and personal property, but there were also some fairly wealthy actors in the service industry. Reuben Frazier, a local blacksmith, reported $4,000 in real and personal property. Generally, artisan-shopkeepers like Frazier, although not as wealthy as the merchants, sustained the service economy that absorbed the bulk of local capital and employed just over 25 percent of the population.[26]

The service industry and the construction industry absorbed 46 percent of local households; relatively little capital or labor was invested in manufacturing or transportation. The major manufacturers were the brickyard and the flour mill, and two teamsters were the only residents directly involved in the transportation industry. It is possible, however, that there were more people working in these industries, since ten households reported the occupation of "common laborer" and six others reported no occupation. In any case, there was no labor shortage in Cañon City, but the demand for local building was not adequate for the further development of either brick manufacturing or construction. It would seem that the construction of the penitentiary would have given these industries a boost, but that was not apparent in 1870.

As shown by the data in Table 7.1, nonlaboring classes in 1870 constituted roughly half of the households and controlled 89 percent of municipal wealth. The bulk of nonlaboring class wealth was controlled by merchants and shopkeepers, although professionals claimed 20 percent of municipal wealth, and "owner-employers" (including manufacturers, farmers, and ranchers) claimed 17 percent. The laboring classes included 14 artisan (craft-title) households, 12 clerical and service households, and 15 households of common laborers, most of whom were employed in the brickyards, flour mills, or neighboring farms. The smallest yet wealthiest segment of the laboring class was the clericals, including two households reporting combined wealth of $3,000 ($1,500 per household). The artisans reported just over half as much per

Table 7.1 Wealth by Class Category for Households in Cañon City, 1870

Class Category	Wealth	Percentage of Wealth	Households	Percentage of Households
Nonlaboring classes	$141,080	89.14	40	49.38
financier	4,800	3.03	3	3.70
owner	27,335	17.27	6	7.41
professional	32,300	20.41	8	9.88
merchant	76,495	48.34	17	20.99
none	150	.09	6	7.41
Laboring classes	17,180	10.86	41	50.62
artisan	10,870	6.86	14	17.28
worker	6,310	3.99	27	33.33
Total	158,260		81	

Source: U.S. Bureau of the Census (1870) Population Schedules for Fremont County, Colorado Territory.

Data come from the population of occupied dwelling units, aggregated to the household level and collapsed into class categories based on occupational title.

capita wealth ($776), the service workers employed in local shops reported no wealth, and the common laborers reported average wealth of $220.67.

It is reasonable to assume that the "artisans" identified in the 1870 Census were independent artisan-shopkeepers and that only one-third of the local population worked for wages. One might argue that the households reporting no occupation were also available for wage labor (given that they reported almost no wealth), but these represent only 7 percent of the population and at least some of these are female-headed households that were unlikely to provide labor for farms, ranches, or manufactures. They might be included, however, as surplus labor for shopkeepers. In any case, just over one-third (34 percent) of the laboring class was self-employed (as "artisan-shopkeepers"), and they (along with the merchants and other shopkeepers) employed an additional 29 percent of local laboring households. The remaining 37 percent of laboring households were employed by manufacturers, farmers, and ranchers.

The municipal census does not, however, provide a very complete picture of the Cañon City economy. Unlike Denver and Pueblo, large wholesale merchants did not control the bulk of municipal wealth in Cañon City. In fact, as indicated in Table 7.1, more wealth and considerably more households were engaged in service than in trade. Local enterprise was, in short, dependent upon the regional farmers who purchased goods and services in local shops. The Wet Mountain and Beaver Creek settlements contained a relatively large population of farmers, ranchers, and their workers, who supplied both the consumer market and the products that sustained Cañon City in this period. Particularly before the railroad arrived, and to a large extent afterward, farming was the predominant industry in Fremont County.

The 1870 Census results on the distribution of households and wealth across occupations for Beaver Creek showed that the Beaver Creek settlement supported nearly twice the Cañon City population and that local residents reported almost twice the municipal wealth, which was controlled not by merchants and shopkeepers but by farmers and ranchers. The four local livestock dealers were relatively well off, but their average wealth did not match that of the farmers and ranchers, who controlled 85 percent of local wealth although they constituted only 34 percent of the population. The town and the county did have one thing in common: Both had a large laboring population that controlled relatively little wealth.

Like the Cañon City laboring classes, the agricultural laborers were a diverse lot, including many penniless laborers who lived with wealthy farmers, but also including some households with modest means (perhaps $1,000) who were apparently working for relatives. Aside from using household labor, it seems that some farmers hired their cousins or brothers, who had established independent households but did not own a farm. A case in point is the Craig family. M. M. Craig (former county justice) was enumerated as a farmer, reporting $1,285 in personal and real wealth. John H. Craig was enumerated as a farm laborer, who lived with his wife, two children, and another laborer named John Benjamin. It is not clear that the Craigs were related, but they both were born in North Carolina (as was Benjamin). In any case, M. M. Craig had four farm laborers living in his house, and he probably employed John Craig and John Benjamin as well, but of the six farm laborers in the two Craig households only John Craig reported any wealth.

Kinship notwithstanding, most of the laboring households on Beaver Creek were farm laborers, and most of them reported little or no wealth. Local farmers were using their families as laborers, but they were not "family farmers."

Cañon City had only six agricultural households in 1870, but one finds a pattern similar to Pueblo. Farm laborers constituted 50 percent of the households and claimed only 1 percent of the wealth. Of the ninety-nine farming households in Beaver Creek, sixty-one (62 percent) were farm laborers, and these families controlled only 10 percent of the wealth in the local farming industry. Conversely, the farmers who made up 38 percent of the families controlled 90 percent of the wealth. Clearly, the farmers were employing laborers; some of them came from New Mexico, but many others were from eastern states.

The employment of Mexican-American laborers was less widespread in Fremont County than in Pueblo. On Beaver Creek, there were few Mexican-American households, and the distinction between "farm workers" and "farm laborers" is not apparent. The only Beaver Creek residents enumerated in the Census with the occupation "works on farm" were childen of "farmers," and since these children were included in the parent household, the occupation does not appear in this analysis. In Cañon City and within the immediate vicinity, however, there were more Mexican-American households. There one finds the distinction between "farm workers" (who never were natives of New Mexico with Hispanic surnames) and "farm laborers" (who sometimes were). Thus the agricultural workers of Fremont County were divided into family and nonfamily segments, and the nonfamily laborers were subdivided by ethnicity.

Overall, it seems reasonable to conclude that farmers dominated Fremont County. In 1870, all three county commissioners were identified in the census as farmers, and their actions indicate that at times they represented the interests of farmers in opposition to the merchants and businesspersons of Cañon City. Generally, the commissioners continued with the business of the 1860s, licensing local merchants, shopkeepers, and lawyers and establishing county roads and bridges in the booster tradition evidenced in Pueblo and elsewhere in Colorado. In 1870, however, they decided that the petitioners should bear the expense of surveying roads and notifying local property owners of the proposed route. Thus the county reduced its commitment to subsidize the cost of establishing county roads, and new tax rates were established, allocating only two and one-half mills for road construction, eight mills for county purposes, and five mills for schools. The local farmers, who by 1870 had gained control of Fremont County, were more concerned with educating their children than with building roads or otherwise promoting economic development.[27]

In April 1872, the county chartered the town of Cañon City, and the first board of trustees began its efforts to establish local government. This was a far cry from the Law and Order Committee, and the first legislative session clearly established the plan to maintain public order in efforts to facilitate boosterism. The board approved a law prohibiting the carrying of concealed weapons and another restraining animals from running at large.[28] The local editor was concerned, however, that municipal authorities were not sufficiently diligent in combating the threat to public order.

> On Saturday night a small building next to the Baptist church, occupied by Bertie Wood, a woman of questionable reputation, who came here last week, was attacked by parties unknown, and all the windows completely demolished by stones and clubs. Offenses against the peace and morals of our community should properly be adjusted before a legal tribunal and not by mob law. . . . Sabbath afternoon the children of the Baptist Sabbath School were compelled to listen to an outpouring of billingsgate that would have blackened the hinges of hell itself. A railroader and a cypian [prostitute], each with revolvers drawn, defied each other and everybody else, within a few feet of the church entrance. During the melee one shot was fired by the man, it passing through the door of the "shebang" but hurting no one.
>
> Mr. Mayor and Councilmen, the people most earnestly entreat you for speedy relief from similar scenes.[29]

At its next meeting on 6 August 1872, the city council appointed town police and passed a new ordinance declaring that "bawdy houses" and "houses of ill fame" were a public nuisance, prohibited within the city limits, and punishable by fines of ten to one hundred dollars. Perhaps this ordinance eliminated prostitution in the city or at least removed the menace from the steps of the Baptist church. Local J.P. and police records have not survived and were not reported in the local newspaper, but after the local police were appointed the editor made no further reference to the problems of prostitution and armed assault.

Nevertheless, records of the territorial District Court suggest a change in local politics after the Civil War. Generally, the concern with crimes against property was sustained, but there was an increasing concern with crimes against public order (or government), even in the county court. The limited docket from the Civil War years does not offer sufficient cases to sustain a generalization, but the accounts of Judge Fowler's court suggest that his efforts were focused on the standard set of assaults and larcenies that accompanied the mining trade. It seems that local efforts to control crime were not, to any appreciable extent, supplemented by the efforts of county or territorial authorities until after the revitalization of the local economy and the booster efforts of 1870. As shown by the data in Table 7.2, only four criminal cases were heard in District Court prior to 1868.

Table 7.2 Criminal Cases by Type of Offense for the Territorial District Court in Fremont County, 1862–1880

	Offense against			
Date	Property	Persons	Government	Total
1862–1863	2 (.50)	2 (.50)	—	4
1868–1873	16 (.43)	9 (.24)	12 (.32)	37
1878–1880	24 (.47)	5 (.10)	22 (.43)	51

Source: Fremont County Courthouse, Cañon City.

Proportion of row total is to the right of the frequency.

Between 1868 and 1873, thirty-seven cases were on the criminal docket. Nearly half of these were larcenies, mostly charges of illegally branding cattle. There were, however, nine crimes against persons—six assaults and three homicides. Aside from the fact that the court was busier after 1867, the most noticeable change is in the prosecution of crimes against government, or public order. The District Court docket contained seven gambling cases, three contempt charges, one malicious mischief, and one charge of malfeasance in office. The police magistrate, appointed in February 1873, was most probably even more concerned with public order, particularly prostitution, but no records from that court have survived. In any case, it appears that the Cañon City boosters were enjoying not only renewed prosperity but a government that maintained public order as well as protecting property.

The concern for public order, the predominant interest of boosters, was championed by the newspaper editor and defended by the city government. Beyond the city limits, however, the interests of the farmers predominated and were defended by the government of Fremont County. Even with the relative increase in crimes against government (or public order), the predominant concern of the county court was crimes against property, particularly livestock theft. Thus local politics reflected the interests of land and trade, and local authorities defended property and public order. The District Court was still not especially busy, and the number of convicts in the local penitentiary who had been convicted by Fremont County authorities was minimal, especially compared to Denver and Pueblo.[30] Local merchants and businesspersons were determined that Cañon City was destined to compete as the commercial and industrial center of Colorado even though Cañon City was, of course, much smaller than

Denver and Pueblo. Thus the local editor urged that the citizens spare no efforts to attract industry and thereby facilitate economic development:

> We are waiting for something to turn up; and while we wait others secure the advantages. It is time for us to get to work and see that our advantages are utilized. When parties come here to invest we should give them every advantage and not drive them from us by the high figures at which we hold our land. We need manufacturing establishments, or reduction works, to make our town prosperous.[31]

The farmers, however, were less concerned with the expansionist goals of municipal actors. They were not avid supporters of wagon road or railroad construction but were more concerned with maintaining their lands, educating their children, and developing an agricultural economy that would be a source of wealth and comfort in retirement and a legacy for the following generations. The farmers desired, in short, a landed estate, perhaps more modest than a plantation but more impressive than a homestead. The traders and land speculators had other ideas, but the farmers' resistance to national capital frustrated the Cañon City actors at every turn. As the editor reported:

> Not long since a farmer said to me, "railroads are a positive damage to us farmers because, by their facilities for transportation they bring corn, wheat and oats into our country so as to spoil the market for our grains."
> . . . O, said the farmer, you can favor railroads on selfish principles: I acknowledge that they help to build towns, and you are interested in that kind of property.[32]

By 1872 Cañon City had not emerged as a major industrial city, but it remained a thriving supply town and trade center for the farmers and ranchers of the surrounding region. It did not match Pueblo in the cattle trade and did not match Denver as a commercial center, but it seemed to be a fairly well established agricultural center. Unlike Greeley, however, Cañon City was not the center of a family farming community. Cañon was a Caucus town, established on the basis of an alliance between land and trade. Labor, although not formally disenfranchised, was not organized for effective political action. In fact, industrial and agricultural labor were geographically and socially isolated from each other, and even the agricultural workers were divided by kinship ties that bound some (but not all) to the farmer.

Local industry was under control, and all that remained was to attract a railroad. Toward this goal, the Board of Trustees was indefatigable in its efforts. In June 1872, Thomas Macon proposed that the Cañon City Board of Trustees grant right-of-way to the Denver and Rio Grande railroad. The appropriate ordinance was passed, but that was not the end of the matter.

The coming of the railroad proved to be a more complicated and controversial matter than Macon and his fellow board members might have foreseen. Both county and town officials soon found themselves choosing sides in a railroad war.

Attracting Eastern Capital

The challenge of the 1870s was for merchants and local businesspersons to attract national capital without threatening local control, especially control of local land. Increasingly, these efforts brought municipal leaders into direct conflict with local farmers, particularly as local actors became involved in the southern Colorado railroad wars.

As already noted, Cañon City leaders were interested in a rail connection that might reestablish the southern route through the Rockies and stimulate the regional coal-mining industry. They did, in fact, have an attractive package to offer the railroad companies. Although Cañon City could not approach Denver in commercial activity, the Royal Gorge did provide a natural passage to the Continental Divide, and that route to Salt Lake City was more practical than the northern Colorado path. Aside from this, Fremont County had rich coal deposits that would prove invaluable to local railroads, once these deposits were effectively exploited. Nevertheless, the Union Pacific had already established a Wyoming route to Salt Lake City, and the Kansas Pacific was still planning to connect with the Union Pacific in Cheyenne rather than build a parallel line to the West. Thus the K.P. decided to build to Denver, despite the advice of William J. Palmer.[33]

Palmer was sufficiently impressed with the possibility of a southern Colorado railroad to quit his job at the Kansas Pacific and establish the Denver and Rio Grande railroad company in October 1870. This company, in conjunction with the Central Colorado Improvement Company, was to develop a railroad empire that would connect Denver with the Arkansas Valley and New Mexico and eventually extend across the southern Rockies, joining the Union Pacific in Salt Lake City. In the short run, Palmer intended to build from Denver to the Arkansas River, near Pueblo, and then westward to the coal mines of Fremont County. In January 1872, regular service between Denver and Colorado Springs was established, and the grading of the road to Pueblo commenced. Before the year was out, the route to the coal mines at Labran was completed, but that was merely the beginning of the railroad problems in Fremont County.[34]

The Denver and Rio Grande faced three major problems in 1872. First, the company was generally distrusted by the Arkansas Valley settlements, including Pueblo and Cañon City. Second, the Atchison, Topeka & Santa Fe was attempting to capitalize on popular support as a competitor for the southern Colorado trade. Third, the Denver and Rio Grande faced financial difficulties that increased dramatically during the financial panic of 1873. These three problems were intimately interrelated. The company raised revenues through land speculation, which was the purpose of the Central Colorado Improvement Company, and through bonds supplied by counties or cities that desired rail service. In order to profit from land speculation, the company developed its railroad towns at the expense of the previously established communities, but such plans often backfired. As previously noted, the development of South Pueblo cost the railroad the county bonds that had been promised, when Judge Hallet determined that the bonds were forfeit after the depot at Pueblo was abandoned.[35]

The financial difficulties that inspired the construction of South Pueblo merely deepened when the bonds were withdrawn, and public relations problems multiplied as the railroad sued for its lost revenues. Raising the transportation rates to defray construction costs did not improve matters. Instead, the company was condemned as both a cheat and a gouger, and local animosity increased. The combination of financial difficulties and diminishing popular support facilitated the efforts of competing lines that were able to capitalize on opposition to the Denver road. Once the Atchison, Topeka & Santa Fe succeeded in securing Pueblo County bonds, the Denver and Rio Grande was forced to extend its railroad network toward New Mexico and Cañon City in order to preempt the "foreign" competition. This strategy caused the D.&R.G. to overextend its financial capabilities, in attempting to build two railroads, neither of which could be supported by local traffic.[36]

In theory, the railroad to Cañon City was to be self-supporting, because the Central Colorado Improvement Company was to develop the local coal mines and reap additional benefits from favorable transportation rates. In May 1872, the Improvement Company agreed to purchase $1,040,000 worth of railroad bonds at 80 percent of par value. In exchange, the railroad agreed to build both a rail and a telegraph connection between Pueblo and Cañon City, reaching the coal fields by May 1873 and Cañon City one year later. Meanwhile, as already noted, the land company purchased as much real estate as it could reasonably afford, both on Coal Creek, where it established the Town of Labran, and in the surrounding county.[37]

By October 1872, the rail connection between Pueblo and Labran was completed, but the Denver and Rio Grande could not afford to pay for the construction and did not manage to assume ownership until 1874. The Union Contract Company could not be paid for its construction efforts, partly because neither Pueblo nor Fremont County had delivered the bonds that they had promised. Apparently the Fremont County bonds were forfeit because of a legal technicality, but it soon became apparent that the Denver and Rio Grande was to receive at best lukewarm support in Fremont as well as Pueblo. Cañon City residents were not satisfied with a railroad as close as Labran but demanded that the rail be completed to the Cañon City limits before any funds would be offered. Having witnessed the development of the railroad town at South Pueblo, Cañon City residents had no intention to languish as the railroad town of Labran prospered.[38]

Receiving no assurances from the Denver and Rio Grande, Cañon City citizens held a public meeting in January 1873 and appointed B. F. Rockafellow, among others, to draft a formal invitation to the Atchison and Topeka to take advantage of the opportunities that a Cañon City railroad might offer. The A.T.&S.F. declined, at least initially, since that company was also suffering financial difficulties in the construction of railroads that local commerce could not support. Palmer, seeing the opportunity to raise much needed revenues, agreed to build to Cañon City in exchange for $100,000 in county bonds. The pros and cons of this proposition were much debated in the local press, as supporters suggested that voters not be swayed by their hatred of Palmer to reject the opportunity for wealth and prosperity that a local railroad would surely bring. The bonds were approved by a majority of merely two votes, and the County Commissioners, fully aware of the divided sentiments, refused to issue the bonds.[39]

As already noted, the issue of railroad bonds divided the merchant and the farmer, hence, the city and the county. As shown by the data in Table 7.3, nearly 80 percent of the Cañon City voters were in favor of the railroad bonds. In the county, outside of Cañon City, nearly 70 percent voted in opposition to the bonds. The county commissioners, all of them farmers, refused to issue the bonds, the second time that the county had frustrated municipal efforts to finance a rail connection despite the results of the bond issue election. This second defeat was particularly disturbing, since the railroad interests had spared no efforts in campaigning for their cause. The local newspaper had even published an appeal to the Mexican-American voters, a pro-bond editorial printed in Spanish.[40] Nevertheless, the farmers of the county held sway.

Table 7.3 Cañon City and Fremont County Vote in Railroad Bond Election of 1873

City/County	Vote for Bonds	Vote against Bonds	Total
Cañon City	173 (.79)	45 (.21)	218
Fremont County[a]	106 (.31)	232 (.69)	338
Total	279 (.50)	277 (.50)	556

Source: Cañon City Times, 26 June 1873:3.
[a]County vote does not include Cañon City vote.

This time Cañon City residents were not content with the decision of the Fremont County Commissioners. On 6 April 1874, the voters of Cañon City approved the subscription of $50,000 in municipal bonds to entice the Denver and Rio Grande. Of 150 eligible voters, 104 cast ballots in favor of the bonds, and only two opposing votes were cast. Despite the reluctance of the county voters, Cañon City residents were more than willing to pay the price for a rail connection, since the business and commercial interests of the city were clearly tied to trade with the mines. The Board of Trustees quickly approved an amendment of the right-of-way granted in 1872, and the Town Clerk prepared the municipal bonds. In July 1874, the *Cañon City Times* reported the arrival of the first passenger car, containing two passengers. The editor noted, "We now have railroad communication with the world and are comparatively happy."[41] Yes, only "comparatively happy," because the Denver and Rio Grande, in characteristic style, had constructed its depot on the edge of town, but the railroad had more or less reached Cañon City.

It soon became apparent, however, that Palmer and company were not planning, in 1874, to build through the Royal Gorge and establish Cañon City as the gateway to the West. The municipal bonds allowed the Denver and Rio Grande to assume control of the line that the Union Contract Company had held since 1872, but further construction in that direction was not a priority at that time. A more pressing problem was the Atchison and Topeka railroad, which was marshalling its forces for war. In March 1874, Pueblo County voters approved $350,000 in bonds to finance the construction of the Pueblo & Salt Lake City Railroad, but this company and various other local enterprises were soon combined to form the Pueblo and Arkansas Valley Railroad in union with the Atchison and Topeka. Palmer viewed these developments with suspicion, anticipating that the A.T.&S.F. intended to establish Pueblo as the center of a railroad empire that would effectively displace the D.&R.G.[42]

Palmer strained his financial resources to construct his road to New Mexico, agreed to pay the Union Contract Company on the most generous terms, and even allowed them to appropriate all receipts on the line to El Moro until May 1878. Such efforts notwithstanding, Palmer could not cover the cost of construction. The construction crews were not being paid, and the bondholders grew impatient. In August 1877, Louis H. Meyer, representing a considerable share of the investors, requested that the financial affairs of the railroad and the construction company be settled separately, by court order. Fortunately for Palmer, Judge Hallet denied the request, noting that the railroad was within its legal rights and did not require the interference of the court.[43]

Meanwhile, the citizens of Cañon City, thoroughly disappointed in the operation of the Denver and Rio Grande, established the Cañon City and San Juan Railroad as a holding company for the A.T.&S.F. and surveyed the Royal Gorge in 1877. Recent silver discoveries at Leadville had brought new life to the old California Gulch settlement, and Cañon City residents were determined to capitalize on the opportunity to reestablish commerce with the mines. They were joined in this ambition by both Palmer, of the D.&R.G., and William B. Strong, who was appointed manager of the A.T.&S.F. in November 1877. Strong initially approached Palmer with the offer to cooperate or perhaps to lease the Denver and Rio Grande. Palmer suggested that they might jointly finance a rail connection with Leadville and thereby defeat the Denver and South Park company, which intended to build a line from Denver. Beneath these overtly cooperative gestures, however, was a definite lack of trust. Palmer and Strong eyed each other suspiciously, each wondering what the other might attempt.[44]

This distrust was not without foundation. In February 1878, Strong received authorization to build toward Santa Fe, and he immediately dispatched his chief engineer, A. A. Robinson, who was to gather a small work force and commence construction at Raton Pass, which was the key to the Santa Fe traffic. Robinson booked passage on the Denver and Rio Grande to El Moro and equipped with a horse, courtesy of Uncle Dick Wooten, proceeded immediately to his destination. John A. McCurtie, of the Denver and Rio Grande, also had orders to take Raton Pass, but when he arrived, on 29 February, Robinson's crew was already hard at work. Thus the A.T.&S.F. won its first battle with the Denver road. Robinson secured a court order to prevent McCurtie and his men from interfering with their construction efforts, and Palmer decided to surrender Raton Pass, on the assumption that he could not fight his wealthy adversary on two fronts. Palmer advised McCurtie to turn his attention to the road toward Leadville.[45]

When McCurtie withdrew from Raton Pass, Robinson sent an agent to Cañon City to preempt the anticipated action by the Denver and Rio Grande. The D.&R.G. was not about to transport the enemy to Cañon City, having learned that lesson at Raton Pass. Nevertheless, the A.T.&S.F. crew was able to secure horse-drawn transport, and they had already organized Cañon City residents to secure the route through the Royal Gorge. The Cañon City and San Juan Railroad Company had surveyed that route in 1877, and agents for that company began a largely symbolic grading operation as soon as they heard that the Denver and Rio Grande crew was on its way. The D.&R.G. arrived with the contracting firm of Carlile, Orman, and Crook (from Pueblo), only to find Cañon City residents engaged in desultory efforts to grade their right-of-way for the Atchison and Topeka. The Pueblo newspaper celebrated the fact that the Denver road had been outsmarted once again, but the issue was far from settled.[46]

The Denver and Rio Grande maintained that it had a prior claim to the Royal Gorge, but the Cañon City and San Juan obtained an injunction, based on the premise that the D.&R.G. had abandoned its construction plans, while the Cañon City company had established its prior claim by surveying the proposed route and beginning the grading operation. In 1878, the local railroad company was maintaining the legal fiction of its independence from the A.T.&S.F., and the tangled legal dispute was presented to Judge Moses Hallet. Hallet initially enjoined both the D.&R.G. and the A.T.&S.F. from building in the Royal Gorge, but later ruled that each might build parallel tracks and share the same tracks where space did not permit two roadbeds. Hallet did determine, however, that the Cañon City road had priority of claim.[47]

Palmer was convinced that the local court was biased against his company, so he appealed the case to the U.S. Supreme Court. Meanwhile, the Atchison and Topeka merged with the Cañon City company, and the A.T.&S.F. prepared to construct its line to Leadville. Palmer tried to convince his stockholders that the Supreme Court would ultimately honor their claim to the Royal Gorge, but the deteriorating financial condition of the D.&R.G. finally convinced the investors to declare a truce. In October 1878, the Denver and Rio Grande was leased to the Atchison and Topeka for thirty years, and it appeared that the railroad war was finally settled. Both Pueblo and Cañon City celebrated the defeat of the Denver road, and Cañon City anticipated a golden future as the transportation and industrial center of the southern Colorado mining districts.[48]

Such dreams of grandeur were once again frustrated. In 1878, despite the apparent defeat of the Denver road and the happy marriage of the Cañon City and Atchison and Topeka enterprises, neither Palmer nor the courts had played their last cards. Palmer was still convinced that he would win his battle in the courts, so he did all in his power to break the lease with the A.T.&S.F. In December 1878, when the D.&R.G. was to be delivered, Palmer refused to surrender his railroad and refused to accept the proffered rent, since he claimed that he had not been offered an acceptable receipt. The D.&R.G. was declared in contempt of court, but the delaying techniques paid off. In April 1879, the Supreme Court granted the Denver road the prior right to build in the Royal Gorge, although the court stipulated that multiple lines could be constructed, with joint tracks wherever necessary.[49]

Both the federal and the state courts were attempting to establish the basis for cooperative ventures between the A.T.&S.F. and the Denver and Rio Grande. This might have seemed reasonable to the learned jurists, particularly since the Atchison and Topeka had leased the Denver road for a period of thirty years. Nevertheless, the lease was not effected in the spirit of cooperation, and, as was the case with the Golden railroad company, the lessee forcibly resisted the terms of the contract. Once the Supreme Court had established the right of the Denver and Rio Grande, McCurtie and his construction crew prepared for battle. While armed men physically occupied the Royal Gorge, the D.&R.G. attempted to get an injunction to prevent the A.T.&S.F. from interfering with their construction efforts. Amid rumors that the judge was to be kidnapped, an injunction was finally issued by Judge Bowen of the Leadville District Court.[50]

Armed with this court order and a large deputation of "peace officers," the Denver and Rio Grande physically seized its depots and rolling stock.

The most spectacular confrontation was in Pueblo, where A.T.&S.F. agents were armed and ready to repel the efforts to seize the South Pueblo depot. The conflicting accounts of this battle suggest parallels to the shoot-out at the O.K. Corral. Some versions even claim that Bat Masterson was present. In any case, the assault was successful, and Palmer was once again in control of his railroad, although the Pueblo District Court did not immediately recognize the legality of his claim. In July, Judge Hallet ordered Palmer to honor his lease and turn the railroad over to the A.T.&S.F. Palmer replied that this was not possible, because the railroad had been turned over to a receiver (an old friend who had agreed to play this part in attempting to deceive the court). This ploy worked for only a very short while. By mid July, the court determined that the receivership was fraudulent and ordered that the lease be honored.[51]

When the Denver and Rio Grande attempted to appeal this decision, Hallet denied the appeal on the grounds that the company was in contempt of court and had no right to appear with any requests whatsoever. Judge Miller supported that ruling and lectured the D.&R.G. lawyers on the error of their ways. As he so forcefully argued, "No judge, no court can sit quietly down and tolerate such abuses of process."[52] In sorting through the legal entanglements, however, Hallet finally recognized the prior claim of the Denver and Rio Grande, as established by the Supreme Court, and he allowed the company to break its lease with the Atchison and Topeka. Hallet was disgusted with the behavior of both parties, so he terminated the lease and placed the "Denver" road in the hands of a court-appointed receiver on 24 July 1879.

The Denver and Rio Grande, although secure in its claim to the Royal Gorge, was still in dire financial straits and still faced competition from the Denver and South Park railroad, which intended to approach Leadville from the north. The solution to both problems came in the form of a familiar figure, Jay Gould, the guardian angel of foundering railroads. Gould and Russell Sage bought large segments of D.&R.G. stock in September 1879, when shares were selling at 22 percent of par. The Denver road then became another piece of the Gould empire. Once he was in control, Gould followed his standard policy of threatening the A.T.&S.F. with a parallel line to Missouri. He also made peace with John Evans, of the Denver and South Park, and secured the D.&R.G. claim to the Leadville trade. Then, in the treaty of Boston, Gould brought all of the major roads under his control, effecting truces between the Union Pacific and Kansas Pacific as well as the Denver and Rio Grande and the Atchison and Topeka. The agreement between those two cancelled the lease, ended all litigation, and paid the A.T.&S.F. $1,400,000 for all its construction efforts. The D.&R.G. abandoned its plans to construct a line to Saint Louis as well as the projected line to New Mexico. The A.T.&S.F. then controlled the trade from Saint Louis to Pueblo, and the D.&R.G. built a rail connection to Salt Lake City.[53]

This plan served the interests of the D.& R.G. stockholders, since the value of their shares rose from twenty-two to seventy-five percent as the "Denver" road secured its claim to the western trade. It also served Gould's interest in developing Pueblo as the transportation and industrial center of the Arkansas Valley. Nevertheless, the Denver and Rio Grande still faced fierce competition as a rail connection to Salt Lake City, and it is not clear that Gould favored the D.&R.G. in its later battles with both the Union Pacific and the Denver and Salt Lake. Gould was in general more interested in consolidating railroads than in building them and was most concerned with his control of the transportation industry. He and others joined the wholesale exploitation of the Colorado railroads, which led the D.&R.G. through continuing financial and legal difficulties.[54] Those adventures extend far beyond present concerns. The railroad wars were over in 1880, so far as Cañon City was concerned, since Pueblo was then established as the central exchange between the Atchison Topeka and the Denver and Rio Grande.

Cañon City After the Railroad Wars

The railroad wars of southern Colorado did not destroy Cañon City, but neither did they establish the transportation and industrial center that the city fathers had envisioned. Even had the Atchison and Topeka won the race to the Royal Gorge, it is not clear that Cañon City would have developed much differently than it did. To some extent, one might argue that the railroads accomplished the goals of their local promoters. The coal and oil industries of Fremont County were developed, and rail transportation undoubtedly helped the local trade. Nevertheless, industry located in Pueblo, and Cañon City remained a service and supply center for agriculture and, to a certain extent, a way station for those traveling to the silver mines in Leadville.

Agriculture in Fremont County continued to thrive, but it did not reach the dimensions of Weld County, or even Pueblo County production. The state auditor reported in 1878 that Fremont County farmers had 64,924 acres under cultivation, and this acreage, with improvements, was valued at $281,288. That same year, local coal mines produced 73,000 tons of coal, or just over 36 percent of the state's total production, which must have been worth close to $300,000. This suggests that coal had displaced agriculture as the major county industry. Clearly, the railroads had provided the basis for the development of the Fremont County coal fields, although they had not established Cañon City as the industrial center of the Arkansas Valley.[55]

The coal mines had been developed in the 1870s by the Central Colorado Improvement Company, the child of the Denver and Rio Grande. The C.C.I.C. was a major partner in the Colorado Coal and Iron Company, which later became the Colorado Fuel and Iron Company. Henry and Willard Teller, of

The railroad depot at Cañon City. Courtesy Colorado Historical Society (F-17640)

Central City, also invested in local coal mines, but they were overshadowed by the C.C.I.C. In 1879, the Colorado Coal and Iron Company produced 70,647 tons of coal in its Fremont County mines, nearly matching the total county production of the previous year. In addition, the C.C.I.C. produced another 49,455 tons at Cucharas and El Moro. The company produced 120,102 tons of coal in 1878 and also manufactured 10,786 tons of coke at the El Moro plant in addition to their Pueblo manufactures and, of course, their railroad.[56]

These figures suggest two conclusions. First, the Denver and Rio Grande and its various affiliates controlled coal production in Fremont County and in southern Colorado more generally. Second, Cañon City was not the industrial center for railroad company enterprises. Perhaps one might attribute this fact to the general animosity that Cañon City leaders expressed toward Palmer and his railroad, but it seems that Palmer was not loved in Pueblo either. In fact, while the Pueblo papers were berating the D.&R.G., Thomas Macon (of Cañon City) was representing the company in court. What distinguished Cañon City was the fact that the C.C.I.C. did not own an adjoining town. South Pueblo was a railroad town, as were El Moro and Cucharas. These were obviously better places to develop the industry that the railroad companies created.

The Colorado Coal and Iron Company owned 13,571 acres of Fremont County coal fields, 83,748 acres of agricultural land and town sites on Coal

Creek, and 1,057 acres on Iron Mountain, south of Cañon City. It also owned 8,121 acres in El Moro, plus the land in and around South Pueblo. In short, Palmer and his investment partners owned most of the extraction and production centers associated with the coal and iron works that sustained their little railroad. In fact, these industrial enterprises generally fared better than the railroads and thereby sustained the town of Pueblo, even when the D.&R.G. was bankrupt.[57] What Palmer and associates did not own was the City of Cañon or the farmlands in the immediate vicinity. Therefore, they did not establish their industrial works in that location.

Fremont County farmers had secured their land claims, first through the claim club, then through the county, and finally in accordance with the federal land survey. Hence industry went elsewhere, where the railroad's land speculation company might find available real estate. Of course, Cañon City had the State Penitentiary, as it does to this day. In fact, the town is now surrounded by a number of more modern penal institutions. Thus Cañon City managed to sustain itself as a prison town and supply town for local farmers and ranchers. It also managed to avoid the fate of Pueblo—the commercial neighbor to an industrial railroad town. Fremont County residents managed to secure their land claims, and Cañon did avoid dependency, in some sense, although it clearly did not control the exploitation of its regional resources. In that sense, it was, and is, a captive town and is thereby a classic example of small-town America.

Cañon City represents an unusual example of a Caucus town, and its history suggests the limitations of analyses that reduce comparative political economy to comparisons of distinctive industries.[58] Cañon City was a mining supply center in 1860, but it was different from Denver and Central City. The trade with the southern mines was short lived, and the miners never managed to fight their way into municipal governance. In a similar vein, Cañon City was a commercial center for the farmers of Fremont County after 1864, but it did not resemble Greeley in 1870. Fremont County farmers exploited a large population of agricultural laborers, who were effectively divided by ethnic and kinship bonds that tied some but not all to the landowners. Even some would-be prospectors and miners provided occasional labor on the farms, thereby further dividing the laboring class. Farmers and merchants allied in Fremont County governance, but the latter (unlike their counterparts in Greeley) continued their expansionist efforts despite the farmers' resistance to national and international capital.

In this regard, the farmers of Fremont County were quite unlike their counterparts in Pueblo. Like the businesspersons of Golden, the farmers resisted the penetration of national capital and refused to sacrifice their control of local enterprise. Unlike the railroad promoters of Golden, however, the Fremont County farmers were able to secure their land rights and survive capital flight. The corporate conglomerates controlled the coal mines and the ore-reduction and manufacturing works near Pueblo as well as the Colorado railroads. Nevertheless, the farmers around Cañon City maintained control of their lands and their laborers, which suggests the relative advantage of the farmer who, lacking capital, might still manage to subsist on the basis of family cultivation efforts. This was, perhaps, the ultimate basis for economic independence that was granted to the American frontier settler.

CHAPTER EIGHT

The Enduring Legacy of the American Frontier

The preceding tale of six cities has been guided by a perspective on the American frontier experience that might help us to understand our past and perhaps to shape our future. This perspective borrows from both the consensus and conflict perspectives but differs markedly from both. The consensus perspective on American economic and political development has quite rightly focused attention on the town booster—the predominant actor in establishing "law and order" and in promoting economic development. Nevertheless, that perspective has largely ignored the developing class structure and the political struggles engendered by efforts to attract national capital and to secure federal government sanction for local governing authorities.[1]

The conflict perspective on the American frontier experience has remedied this deficiency to some degree but still leaves a considerable gap between local histories that focus on the conflicting interests that clashed on economic and political development and national histories that focus on the exploitation of the western hinterland by the commercial and financial interests of the Northeast. The local histories tend to ignore the process of capital penetration and federal government expansion that was fostered by the entrepreneurial efforts of western pioneers. The national histories tend to ignore class structure and class conflict, both on the western frontier and in the Northeast. In this regard, the conflict perspective provides a less comprehensive and cohesive body of theory and analysis than the competing consensus perspective.[2]

My comparative analysis of Colorado frontier towns is guided by the effort to provide a more comprehensive and coherent perspective, building on the conflict tradition but also recognizing its limitations and therefore borrowing generously from the insights offered by the consensus approach. In this regard, my analysis deviates sharply from some of the neo-Marxist perspectives on social class and on the relationship between social class and political partisanship.[3]

First and foremost, I view class relations as both productive and commercial relations rather than simply focusing on the exploitation of productive labor. Aside from simplifying efforts to classify merchants, shopkeepers, and professionals, this expanded concept of social class allows one to recognize the significance of the relations between commercial and industrial classes, particularly in the process of economic development. In this regard, the preceding analysis has focused on the boosters and their efforts to attract labor and capital in the interest of short-term profits. Thus the concerns of world system theory are incorporated into this perspective on the American frontier, although, unlike world system theory, this analysis does not ignore local class structure or reduce the relations between merchants and industrial laborers to the inevitable process of establishing dependency through the exploitation of wage labor.[4]

Neither commerce nor the state is viewed as the instrument of capitalist oppression. Instead, both economic and political institutions are viewed as unstable coalitions representing the short-term interests of various classes that possess both the economic resources and the political organization required to defend their control of a local political economy. Because neither national nor local capitalists had the capacity to control the nineteenth-century political economy, a variety of class-based interests contested the establishment and development of economic and political institutions. The state (both locally and nationally) was neither a semiautonomous administrative body nor an autonomous political structure. It was essentially the target of class-based political struggle and was controlled, in varying degrees with varying success, by coalitions of class-based partisans, united in response to a perceived threat or opportunity.[5]

This does not imply that the exploitation of labor and the penetration of capital were not the predominant cause of class-based political struggle. The point is simply that opposition to monopoly capital investment was contingent upon economic resources and political experience as well as the clear and present danger of monopoly capital investment. Furthermore, the expression of local opposition was mediated by emerging and existing political parties that were competing in their efforts to capture class-based support in the interest of gaining control of local and national government.[6]

One might argue that support for either the Republican or Democratic Party is evidence of cooptation, but that is true only to the extent that radical social change requires extrainstitutional struggle.[7] In the short run, both the partisans and the parties should be viewed as rational actors, responding to short-term opportunities and threats within the limits of their economic resources, political organization, and experience. Nineteenth-century classes and parties acted on the basis of their short-term interests as they perceived them, based on their economic and political history and class-based experience. The miners of 1880 were able to draw on the experience of the mining frontier, even if there were virtually no pioneer miners left. The oral history of a class (or party) is part of its political tradition, despite the fact that this history is always subject to reinterpretation (or distortion) based on changing consciousness and shaped by changing circumstance and ongoing political struggle.[8]

Consequently, it is pointless to evaluate class-consciousness from the perspective of long-term consequences. False consciousness is a useless concept, since class circumstance and consciousness are shaped by their ongoing interrelations. Class is both an objective circumstance and a subjective experience. Most important, however, it is a process of political struggle in which changing circumstance is both cause and effect. Simply stated, changing economic circumstance (capital penetration, for example) often inspires political struggle (assuming resources and organization) that in turn affects economic circumstance.[9] In frontier Colorado, for example, efforts by Denver merchants and shopkeepers to control the price of gold were experienced by the gold miners as a threat to their economic circumstance. Consequently, they organized and effectively reestablished the traditional price.

Not all class-based politics is reactive, however. Generally, it involves a complex set of actions and reactions as competing or conflicting claims are established and contested. In the Gregory Mining District, for example, Gregory and his partners established some form of political organization to secure their control of local claims. Then the influx of newcomers inspired political reorganization, as old-timers and newcomers struggled to establish political institutions that would defend the rights of discovery, purchase, sale, and preemption. In the process, they developed not only political organization but the experience of class-based struggle, which prepared them for subsequent resistance to actions that might threaten the miners' control of the mines.

Conceptually, it is possible to separate the objective component of class circumstance from the subjective experience that inspires political action. The gold miners of frontier Colorado were, for the most part, independent artisans who claimed usage rights to gulch (or placer) claims, physically labored in the production of gold dust, and exchanged the product for the means of production (tools) and subsistence (food and luxuries such as liquor). Their class position is thus defined by their physical labor in petty-commodity production and by their commercial relations with merchants and shopkeepers, as sellers of gold and buyers of goods and services.

The fact that miners exchanged gold dust for goods and services in Central City and Denver is an important component of their class circumstance. Their experience and their collective political struggles were shaped by their commercial relations as well as by their productive efforts. To deny this assertion is to challenge the stated position of the miners, who claimed to represent the interest of labor in opposition to the price-fixing conspiracy of the Denver merchants. Clearly, the experience of producing and selling gold dust provided the basis for the claim that the producer was entitled to establish the price of the product. This claim was enforced by the threat of a producer cooperative, thereby convincing the merchants to concede the producers' right to establish commodity prices. This same right was claimed by the Denver blacksmiths, bakers, and printers and was not contested by the miners. Apparently, the commodity producers recognized each other's right to sell their products at a standard price.

This price-fixing right, based on a simple distinction between laboring versus nonlaboring classes, expresses the essential rules that govern commercial relations in artisanal petty-commodity production. Those who physically labor in the production of commodities have the right to set commodity prices. The baker can set the price of bread but not the price of gold. Of course, if prices are represented in a common metric, such as dollars, setting the price of bread essentially determines the relative value of gold. Nevertheless, the dispute between baker and miner is not based on efforts to undermine the economic resources of the other. In theory, the relative price will be established by haggling, within the limits of supply and demand. If all the bakers sell at the same price, the miners have two alternatives—eat something else or bake their own bread. In either case, the miner forgoes relations with the baker by refusing to pay the prevailing price.

The same general principle can be applied to the relations between merchants and miners, except that the merchant does not physically labor in producing the commodities offered for sale. The merchant sells commodities that are produced elsewhere and thereby claims price-fixing rights. If the producers or transporters of these commodities are economically independent and politically organized, they might set the wholesale (merchant's) price for their goods and services. Nevertheless, the merchant sets the local retail price and thus violates the principle of producers' rights. More generally, nonlaboring classes (including employers) that set the price for goods produced by others violate the principle of the producers' rights, as defended by the commodity producers of frontier Colorado.

This does not imply that the merchant was exploiting the miner any more than the baker was. Clearly, the miners of Colorado were both willing and able to defend themselves against price-fixing efforts by merchants. They were not, however, inclined to forgo commercial relations and sustain a subsistence economy in which local artisans produced all the products consumed in local industry, including the means of subsistence. One might argue that this is evidence of false consciousness, or petty-bourgeois consciousness, but such allegations obscure more than they clarify. Merchants did not coopt or coerce productive labor. Quite the contrary—they attempted to entice labor to cooperate in economic and political development in the interest of potential profits.

One might argue that the pursuit of wealth, as opposed to the attachment to craft, is petty-bourgeois. Nevertheless, in a capitalist economy a short-term interest in money is hardly irrational, given the need to purchase the means of subsistence. It may be that the nineteenth-century laboring classes fall short of our "artisanal" ideal. In varying degrees, however, they identified themselves as producers, sometimes explicitly as workers, in contrast to their nonlaboring associates. In some cases, they organized themselves on that basis in order to establish or sustain their control of the local economy. In this regard, the miners, artisan-shopkeepers, and farmers of the Colorado frontier defended their interests as members of the laboring classes in their artisanal, petty-commodity-production economies.[10]

As evidenced in the discussion of Caucus towns, laboring-class political organization was not inevitable. In some towns and counties, labor worked for wages and never enjoyed the economic resources and political organization required to defend their class-based interests. In these political economies, the principle of commodity-producer rights (or the rights of labor) was largely ignored, and the rights of property overwhelmed the rights of persons. The price of water, the tolls on wagon roads, and the price of cattle and vegetables raised by hired hands were determined not by the laborers but by the employers. In fact, lacking effective political organization, the workers could not even establish the price of their labor. Unlike the artisanal commodity producers, these workers were economically exploited and politically disenfranchised. In this regard, they were less successful in class-based political struggle and were consequently less actively engaged in developing an expressed class interest.

The extent to which these laboring classes were not actively defending their interest can be attributed to divisions within the laboring classes that were exploited by nonlaboring antagonists, most notably employers. Not only did southern Colorado farmers and ranchers exploit kinship and ethnic distinctions, institutionalized in the difference between "workers" and "laborers," but these distinctions were reproduced in the political struggles of the independent artisans. The miners who opposed the Provisional Government as a clear and present threat to their control of the mines explicitly distinguished themselves from the residents of Woodville—including those who were employed in the construction of Wood's irrigation ditch. This is, perhaps, even more apparent in the heated debate between the Grangers and Greenbackers of Greeley. In both cases, however, this distinction represented an apparent difference in both economic circumstance and political organization.

These divisions within the laboring classes facilitated efforts to divide and conquer opposition to capital penetration and proletarianization. This was not, however, a conspiracy perpetrated by a united nonlaboring class. The interests of laboring and nonlaboring classes were in some cases contradictory. If nonlaboring classes were united in private, Caucus governance and thereby defended the rights of property as the basis for exploiting wage labor, their expressed interests and actions were diametrically opposed to the interests of labor. Nevertheless, the exploitation of wage labor was not a clear and present threat to the independent artisans of frontier Colorado. So long as local Carnival governance was sustained as the vehicle for defending the interests of local laboring classes, the interests and actions of capitalists in other communities were not a pressing concern.

Both laboring and nonlaboring classes defended local autonomy—specifically, local control of political and economic institutions—in opposition to outsiders, notably eastern capitalists. Since the economic independence of the frontier artisans was not seriously challenged prior to the intrusion of monopoly capital, the conflict between labor and capital was confounded with the conflict between local and national interests. Regardless of how one might distinguish the objective interests of the Colorado laboring classes, their experience fostered both intraclass cleavage and interclass alliance, which is apparent in the partisan struggles of early statehood.

Class Circumstance, Struggle, and Partisanship

Colorado capitalists, newspaper editors, and leading politicians were concerned in 1880 that there might be a statewide labor uprising. In January, the coal miners of Erie, in largely agricultural Weld County, had been successful in their strike for an increase in the piece rate (or tonnage price) paid by local mineowners. Then in May the Leadville silver miners in mountainous Lake County walked off the job, disputing working conditions and prevailing wages. They organized a general strike, involving thousands of miners, which brought mineral production to a virtual halt, provoked violent confrontations, and finally inspired the governor to declare martial law. Meanwhile, in Denver, bricklayers and carpenters called a general strike while printers for the *Rocky Mountain News* (the Democratic newspaper) walked out over a contract dispute. At the same time, the Greenback Party was pressing its demands for cheap money and attempting to form a labor alliance.[11]

Skilled trades were unionized and prepared for combat. Miners were organizing and beginning to search for allies in the cities, while farmers had organized Grange cooperatives and had offered this solution to the laboring classes. As early as 1873, the Colorado farmers had asserted that "there will be no remedy until the farmers and laborers unite, each class for itself, and do their own business, being their own managers, producers dealing with producers, exchanging what each produces, and then the idlers will be choked off."[12] The potential for a general labor uprising in 1880 was tremendous. Why, then, was there no such uprising? Why did the various fractions of the Colorado laboring classes not unite in a general strike, a labor cooperative, or a Greenback-Labor Party?

Accounts of late-nineteenth-century political struggles suggest at least three different arguments, each of which must be addressed in the context of three related questions. First, did any of these struggles constitute a radical challenge to the American political economy? Second, was one or more of these struggles sufficiently organized and internally coherent to constitute a social movement or, at least, a political party? Third, what was the class base of each of the contending interests? Was this in fact class conflict and, if so, which classes were involved?

One might argue that the Greenbackers were a radical political party organized to represent the interests of the laboring classes. As conflict escalated, however, the party developed central authority structures, and an oligarchy representing the interests of capitalists took control. These capitalists reoriented the party from radical, "extrainstitutional" struggle to liberal, electoral reforms. The "free silver" platform attracted both miners and mine-owners as well as the remnants of the Greenback constituency, notably indebted farmers. Thus the Silver Democrats coopted the Populists in 1896 and offered their standard solution to the labor problem—opposing unions and other monopolies while blaming the Chinese and the Republicans for the declining position of Anglo labor.[13]

Alternatively, one might argue that the Colorado labor movement, including the farmers' movement, developed too quickly, without a local institutional base capable of socializing members into the movement culture. Leadville was an instant city, virtually unpopulated in 1875 but housing 25,000 by 1880. This rapid growth undermined efforts to develop a movement culture in Leadville, and the isolation of mining communities more generally further hampered movement development. Farmers and urban workers might have been better organized, but they were isolated from the miners and from each other. Hence, the labor movement lacked a movement culture and was therefore coopted by the Democrats, as was the Populist Movement. The critical problem from this perspective was not diverging class interests but inadequate grass-roots political organization.[14]

It might also be argued that differences in the economic circumstance and political experience of miners, skilled trades, and farmers would have prevented the development of a radical laboring class even if they had been better organized. Farmers had organized as a class "for itself," but this was not a working-class movement. The Colorado laboring classes (urban workers and miners) had not yet organized themselves as a working-class party and had no interest in joining the farmers. The farmers supported a petty-bourgeois reform movement, incapable of addressing the concerns of the laboring classes or effecting significant social change. Colorado farmers, like their counterparts in Kansas, were essentially artisan-shopkeepers, whose political reform efforts were more likely to serve capital than labor. Miners and skilled trade workers did not support the Greenbackers, not because of false consciousness but because the party had nothing to offer to the the rational, self-interested laborer.[15]

Each of these explanations might be defended, but each is also seriously deficient. First, the miners of Colorado were not coopted by the mineowners. In fact, the strikes of 1880 were merely the opening battle in a protracted struggle that continued through the violent confrontations at Cripple Creek in 1904 and Ludlow Station in 1914, which ultimately broke the back of the radical mining unions. Second, Colorado miners, skilled trades, and farmers each had a tradition, dating back to 1859, of collective political action in defense of class interest. In varying degrees, they established producer cooperatives or negotiated favorable trade agreements. Thus they developed independent institutions (mining camp governments, trade unions, and agricultural cooperatives) and a movement culture.[16]

Finally, the Greenback Party of Colorado was supported by both poor farmers (tenants or indebted owners) and coal miners as economic hardships drove individuals from agriculture to mining in search of subsistence. In this regard, the class distinction between miners and farmers was less apparent to the Greenbackers than might be suggested by some contemporary class theorists. The most proletarianized fractions of the farming and mining population supported the Greenback Party. The party was not supported, however, by silver miners and skilled trades workers or by farmers who were not indebted or reduced to tenancy. These "wealthy" farmers were more likely to join the Grange and were, in that regard, petty-bourgeois reformists.

Nevertheless, the initial and most successful class-based political struggles by miners and skilled trades were, in many ways, indistinguishable from the Grange. Frontier miners, blacksmiths, bakers, and printers had organized in defense of their class-based interest as laboring commodity producers. This was a critical step in establishing the tradition of class-based political struggle and public, Carnival government, which facilitated subsequent efforts to organize in opposition to capital. It was, in this regard, not simply proletarianization but the experience of successfully defending class interest and thereby establishing popular political institutions that combined to produce radical laboring class struggle in the early years of statehood.

The successful class-based political challenges of the frontier miners and urban skilled trades workers were essentially petty-bourgeois reform movements that united laborers who had the economic resources required to exercise "structural" power, based on their position as commodity producers within their respective industries. Ultimately, however, proletarianization reduced their economic resources while at the same time engendering radical class consciousness. The problem was that once they were prepared to attack the instituted order they no longer had the capacity.[17]

By 1880, Colorado miners, skilled trades, and farmers were mobilized in opposition to capital, but distinctive differences in their economic resources (hence, structural power) resulted from industrial differences in the timing and nature of capital investment and proletarianization. There were also differences in their prior experience in class-based political organization, in "revolutionary" memories, and in repertoires of collective action. Their capacity to mobilize allies by defining their conflict as "labor versus capital" or "us versus them" also differed. Finally, they had differing abilities to utilize radical tactics—extrainstitutional forms of cooperation to challenge the institutional structure. At various times, in varying degrees, the Colorado laboring classes had the resources, experience, and opportunity to mobilize. They were thereby capable of radical struggle. At no time, however, did all of the fractions of the laboring classes join in the same struggle, because proletarianization and resistance proceeded in different forms, at different times, across industries, thereby dividing the laboring classes. Furthermore, the conflict between labor and capital was inextricably intertwined with the struggle between local autonomy and incorporation into the national political economy, which engendered inter-class alliances.

In any case, the labor uprisings and political struggles of 1880 were engendered not by economic decline and social dislocation but by economic prosperity and class-based political organization. After the Civil War, prospectors and miners returned to work the mountain streams of the Rockies, in some cases as independent prospectors on unclaimed land, in other cases as renters or wage workers. Before the silver rush, miners moved freely from one situation to another. Skilled Cornish miners were able to exploit the abandoned gold mines of the Central City region and could consolidate their holdings through purchase or lease and take advantage of improved ore-reduction technology.[18]

Elsewhere, in the abandoned gold fields near what would become Leadville, prospectors and miners found reasonable quantities of silver ore as early as 1873, but the combined effects of economic depression and inadequate transportation limited the potential for exploiting these claims. As Colorado recovered from the depression, prospecting and mining increased, and miners began organizing, much as they had in 1859. The Central City newspaper reported miners' meetings in 1878 and reported that miners near Leadville had organized in opposition to claim jumpers in 1879. In March 1880, the editor reported that Leadville miners were defying the local courts and attempting to establish the authority of the assembled miners in adjudicating claim disputes. Thus the Leadville miners recapitulated the experience of their frontier counterparts in attempting to establish their control of the silver mines.[19]

As capital and labor poured into the Leadville region, however, the prospects for independent subsistence declined dramatically. The miners' struggle shifted from claim disputes to wages and working conditions as experienced miners made the familiar shift from prospecting to wage labor. They were joined by newcomers, who were then educated in the western mining tradition. Colorado mining strikes were not new, of course. In 1870, Clear Creek County gold miners had organized an unsuccessful strike, demanding higher wages. By 1880, however, miners were more successful because the economic boom offered the opportunity to demand concessions while capital investment facilitated mobilization by concentrating workers in large corporate enterprises. Eastern capital investment also facilitated efforts to recruit allies on the basis of labor solidarity and resistance to "outsiders." Even within the nonlaboring classes, there was concern for the extent to which "the bears" of Wall Street had gained control of the mines and were more interested in speculation than in the development of Colorado industry.[20]

In Leadville and even in Denver, there was sympathy for the miners among the unionized skilled trades. After the walkout in May, efforts to blame the union for intimidating miners who were prepared to work did not convince some union workers who had been accused of similar tactics. After the strike was settled by martial law, members of the Leadville Typographical Workers Union were among the "trouble makers" who were compelled to leave town. The brickmaker, carpenter, and printer strikes in Denver were not sympathy strikes, but the workers were no doubt inspired by the efforts of the miners. The Democratic editor explicitly addressed local sympathy in an editorial warning the Denver strikers that intimidation tactics would not be tolerated. The paper also reported that Michael Mooney, the leader of the Leadville miners' union, came to Denver as soon as the strike was settled. He addressed a large assembly of "Workingmen in Denver," explaining the lessons of the Leadville strike. Meanwhile, the Greenback-Labor party published its campaign platform, including a condemnation of the Leadville capitalists and the imposition of martial law.[21]

The Greenback Party was the only partisan supporter of the Leadville union, so one might expect that it would have emerged as the labor party of 1880, uniting poor farmers, coal and silver miners, and skilled trades. Election results suggest that this did not happen to any appreciable extent. Not only were the Greenbackers soundly defeated by the Republicans, but they captured virtually no votes in the older mining districts of Gilpin County (1 percent of the county total) and Clear Creek County (4 percent) or in the new silver mines of Lake County where Leadville is located (2 percent). The Greenback Party received no votes in Pueblo and only limited support in Denver (2 percent in Arapahoe County).

In fact, the only substantial Greenback vote was concentrated in three contiguous counties—Boulder, Weld, and Larimer—located between Denver and Wyoming (to the north) and extending from the eastern slope of the Rockies to the Kansas border. Although one might conclude that farmers supported the Greenbackers, since Boulder, Weld, and Larimer counties were the leading producers of wheat in the state, the majority of the Greenbackers in Weld and Boulder counties actually were coal miners or, perhaps, laborers who worked both on farms and in the mines.[22]

In 1878, the pattern of county election returns had been quite similar to the 1880 results, with virtually no Greenback support in Arapahoe County, which then included Denver, and modest support in Boulder and Weld. The Greeley editor explained that the Greenback vote was limited to "Erie, in this county, and Sunshine in Boulder," which were the major coal producers in the region. Erie residents cast 72 percent of the popular vote for the Greenback representative and 82 percent for their gubernatorial candidate, compared to 21 percent (for Congress) and 23 percent (for governor) in Greeley. Poor farmers also supported the Greenbackers, but they were a distinct minority, particularly in Greeley. In Weld and Boulder counties, it was the coal mining districts that were the base of Greenback support.[23]

The Greenbackers did not enjoy similar support in other coal mining counties. In 1879, Boulder was the leading producer of Colorado coal, followed by Fremont, Las Animas, Weld, Jefferson, and Huerfano counties. The coal-producing counties other than Boulder, Weld, and Larimer were controlled by the Democratic Party, so what distinguished the election returns in those three counties was not simply the Greenback vote but the lack of Democratic Party support. These were the only counties that offered the Democrats less than 40 percent of the popular vote.[24]

One might argue that these returns reflect mass defections from the Democratic Party, but none of these three counties had voted Democratic in 1876 when there was no Greenback candidate for governor. In contrast, Fremont, Jefferson, Huerfano, and Las Animas counties had supported the Democrats in 1876 and 1878. They were traditional strongholds of the Democratic Party.[25]

The significance of this fact can be grasped by crudely distinguishing the Democratic and Republican parties and the class-based support that they were able to secure. Both parties opposed labor unions, but the Democrats opposed unions as part of their general opposition to monopolies, tariffs, Chinese immigration, and the various conspiracies of Republicans and eastern capitalists. In this regard, the Democrats were the party of local (versus national) capitalists and unorganized, unskilled workers, who believed that the Chinese laborers and the national capitalists were the source of their current difficulties.

The Republicans supported tariffs to promote industrial growth and opposed unions because "there can be no such thing as a war between capital and labor which will not be in the end detrimental to both." Also, the Republicans opposed the idea of organizing workers as a class of "mere wage laborers, and taking away the ambition to become an owner of property."[26] Thus the Republicans appealed to the Colorado boosters (including the wealthiest wholesale merchants and bankers) and the workers who still considered themselves at least quasi-independent and capable of negotiating labor-capital disputes.

The Democrats controlled southern Colorado, partly because of traditional loyalties but also because the local capitalists had enjoyed a tradition of unchallenged control in the southern Colorado political economy, relying initially on Mexican labor and later on immigrants from eastern Europe. As indicated in the histories of Cañon City and Pueblo, these were Caucus towns. The laborers of southern Colorado in general did not have the experience of political organization and class conflict that the northern miners and farmers had enjoyed. The same was true in Jefferson County, the home of the Colorado Central Railroad. Hence, these workers were effectively exploited by local capitalists, and they remained faithful to the Democratic Party.[27]

The most proletarianized segments of the Colorado laboring classes generally supported the Greenbackers. The exception to this rule was the farm laborers and coal miners who were economically exploited and politically disenfranchised in the Caucus towns of frontier Colorado. The miners and poor farmers of Weld County benefited from the traditions and institutions established by the Greeley farmers in their political struggles of 1870. Even though the Greeley farmers did not support the Greenbackers, they had in fact facilitated the organizing efforts of the Weld County Greenbackers by establishing the local tradition of class-based political struggle and popular participation in government. The laboring classes of Fremont and Jefferson counties did not have a tradition of class-based struggle or popular government. Consequently, they were not effectively organized by the Greenback Party.

Despite the coal miners and poor farmers who supported the Greenbackers, the Republicans maintained control of northern Colorado. They retained the loyalty of the "wealthy" farmers of Greeley, the semiautonomous miners of Gilpin County, and the skilled trades workers of Denver. Each of these fractions of the Colorado laboring classes distanced themselves from the unskilled coal miners and indebted farmers. In contrast to those impoverished workers, the "privileged" segments of the laboring classes distinguished themselves by their ability to negotiate with local capital and thereby maintain relative independence. Thus class circumstance and political experience reinforced their loyalty to the Republican Party.

The silver miners of Leadville also distinguished themselves from the agricultural workers and the coal miners. Compared to the southern laborers, the Leadville miners did seem to enjoy a privileged status, although they were less successful than the coal miners of Erie, who gained wage (or piece rate) increases after their 1880 strike. The Leadville strike was settled without a wage increase but with the mineowners' agreement to pay the traditional wage of three dollars per day for an eight- (versus ten-) hour shift. The eight-hour shift was optional, but most companies complied with the agreement.[28]

In this regard, one might seriously question the Leadville miners' support for the Democratic Party, but their experience between 1878 and 1880 suggested that eastern monopoly capital was the enemy, just as the Democrats claimed. Furthermore, since it was the Republican governor who had declared martial law, the miners were inclined to believe that the Republicans and the eastern capitalists were allied in a conspiracy against local labor and capital. Between 1878 and 1880, Leadville miners repeatedly confronted the Republican government's defense of monopoly capital in their efforts to fight for control of local claims and, later, during the strike. Even before the strike, however, the local Democrats were increasingly successful in wresting control from the Republicans, even within the city. While the boosters of Pueblo and Cañon City were consolidating the Republican votes of the municipal residents, the municipal legislature of Leadville was almost evenly divided, as Democrats were able to appeal to local antibooster and anti-Republican sentiments.[29]

The Leadville miners were inclined to blame the Republicans and the monopoly capitalists for the conspiracy against local entrepreneurs. Consequently, they supported the Democratic platform of free silver and local opposition to Republican politicians and eastern monopoly capitalists. In any case, as wage laborers, they had little sympathy for the Greenbackers. Cheap money might interest indebted farmers or coal miners who aspired to yeoman farmer status, but it did not interest the silver miners. Thus did class circumstance and political experience distinctively shape the consciousness of various fractions of the Colorado laboring classes and thereby foreclose the possibility of a Greenback-Labor Party.

THE LESSONS OF HISTORY

Ultimately, the wealthy farmers and skilled trades workers who supported the Republicans and the Leadville miners who supported the Democrats were attempting to defend their interests as members of the laboring classes. They struggled in opposition to capitalists, who appropriated their surplus labor and who undermined the distinction between these privileged segments of the laboring classes and the common laborers who supported the Greenbackers. Nevertheless, the experience of each fraction of the Colorado laboring classes was distinctively different.

The farmers became Grangers because they were fighting their battle in the commodity market, where middlemen claimed most of the available surplus. These farmers did not see their future as indebted tenants or common laborers and thus did not support the Greenbackers. The farmers wanted more money for their crops, but they did not want an inflated currency. Unlike the Greenbackers, they were not struggling against debt to finance their independence. The wealthy farmers had won their battle to control their land and water and had, in Greeley at least, managed to negotiate successfully with local merchants. Ultimately, they even gained concessions from State and federal politicians, concessions that were purportedly designed to help the family farmer.

In a similar vein, silver miners and skilled trades did not support cheap money policies since they were concerned with the buying power of their wages. The skilled trades were fighting for better wages, just as the Leadville miners were, but they were fighting different enemies. The workers in Denver were negotiating with local building contractors and were, to some extent, successful in gaining concessions during the construction boom. The miners were fighting corporate capital, and their bloodiest battles were still ahead. Unlike other fractions of the Colorado laboring classes, they were fighting monopoly capital in the labor market. After losing the first battle in 1880, they supported the Democratic campaign against the monopolists, at least initially. Later, however, Republican "law and order" and the union-busting efforts of monopoly capital convinced the miners that more radical alternatives were necessary. The Rocky Mountain miners supported the Western Federation of Miners and became the western base for radical union organizing. In this regard, they were not coopted but repressed, much as the Democrats had promised. The Democrats were wrong in one detail, however, since the miners were not crushed by imported Chinese labor but were instead beaten to death by imported thugs.[30]

One might conclude that the Colorado labor uprising of 1880 was defeated by the petty-bourgeois reformist stance of the farmers, the trade union mentality of the skilled trades, and the cooptation of the miners by the Silver Democrats, who were controlled by an oligarchy of local capitalists, most notably owners of silver mines. Nevertheless, the most successful struggles of the Colorado laboring classes were petty-bourgeois commodity-market disputes, and these were a critical stage in the process of class formation.

The experience of class-based political struggle by frontier laboring commodity producers created both a political tradition and an institutional structure that facilitated subsequent resistance to monopoly capital. These commodity reform movements reflected and reinforced a class consciousness that was limited by the segmentation of the Colorado laboring classes. Farmers, skilled trades, and even miners continued to distance themselves from unskilled wage laborers and to cooperate with the major political parties in efforts to maintain their privileged status. In these efforts, the farmers and skilled trade workers were able to gain some short-term concessions in exchange for supporting the Republican campaign to crush the increasingly radical mining unions.

One might conclude that the frontier laboring classes, not unlike the farmers and the industrial workers of today, suffered from false consciousness. They did not unite with the most proletarianized segments of the laboring classes but instead fought to maintain their relatively privileged position. It is my conclusion, however, that we should not expect the laboring classes to foretell their futures or to organize on the basis of our theoretical projections toward an ultimate resolution of their problems. Capital penetration and proletarianization proceed unevenly across industrial sectors. The political formation of classes will therefore proceed at different rates, in different forms, reflecting the diverging experiences of distinctive fractions of the laboring classes. We must expect them to be engaged in different battles, focusing on immediate concerns, without regard to allies fighting battles on distant shores.[31]

NOTES

CHAPTER 1. CLASS STRUCTURE AND CONFLICT IN FRONTIER COLORADO

1. See Greeley history, in chapter 4, on Grangers, Greenbackers, and irrigation disputes; *Weekly Register* (Central City), 2 January 1880, 2, on coal strike; *Rocky Mountain News* (weekly, Denver), 23 June 1880, 1, on Leadville strike; *Weekly Register*, 25 June 1880, on strikes in Denver; *Rocky Mountain News*, 11 and 23 February 1880, 4, on intimidation tactics in enforcing collective bargaining.

2. Frank Hall, *History of the State of Colorado*, 4 vols. (Chicago: Blakely, 1889–1895) 2; 411–423, and Jerome C. Smiley, *History of Denver* (Denver: Old Americana Publishing Co., 1901), 589–599, on Colorado Central railroad war; Robert G. Athearn, *The Denver and Rio Grande Western Railroad* (Lincoln: University of Nebraska Press, 1977), 79–83, on Denver and Rio Grande; *Rocky Mountain News*, 28 April 1880, and Alvin Theodore Steinel, *History of Agriculture in Colorado* (Fort Collins, CO: State Agricultural College, 1929), 134, on fencing and disputed land claims.

3. Frederick Jackson Turner, "The Significance of the Frontier in American History," reprinted in Rogers Taylor (ed.), *The Turner Thesis* (Lexington, MA: D.C. Heath & Co., 1972); Richard Hogan, "The Frontier as Social Control," *Theory and Society* 14 (Jan. 1985): 35–51.

4. Marshall Smelser, *The Democratic Republic, 1800–1815* (New York: Harper and Row, 1968).

5. Ovando J. Hollister, *The Mines of Colorado* (Springfield, MA: Samuel Bowles, 1867), 371–374, on federal law; Gavin Wright, *The Political Economy of the Cotton South* (New York: W. W. Norton, 1978), 137, on Homestead Act.

6. Daniel J. Boorstin, *The Americans: The National Experience* (New York: Vintage Books, 1965), on boosters; Stanley Elkins and Eric McKitrick, "A Meaning for Turner's Frontier," *Political Science Quarterly* 69 (1954): 321–353, 565–602, on homogeneity; Ralph Mann, *After the Gold Rush* (Stanford, CA: Stanford University Press, 1982), on voluntary associations; Carl Abbott, *Boosters and Businessmen: Popular Economic Thought and Urban Growth in the Antebellum Middle West* (Westport, CT: Greenwood Press, 1981), and Lyle Dorsett, *The Queen City* (Boulder, CO: Pruett Publishing Co., 1977), on elite solidarity; see also D. H. Doyle, *The Social Order of a Frontier Community* (Urbana: University of Illinois Press, 1978).

7. Boorstin, *The Americans*, 171–178; Abbott, *Boosters and Businessmen*, 198–208.

8. Allan Bogue, "Social Theory and the Pioneer," *Agricultural History* 34 (1960): 21–34; Robert Dykstra, *The Cattle Towns* (New York: Knopf, 1968); Richard Franklin Bensel, *Sectionalism and American Political Development, 1880–1980* (Madison: University of Wisconsin Press, 1984); Stephen Skowronek, *Building a New American State: The Expansion of National Administrative Capacities, 1877–1920* (New York: Cambridge University Press, 1982).

9. Michael Burawoy, "Introduction," in Burawoy and Theda Skocpol (eds.), *Marxist Inquiries*, supplement to the *American Journal of Sociology* 88: S1–S32, on ideological rifts; Robert Dykstra and William Silag, "Doing Local History: Monographic Approaches

to the Smaller Community," *American Quarterly* 37 (1985), no. 3: 411–425; Immanuel Wallerstein, *The Modern World System III: The Second Era of Great Expansion of the Capitalist World Economy, 1730-1840s* (San Diego, CA: Academic Press, 1988); and Thomas Hall, "Incorporation into the World System: Toward a Critique," *American Sociological Review* 51 (June 1986): 390-402.

10. Boorstin, *The Americans*, on boosters; Hollister, *The Mines of Colorado*, 131, on eastern capital investment in Colorado mining.

11. Scott G. McNall, *The Road to Rebellion; Class Formation and Kansas Populism* (Chicago: University of Chicago Press, 1988); William G. Roy, "The Interlocking Directorate Structure of the United States," *American Sociological Review* 48 (April 1983): 248–256, on corporate, monopoly capital formation.

12. Eric Olin Wright, *Classes* (London: New Left Books, 1985), on new class theory; Michael Schwartz, *Radical Protest and Social Structure: The Southern Farmers' Alliance and Cotton Tenancy, 1880–1890* (1976; reprint ed., Chicago: University of Chicago Press, 1988), on the crop lien system.

13. Auraria Town Company Records, 8 November 1858, Colorado State Historical Society, Denver.

14. *Rocky Mountain News*, 15 January 1860, 2.

15. Thomas Maitland Marshall, *Early Records of Gilpin County, Colorado* (Boulder: University of Colorado Press, 1920).

16. Marshall, *Early Records*, 17, quoting miners; *Rocky Mountain News*, 9 May and 18 April 1860, on blacksmiths and printers; *Colorado Republican* (weekly, Denver), 25 May 1861, on bakers.

17. Smiley, *History of Denver*, 373 and 443, on lot jumpers; see Golden history, chapter 5, on political struggles.

18. B. Richard Burg, "Administration of Justice in Denver People's Courts: 1859-1861," *Journal of the Old West* 7, no. 4 (October 1968): 510–521; Richard Hogan, "Carnival and Caucus: A Typology for Comparative Frontier History," *Social Science History* 11, no. 2 (summer 1987): 139–167.

19. *Rocky Mountain News*, 26 December 1860, on popular sovereignty; Proceedings of Denver Municipal Government, September 1860, on microfilm in the Western History Department, Denver Public Library; see also Hogan, "Carnival and Caucus."

20. Hogan, "Carnival and Caucus."

21. Frederick Merk, *History of the Westward Movement* (New York: Knopf, 1978), 116, 229–230; Malcolm J. Rohrbough, *The Land Office Business: The Settlement and Administration of American Public Lands, 1789–1837* (New York: Oxford University Press, 1968), 142, on squatter and debtor resistance to federal Land Office; Gavin Wright, *The Political Economy of the Cotton South*, 137, on Homestead Act of 1862.

22. Bensel, *Sectionalism and American Political Development*, on exploitation of South and West; Barrington Moore, *The Social Origins of Dictatorship and Democracy* (Boston: Beacon Press, 1966), on the impossibility of planter-industrialist "revolution from above"; Schwartz, *Radical Protest and Social Structure*, on crop lien system.

23. Hogan, "The Frontier as Social Control," on inducing frontier entrepreneurs.

Chapter 2. Denver

1. The initial settlement of Denver, Auraria, and Saint Charles as well as earlier prospecting and settlement efforts are discussed, in detail, by Jerome C. Smiley, *History of Denver* (Denver: Old Americana Publishing Co., 1901), chapters 19–22; Saint Charles Town Company records are in the Western History Department of the Denver Public

Library (CoD); see also Frank Hall, *History of the State of Colorado*, 4 vols (Chicago: Blakely, 1889–1895), 4: 19–22. The Saint Charles Company was not dispossessed without recompense. Smiley, *History of Denver*, 202–205, 215–219, notes that members of the Saint Charles Company were admitted to Denver Company and vice-versa; Lyle Dorsett, *The Queen City: A History of Denver* (Boulder, CO: Pruett Publishing Co., 1977), 6, reports that members of the Saint Charles Company were given $250 and shares in the Denver corporation. Records of the town companies are in CoD; typed transcriptions are in the Colorado Historical Society (CoHi) in Denver.

2. Dorsett, *The Queen City*, 29.

3. Leroy Hafen (ed.), *Reports from Colorado* (New York: Lewis Historical, 1948), 19 (on Wildman's family), and 66–83 (on Wildman).

4. Smiley, *History of Denver*, 302 and 336, reports prices and wages in Denver. Average wage estimates correspond to wage rates reported in local business records, located in the Western Business History Collection (CoHi). Wildman, in Hafen, *Reports from Colorado*, offers comparable figures, as does Duane Smith, *Rocky Mountain Mining Camps* (Lincoln: University of Nebraska Press, 1974). Stephen Leonard's dissertation, "Denver's Foreign Born Immigrants, 1859–1900 (Claremont Graduate School, History, 1971), 13, offers census data to show that Denver wages were still inflated as late as 1890.

5. There were forty-nine such households in this sample, so the average wealth for laboring households (including these forty-nine) would be $108,045/261 = $413.97.

6. The career of the People's Court is reported by B. Richard Burg, "Administration of Justice in Denver People's Courts: 1859–1861," *Journal of the Old West* 7, no. 4 (October 1968); 510–521; trials were routinely reported in the *Rocky Mountain News* (weekly, Denver), beginning with the first edition, 23 April 1859.

7. *Rocky Mountain News*, 23 April 1859, 3; Smiley, *History of Denver*, 307.

8. Smiley, *History of Denver*, 308.

9. Ibid., 684–686. Smiley claims the club was organized in the winter, but club records (CoHi) include the claim of the Denver Town Company recorded and signed by the club secretary in May 1859. Also, the *Rocky Mountain News*, 13 August 1859, announced a club meeting.

10. Arapahoe County Land Claim Club Records, May 1859 (CoHi).

11. *Rocky Mountain News*, 28 May 1859, 2.

12. Ibid.

13. Ibid., 28 May 1859, 3.

14. Hafen, *Reports from Colorado*, 60.

15. *Rocky Mountain News*, 12 September 1859, 3.

16. *Rocky Mountain News*, 21 December 1859; city council proceedings (CoHi); Smiley, *History of Denver*, 318.

17. Occupations located in Denver business directory, 1859 (CoHi) and Fifty-Niners Directory (CoD).

18. *Rocky Mountain News*, 25 January 1860, 2.

19. *Rocky Mountain News*, 1 February 1860, 3, and special edition of 3 February 1860; see also *Western Mountaineer* (weekly, Golden), 8 February 1860, 2–3.

20. *Rocky Mountain News*, 1 February 1860, 3, and special edition of 3 February 1860; see also *Western Mountaineer*, 8 February 1860, 2–3.

21. *Rocky Mountain News*, 3 February 1860, 1.

22. Ibid., 15 February 1860, 3.

23. *Western Mountaineer*, 24 July 1860, 6, reports the organization of the Denver Vigilance Committee more than five months after the trial of William Harvey. The Golden editor might have been mistaken, or there might have been another vigilance

committee organized earlier that year. Burg, "Administration of Justice," 514, reports on the trial of Harvey and other Bummers, referencing the special edition (3 February 1860) of the *Rocky Mountain News*. Burg implies that this was an action of the People's Court, although he notes the somewhat irregular composition of the court and does not explicitly use the term *people's court*, as he does in most of his other accounts.

24. The chaos of 1860 is reported in Smiley, *History of Denver*, 338–350; in Burg, "Administration of Justice"; and in the editions of the *Rocky Mountain News*, from January to October of 1860. These accounts are very similar; reports in the *Rocky Mountain Herald* differ mostly in interpretation.

25. The Denver Vigilance Committee is distinguished from "vigilantes" because it held trials and did not simply "lynch" the accused.

26. *Rocky Mountain News*, 25 July 1860; Smiley, *History of Denver*, 348.

27. *Rocky Mountain Herald* (daily, Denver) 3 September 1860; *Western Mountaineer*, 6–13 September 1860; Smiley, *History of Denver*, 347–349.

28. Smiley, *History of Denver*, 348.

29. *Rocky Mountain Herald* (daily), 3 September 1860, 2, reports names of posse members. At least four of the nine served as judges or attorneys for the People's Court (Smiley, *History of Denver*, 339–348).

30. *Rocky Mountain Herald* (daily), 11–15 September 1860; *Rocky Mountain Herald* (weekly, Denver), 28 July 1860; *Western Mountaineer*, 6–13 September 1860; Smiley, *History of Denver*, 348; Burg, "Administration of Justice," 518.

31. Some of the confusion in the literature is based on assertions regarding who belonged to the Denver Vigilance Committee and who was opposed to vigilante justice. See, for example, *Rocky Mountain Herald* (daily), 11–15 September 1860; *Rocky Mountain Herald* (weekly), 28 July 1860; *Western Mountaineer*, 6–13 September 1860; Burg, "Administration of Justice," 518. Eugene Frank Ryder's dissertation, "The Denver Police Department" (University of Denver, History, 1971), 13, relies on Burg and on reports in the *Rocky Mountain Herald*. These sources provide contradictory evidence. Smiley, *History of Denver*, 348, offers a secondhand account, based on discussions with one of the vigilantes. His account implies that the leading citizens of Denver (the boosters) were involved in the lynching and the Denver Vigilance Committee but that they defended these as stop-gap measures and generally preferred "legal" alternatives. Thus they opposed vigilante justice in efforts to establish republican forms of government. This seems the most reasonable conclusion.

32. *Rocky Mountain News*, 12 September 1860, 1.

33. Ibid., 26 September 1860, 3.

34. Ibid., 24 October 1860, 2 (quote); 3 October 1860, 2 (reports election).

35. Blacksmiths' meetings and price-fixing efforts (*Rocky Mountain News*, 9 May 1860) were not included in the newspaper data presented in Tables 2.2, 2.3, and 2.4 because they did not occur in the first year of the paper's publication (which ended in April 1860). The bakers' price-fixing efforts of 1860 were implied in a later report of a decision to raise the price of bread (*Rocky Mountain Herald* (weekly) 25 May 1861). That report implied that the bakers had previously adopted a standard price list, although explicit reference to the initial decision was not found in the newspaper reports. It is possible that the bakers were not organized until 1861.

36. *Cañon City Times* (weekly, Cañon City), 27 October 1860, 3.

37. Denver City Council proceedings 8–17 October 1860 (CoHi).

38. Burg, "Administration of Justice," 518; Council proceedings 11 December 1860 (CoHi).

39. Burg, "Administration of Justice," 520; *Rocky Mountain News*, 12 December 1860, 1.
40. *Rocky Mountain News*, 26 December 1860, 1.
41. Council proceedings 9 November 1860 (petition) and 12 March 1861 (prostitution) (CoHi).
42. The Denver company sold unclaimed lots at public auction, in 1860, before surrendering its authority to the municipal government. One such auction was advertised in the *Rocky Mountain Herald* (weekly), 26 May 1860; on legislation, see Smiley, *History of Denver*, 443.
43. Smiley, *History of Denver*, 373.
44. Ibid., 443–451.
45. Ibid., 428 and 436 (on the lynching).
46. Ibid., 428.
47. Hall, *History of the State of Colorado*, 3: 395–396.
48. Smiley *History of Denver*, 581–582.
49. Ibid., 585–586.
50. Ibid., 586–590.
51. Ibid., 593.
52. Ibid.., 542 (sale to Gould) and 593 (land grants); Evans's donation is recorded in the minutes of the Arapahoe County Commissioners 11 July 1870 (County Building, Denver).
53. The Clear Creek miners' strike was reported in the *Rocky Mountain News*, 16 March 1870.
54. *Greeley Tribune* (weekly), 24 September 1873, 2.
55. Carl Ubbelohde, Maxine Benson, and Duane Smith, *A Colorado History* (Boulder, CO: Pruett, 1972), 249–256, on union affiliations.
56. *Denver Weekly Times*, 26 May 1880, 1, refers to the actions of police and a judge, who was not terribly busy, prosecuting "drunks, vags, disturbances of the peace, and assaults." District and federal court dockets were routinely reported, but this story might have referred to a local police court. In the State Archives, in Denver, there are police court records from 1885 but none from 1880.
57. *Rocky Mountain News*, 2 January 1880, 1.
58. Ibid., 28 January 1880, 3, and 11 February 1880, 4 (on printers' strike).
59. Ibid., 8 September 1880, 6.
60. Ibid., 27 October 1880, 4, and 3 November 1880, 2.
61. Ibid., 29 September 1880, 8.
62. Ibid., 3 November 1880, 5.
63. *Denver Weekly Times*, 18 February 1880, 3.
64. Ibid., 18 February 1880, 3.
65. Ibid., 16 June 1880, 1 (Leadville) and 2 (brick makers' strike).
66. Ibid., 3 November 1880, 2.
67. Ubbelohde et al., *A Colorado History*, 229 and 254–256.

CHAPTER 3. CENTRAL CITY

1. Ovando J. Hollister, *The Mines of Colorado* (Springfield, MA: Samuel Bowles, 1867), 59–63; Thomas Maitland Marshall, *Early Records of Gilpin County, Colorado* (Boulder: University of Colorado Press, 1920), xii; D. C. Kemp, *Colorado's Little Kingdom* (Denver: Sage Books, 1949), 26–27; Jerome Smiley, *History of Denver* (Denver: Old Americana Publishing Co., 1901), 260–262.

2. Hollister, *The Mines of Colorado*, 76 (quote). One of Gregory's partners (D. K. Wall) had been a miner and rancher in California and might have helped to draft the laws. See Kemp, *Colorado's Little Kingdom*, 25–27.

3. Colorado School of Mines, "Gold Placers in Colorado," *Quarterly of the Colorado School of Mines* 69, no. 3-4 (Golden: Colorado School of Mines, 1974); 3–4, 11, 69; see also Kemp, *Colorado's Little Kingdom*, 31–33.

4. Hollister, *The Mines of Colorado*, 63, 66–67; Marshall, *Early Records*, 10–15; Kemp, *Colorado's Little Kingdom*, 69–72.

5. Records of Gilpin County mining districts are in the courthouse in Central City. Marshall (*Early Records*) has published an accurate and extremely complete record of laws and meetings. Daniel Ellis Conner, *A Confederate in the Colorado Goldfields* (Norman: University of Oklahoma Press, 1970), 70, 93, discusses Fairplay. "Newcomer" controversies in other districts were reported in the *Rocky Mountain News* (weekly, Denver), 17 September 1859, and in Conner, *A Confederate*, 76.

6. Marshall, *Early Records*, 12–15.

7. John Denis Haeger, *The Investment Frontier* (Albany: State University of New York Press, 1981), discusses conservative nineteenth-century investors. Colorado mining investments are discussed in detail by Joseph E. King in *A Mine to Make a Mine* (College Station: Texas A&M Press, 1977).

8. Kemp, *Colorado's Little Kingdom*, 29; Frank Fosset, *Colorado* (1880; reprint ed., Glorieta, NM: Rio Grande Press, 1976), 300; Hollister, *The Mines of Colorado*, 63.

9. Colorado School of Mines, "Gold Placers in Colorado," 11.

10. *Rocky Mountain News* (weekly, Denver), 10 November 1859, 4; see also Marshall, *Early Records*: 17–18.

11. Marshall, *Early Records*, 16–18.

12. Ibid., 51–52.

13. Hollister, *The Mines of Colorado*, 93.

14. Nolie Mumey, *Laws of Nevadaville* (Boulder, CO: Johnson Publishing Co., 1962).

15. *Rocky Mountain News*, 25 January 1860, 1.

16. *Rocky Mountain News*, 28 December 1859, reports opposition to provisional government; 26 September 1860 reports offer to extend mining camp government (quote). Tax revolt and petition are discussed by Carl Abbott, *Colorado: A Centennial History* (Boulder: University of Colorado Press, 1976), 65, and by Frank Hall, *History of the State of Colorado*, 4 vols. (Chicago: Blakely, 1889–1895) 1: 212.

17. Marshall, *Early Records*, 131; see also *Rocky Mountain News*, 10 October 1860, 2, on mining companies at Spring Gulch.

18. Marshall, *Early Records*, 131–143.

19. Ibid., 129–130 (on flooding), 134 (on lack of water); Smiley, *History of Denver*, 288–289, 318–319 (on ditch company charter, etc.).

20. Marshall, *Early Records*, 40–45; see *Rocky Mountain Herald* (daily, Denver), 21 May 1861, on ditch war.

21. King, *A Mine to Make a Mine*, 11; see also Haeger, *The Investment Frontier*, on conservative mortgage practices.

22. Fossett, *Colorado*, 300.

23. King, *A Mine to Make a Mine*, 6–9; Fossett, *Colorado*, 300.

24. Fossett, *Colorado*, 300; Hollister, *The Mines of Colorado*, 145–149.

25. Fossett, *Colorado*, 304.

26. Hollister, *The Mines of Colorado*, 133.

27. See, for example, Hollister, *The Mines of Colorado*; King, *A Mine to Make a Mine*; or Fossett, *Colorado*.

28. Colorado School of Mines, "Gold Placers in Colorado," 70–75.

29. Smiley, *History of Denver*, 488–493; Carl Ubbelohde, Maxine Benson, and Duane Smith, *A Colorado History* (Boulder, CO: Pruett, 1972), 100.
30. Marshall, *Early Records*, 39–40.
31. Ibid., 46–47.
32. Ibid., 86–87, 100; Eureka District records are in Denver Public Library (CoD).
33. District Court records are located in the Denver Federal Center, although some records are also in the State Archives, Denver.
34. Kemp, *Colorado's Little Kingdom*, 35–37; John Guice, *The Rocky Mountain Bench* (New Haven, CT: Yale University Press, 1972), 63–64; Smiley, *History of Denver*, 708.
35. Kemp, *Colorado's Little Kingdom*, 35–36; Abbott, *Colorado*, 69.
36. Smiley, *History of Denver*, 493–499.
37. Hollister, *The Mines of Colorado*, 363–365.
38. Occupations for municipal officers come from 1870 U.S. Census and 1871 Gazeteer (CoD). King, *A Mine to Make a Mine*, 106, identifies lawyer in fraud case.
39. H. William Axford, *Gilpin County Gold* (Chicago: Swallow Press, 1976), 13; Ubbelohde et al., *A Colorado History*, 117.
40. See King, *A Mine to Make a Mine*, 106, on mining swindles; Fossett, *Colorado*, 314, 334 on Scudder.
41. Fossett, *Colorado*, 288–291.
42. Proceedings of Board, Central City Hall.
43. Ubbelohde et al., *A Colorado History*, 139–141 refer to the "statehood faction."
44. Ibid., et al., *A Colorado History*, 139–147, discuss the struggle for and against statehood.
45. Smiley, *History of Denver*, 596.
46. Ibid.
47. Axford, *Gilpin County Gold*, 60–61.
48. Kemp, *Colorado's Little Kingdom*, 112–116; see also Stephen Leonard, "Denver's Foreign Born Immigrants," 1859–1900 (Ph.D. dissertation, Claremont Graduate School, History, 1971).
49. *Weekly Register-Call* (Central City), 15 June 1878, 1.
50. Ibid., 8 June 1878, 2.
51. Ibid.
52. Axford, *Gilpin County Gold*, 65.
53. *Weekly Register-Call*, 20 February 1880, 1.
54. Ibid., 5 November 1880, 1 (on Denver), 4 (on Central City).
55. Ibid., 10 December 1880, 1.

Chapter Four. Greeley

1. Frank Hall, *History of the State of Colorado*, 4 vols. (Chicago: Blakely, 1889–1895) 4: 337–338, on Fort St. Vrain. See also the discussion in chapter 1.
2. *Rocky Mountain News* (weekly, Denver), 23 April 1859.
3. Saint Vrain Claim Club records are in the Colorado State Historical Society (CoHi); see also Hall, *History of the State of Colorado* 4: 338–339. A number of the St. Vrain club members are listed in Junius E. Wharton, *History of the City of Denver* (Denver: Byers and Dailey Printers, 1866), and in S. W. Burt and E. L. Berthoud, *Rocky Mountain Gold Regions* (Denver: Rocky Mountain News Publishing Company, 1861), as Denver merchants or businessmen.
4. Claim club records (CoHi).

5. Hall, *History of the State of Colorado* 4: 338–339; according to the claim club records (CoHi), Ellen later sold her claims to H. J. Graham.
6. Claim Club records (CoHi); Hall, *History of the State of Colorado* 4: 339.
7. County Commissioners proceedings (Weld County Centennial Center in Greeley).
8. County Commissioners proceedings (Weld County Centennial Center in Greeley).
9. The ranchers were identified in an 1871 Gazeteer, located in the Western History Department of the Denver Public Library (CoD); in the 1870 Census; and in the 1867 Cattlemen's Association Records, in the Colorado State Historical Society (CoHi).
10. David Boyd, *A History of Greeley and the Union Colony of Colorado* (Greeley: Greeley Tribune Press, 1890), offers a biography of Nathan Meeker in Chapter 1.
11. James F. Willard, *The Union Colony at Greeley, Colorado: 1869-1871* (Denver: W. F. Robinson Printing Company, 1918), 1.
12. Willard, *The Union Colony at Greeley*, 3 (quote), see also pages 1–4; Boyd, *A History of Greeley*, 32.
13. Willard, *The Union Colony at Greeley*, reports the minutes of the New York meeting, 6–12.
14. Ibid., 4.
15. Ibid., 6–12.
16. Ibid.
17. Ibid., xxi.
18. Willard, *The Union Colony at Greeley*, xxiii, 27–30; Boyd, *A History of Greeley*, 40-41; *Rocky Mountain News*, 1 June 1870.
19. Boyd, *A History of Greeley*, 41–58.
20. *Rocky Mountain News* (weekly, Denver) 1 June 1870; Willard, *The Union Colony at Greeley*, 27–30.
21. Colony records are in the Greeley Municipal Museum (also reproduced in Willard, *The Union Colony at Greeley*, 171).
22. Proceedings (reproduced in ibid., 18–25).
23. Boyd, *A History of Greeley*, 45–58; Hobbes's allegations were reprinted in *Rocky Mountain News* (weekly, Denver) 27 June 1870 and reproduced in Willard, *The Union Colony at Greeley*, 72–275.
24. Among the Weld County Farwells, C. B. was a Weld County commissioner in 1863 (Commissioners records, Centennial Building in Greeley), Joseph and Cyrus D. were enumerated in the 1870 Census, and C. D. was elected to the executive council (Willard, *The Union Colony at Greeley*, 379).
25. Willard, *The Union Colony at Greeley*, 31 (on cavalry); Carl Ubbelohde, Maxine Benson, and Duane Smith, *A Colorado History* (Boulder, CO: Pruett 1972), 112; note that the battle of Summit Springs (1869) established Anglo supremacy on the plains, but Colorado editors continued to discuss "the Indian problem."
26. Union Colony Records (Greeley Municipal Museum; reprinted in Willard, *The Union Colony at Greeley*, 34).
27. Colony Records, reprinted in ibid., 37.
28. Ibid., 274–278.
29. Ibid., 267.
30. Ibid., 51–52.
31. Ibid., 50–52.
32. Minutes—ibid., 53–55.
33. Hall, *History of the State of Colorado* 1: 538.
34. Willard, *The Union Colony at Greeley*, 364–368.
35. Proceedings of Executive Committee (Greeley Municipal Museum; reprinted in ibid., 53, 81).

36. Boyd, *A History of Greeley*, 59–61; see also proceedings of Municipal Board of Trustees (City Hall); *Greeley Tribune* (weekly), 3 May 1871.
37. Willard, *The Union Colony at Greeley*, 107.
38. It was possible to hold more than one membership and more than one farm lot, but this required additional capital improvements. Minutes (24 February 1871, reprinted in ibid., 96); Greeley Municipal Museum has list of shareholders and those holding water deeds.
39. Willard, *The Union Colony at Greeley*, 373–381.
40. *Greeley Tribune*, 3 May 1871, 2.
41. Ibid., 19 April 1871.
42. Ibid.
43. Ibid.
44. Willard, *The Union Colony at Greeley*, 360–368.
45. Ibid., 23, 373–374.
46. *Greeley Tribune*, 3 May 1871.
47. Ibid.
48. Ibid.
49. Greeley Trustees Proceedings (City Hall).
50. Colony Proceedings (Willard, *The Union Colony at Greeley*, 111–113).
51. Ibid., 296–298; see also court records in Weld County Courthouse, in Greeley (some of these records have been or are being moved to a silo for storage).
52. Dean Fenton Krakel, *South Platte Country* (Laramie, WY: Powder River Publishers, 1954), 174–176.
53. Krakel, *South Platte Country*, 183; Alvin Theodore Steinel, *History of Agriculture in Colorado* (Fort Collins, CO: State Agricultural College, 1929), 113.
54. U.S. Census of 1870.
55. Steinel, *History of Agriculture*, 121.
56. Boyd, *A History of Greeley*, 119–120.
57. Agricultural Fair: Steinel, *History of Agriculture*, 113; Board of Trade: Hall, *History of the State of Colorado*, 1: 517–518. Byers, on Irrigation Convention: Boyd, *A History of Colorado*, 98.
58. Boyd, *A History of Colorado*, 12; Hall, *History of the State of Colorado* 4: 349.
59. *Greeley Tribune*, 22 October 1873, 2 (quote); Boyd, *A History of Colorado*, 89–118; Hall, *History of the State of Colorado* 4: 349–350.
60. *Greeley Tribune*, 5 July 1871, 4 and 11 November 1872, 1 (on land sales); Boyd, *A History of Colorado*, 68–69 (on fence); *Greeley Tribune*, 19 March 1873, 2 (ditches).
61. *Greeley Tribune*, 27 December 1872, 1.
62. Ibid.
63. Ibid., 22 January 1873, 2.
64. Ibid., 11 June 1873, 2.
65. Ibid., 27 August 1873, 2.
66. Ibid.
67. Boyd, *A History of Colorado*, 69–70.
68. Hall, *History of the State of Colorado*, 4: 347–348; Krakel, *South Platte Country*, 23.
69. *Greeley Tribune*, 21 January 1874, 2.
70. Boyd, *A History of Colorado*, 120–123; Hall, *History of the State of Colorado*, 4: 350.
71. Boyd, *A History of Colorado*, 123–127.
72. Hall, *History of the State of Colorado*, 4: 350.

73. Boyd, *A History of Colorado*, 172.
74. Ibid., 268–269.
75. Richard Goff and Robert H. McCaffree, *Century in the Saddle* (Boulder, CO: Johnson Publishing Co., 1967), 22–25.
76. Ibid., 24–35.
77. On struggles between breeders and herders and on eastern capital, see Walter Prescott Webb, *The Great Plains* (New York: Grosset and Dunlap, 1931), 230–232.
78. See ibid., 237; see Lawrence Goodwyn, *The Populist Moment* (New York: Oxford University Press, 1978); on the National Farmers Alliance, see Michael Schwartz, *Radical Protest and Social Structure: The Southern Farmers' Alliance and Cotton Tenancy, 1880-1890* (1976; reprint ed., Chicago: University of Chicago Press, 1988).
79. Willard, *The Union Colony at Greeley*, 6.
80. *Greeley Tribune*, 7 January 1874, 4.
81. Ibid., 5 January 1876, 2; 12 January 1876, 2 (reply to Clark).
82. Ibid., 7 August 1878, 2.
83. Ibid., 2 October 1878, 2.
84. Boyd, *A History of Colorado*, 243 (Law and Order League); see also Hall, *History of the State of Colorado*, 4: 344.
85. Ubbelohde et al., *A Colorado History*, 257–268; 316 (migrant workers); see also Lyle Dorsett, *The Queen City: A History of Denver* (Boulder, CO: Pruett Publishing Co., 1977), 225–226.
86. On the National Farmers' Alliance, see Schwartz, *Radical Protest and Social Structure*.

PART TWO. CAUCUS TOWNS OF COLORADO

1. This is, essentially, an application of Charles Tilly, *From Mobilization to Revolution* (Reading, MA: Addison-Wesley, 1978), 133–138, using monopoly capital investment as the "threat" to local actors' interest in maintaining their control of the local economy. In a similar manner, the tradition of class-based political struggle could be viewed as providing a "repertoire" of collective action. The established form of government (Carnival or Caucus) could be viewed, in Tilly's terms, as providing the "opportunity" for laboring or nonlaboring class political action. My argument also builds on Rubenstein, *Rebels in Eden*, chapter 3, regarding the combined effects of semi-autonomous local residents being exploited by nonresident investors. Rubenstein's discussion of "neo-colonialism" is, in this regard, particularly appropriate, since the frontier political economy institutionalized the contradictory interests of local autonomy and incorporation into the national political economy, which undermined local control of economy and government.
2. In this regard, I am inclined to differ with Jeffery Paige, *Agrarian Revolution*, who tends to minimize the importance of political experience and resources in his structural model of rebellion and revolution. Rubenstein, *Rebels in Eden*, offers a more compatible analysis in his discussion of "quasiindependence and local power" in chapter 4.
3. This is an extension of Rubenstein, *Rebels in Eden*, and Schwartz, *Radical Protest and Social Structure*, applying the same model of "internal colonialism" and "structural, extra-institutional power" to explain local capitalist rebellion. All too often, neo-Marxist theories have ignored capitalist rebellion, except in the context of bourgeois revolt, but Moore, *The Social Origins*, offers some interesting ideas on this topic, particularly with regard to "revolution from above."

4. Patrick H. Mooney, *My Own Boss? Class, Rationality, and the Family Farm* (Boulder, CO: Westview Press, 1988), chapter 2, distinguishes four classes of farmers, combining Marxian and Weberian class theory. In a similar fashion, the diverging class and party positions of the Greeley and Cañon City farmers will be discussed in the concluding chapter.

CHAPTER 5. GOLDEN

1. Marshall Sprague, *Colorado: A Bicentennial History* (New York: Norton, 1976, 52); Lyle Dorsett, *The Queen City: A History of Denver* (Boulder, CO: Pruett, 1977, 1–25); Jerome C. Smiley, *History of Denver* (Denver: Old Americana Publishing Co., 1901), 284, 367, 493, 590, 970.
2. Records of the Mechanics Mining and Trading Company are in the Colorado State Historical Society (CoHi) in Denver.
3. Smiley, *History of Denver,* 284–285 (on Arapahoe and Golden), 261 (on D. K. Wall).
4. Records of Mechanics Mining and Trading Company (CoHi).
5. Records of all three Denver town companies are in CoHi.
6. Smiley, *History of Denver,* 284–285; *Western Mountaineer* (weekly, Golden), 7 December 1859.
7. *Western Mountaineer,* 7 December 1859, 3 (advertisements) and 4 (wagon road).
8. Smiley, *History of Denver,* 319; *Western Mountaineer* reported the organization and operation of these companies, beginning with the first edition (7 December 1859).
9. *Western Mountaineer,* 7 December 1859, 1.
10. Ibid., 7–14 December 1859.
11. Smiley, *History of Denver,* 319; S. W. Burt and E. L. Berthoud, *Rocky Mountain Gold Regions* (Denver: Rocky Mountain News Publishing Co., 1861, 87); *Western Mountaineer,* 7–14 December 1859.
12. Burt and Berthoud, *Rocky Mountain Gold Regions,* 87; Smiley, *History of Denver,* 319; *Western Mountaineer,* 7–14 December 1859.
13. *Rocky Mountain News* (weekly, Denver) 10 September 1859.
14. *Rocky Mountain News,* 17 September 1859.
15. *Western Mountaineer,* 21 December 1859.
16. Ibid., 25 January 1860 (cemetery), 1 February 1860 (property owners' meeting), 8 February 1860 (Golden City Association), 21 March 1860 (citizens' meeting).
17. Ibid., 21 March 1860 (citizens' meeting), 3 April 1860 (election); Association records (CoHi).
18. *Western Mountaineer* reports election and first meeting of new board in 28 June 1860 edition; subsequent references are in 5 and 12 July 1860 editions; see also *Western Mountaineer,* 8 February 1860 (court cases), 6 September 1860 (People's Court).
19. Junction District and Middle Park club records are in the County Clerk's office in Golden. Golden City Association records are at the Colorado State Historical Society (CoHi) in Denver.
20. *Western Mountaineer,* 25 April 1860 (election), 28 June 1860 (council), 6 September 1860 (People's Court).
21. *Rocky Mountain News,* 10–17 September 1859.
22. *Western Mountaineer,* 29 March 1860 (theft from Loveland), 1–8 November 1860 (toll house theft).
23. The lynching is reported in the *Rocky Mountain News,* 17 November 1860.

24. *Western Mountaineer,* 25 October 1860 (*McCleery* vs. *Kansas Territory*), 6 and 27 September 1860 (assaults).
25. Ibid., 4 April 1860.
26. *Rocky Mountain News,* 3 September 1859 (Golden convention); Smiley, *History of Denver,* 310–317, on Golden delegates.
27. Corporate charters are reprinted in Smiley, *History of Denver,* 319 and *Western Mountaineer,* 21 December 1859; *Western Mountaineer,* 8 January 1860 (estrays), 1 February 1860 (irrigation).
28. *Rocky Mountain News,* 14 December 1859 and *Western Mountaineer,* 14 December 1859; see also Smiley, *History of Denver,* 319; Saint Vrain club records (CoHi); Ovando J. Hollister, *The Mines of Colorado* (Springfield, MA: Samuel Bowles, 1867), 75 (Casto) and 87 (Golden bypass).
29. Casto's letter and Golden's reply are published in *Western Mountaineer,* 18–25 January 1860; see also Loveland's advertisement in ibid., 15 February 1860, and report of McCleery trial in 1 November 1860.
30. Ibid., 3 March 1860 (citizen meeting), 12 July and 16–23 August 1860 (toll road dispute).
31. Ibid., 4 April 1860 (court case), 11 April 1860 (Golden's attack), 25 April 1860 (club organizes), 2 August 1860 (Carter's warning).
32. Junction District Claim Club records are in the vault at the Jefferson County Clerk's office in Golden.
33. Claim club records (Jefferson County Clerk).
34. Smiley, *History of Denver,* 493 (Territorial government); Jefferson County Commissioner records are in the County Building in Golden.
35. Junction club records in County Clerk's Office, Golden.
36. Smiley, *History of Denver,* 493.
37. County Commissioner records (County Building, Golden).
38. Territorial District Court records in County Clerk's Office, Golden.
39. Thomas Maitland Marshall, *Early Records of Gilpin County, Colorado* (Boulder: University of Colorado Press, 1920), 129–145, offers records of the election; see D. C. Kemp, *Colorado's Little Kingdom* (Denver: Sage Books, 1949), 37, on Judge Muir; see also the discussion in the Central City chapter.
40. City government records are in the Golden City Hall; *Colorado Transcript* (weekly, Golden), 19 December 1866.
41. Frank Hall, *History of the State of Colorado,* 4 vols. (Chicago: Blakely, 1889–1895) 2: 504, discusses Loveland's purchase; see chapter 1 on the "Lot Question" in Denver.
42. Smiley, *History of Denver,* 581–583.
43. Ibid., 596–597; Hall, *History of the State of Colorado* 2, 95–99.
44. *Colorado Transcript,* 19 December 1866.
45. County Commissioner records (County Clerk).
46. City Council records (City Hall); ordinances were published in the *Colorado Transcript,* beginning in January 1871.
47. Ibid., 5 April 1871.
48. Smiley, *History of Denver,* 584–585.
49. Ibid., 583–594; Dorsett, *The Queen City,* 57–59.
50. Hall, *History of the State of Colorado,* 2: 93–94.
51. Ibid., 2: 94–99; Smiley, *History of Denver,* 597.
52. Hall, *History of the State of Colorado,* 2: 109–110, 395; Smiley, *History of Denver,* 598.
53. Hall, *History of the State of Colorado,* 2: 395.

54. Ibid., 2: 397–399.
55. Ibid., 2: 411–423; Smiley, *History of Denver*, 598–599.
56. Hall, *History of the State of Colorado* 2: 397–399.
57. Ibid., 2: 400–402.
58. Ibid.; Smiley, *History of Denver*, 542.
59. Hall, *History of the State of Colorado* 2: 400–402.

CHAPTER 6. PUEBLO

1. Janet LeCompte, *Pueblo, Hardscrabble, and Greenhorn* (Norman: University of Oklahoma Press, 1978), offers an outstanding history of the fur-trading years.

2. Frederick Merk, *History of the Westward Movement* (New York: Knopf, 1978), 229–239, discusses federal land policy, use, and abuse. Frank Hall, *History of the State of Colorado*, 4 vols. (Chicago: Blakely, 1889–1895) 3: 444–445, 449, discusses the Fountain City settlement, as does O. L. Baskin (ed.), *History of the Arkansas Valley, Colorado* (Chicago: Baskin, 1881), 766; see also volume 6 of George Baxter's papers in the Colorado State Historical Society (CoHi) in Denver. See also Milo E. Whittaker, *Pathbreakers and Pioneers of the Pueblo Region* (Pueblo: Franklin Press, 1917), 41-43.

3. Baskin, *History of the Arkansas Valley, Colorado*, 766; Baxter, vol. 6 (CoHi).

4. Baskin, *History of the Arkansas Valley, Colorado*, 767–769; Cook County, Illinois, was notorious for voting fraud during the reign of Chicago Mayor ("Boss") Richard Daley. It was said that even the dead turned out to vote for the Daley ticket.

5. Baxter, vol. 6 (CoHi); Baskin, *History of the Arkansas Valley, Colorado*, 769–770; *Cañon City Times* (weekly), 15 July 1861.

6. Baskin, *History of the Arkansas Valley, Colorado*, 769–770; *Cañon City Times*, 12 January 1861 (Pueblo Town Company).

7. Hall, *History of the State of Colorado* 3: 450; Baskin, *History of the Arkansas Valley, Colorado*, 769.

8. *Rocky Mountain News* (weekly, Denver), 27 August 1859; *Cañon City Times*, 7 October 1861; Hall, *History of the State of Colorado* 3: 450.

9. Jerome C. Smiley, *History of Denver* (Denver: Old Americana Publishing Co., 1901), 319; *Cañon City Times*, 5 January 1861 (estrays), 23 May 1861 (trial).

10. *Cañon City Times*, 5 September 1861 (lynching), 29 August 1861 (vigilance committee).

11. Ibid., 29 September 1860 (Indian treaty); 3 November 1860 (killing Navajos in New Mexico).

12. John Guice, *The Rocky Mountain Bench* (New Haven, CT: Yale University Press, 1972), 69, discusses Judge Bradford; Hall, *History of the State of Colorado* 3: 453, discusses vigilantes.

13. Whittaker, *Pathbreakers and Pioneers*, 144–156; see also Smiley, *History of Denver*, 374–375, on the Reynolds Gang; Baxter, vol. 6 (CoHi).

14. Baskin, *History of the Arkansas Valley, Colorado*, 775 (Stevenson quote), 771–775; Whittaker, *Pathbreakers and Pioneers*, 54.

15. County Commission records are in the Pueblo County Courthouse in Pueblo.

16. U.S. Surveyor General's records are in the Federal Record Center in Denver.

17. The irrigation company records are in the Colorado State Historical Society (CoHi), in Denver; Arkansas Valley Claim Club records are in the Fremont County Courthouse in Cañon City.

18. Stanley Hoig, *The Sand Creek Massacre* (Norman: University of Oklahoma Press, 1961); see also discussion in the Denver history, chapter 2.

19. Whittaker, *Pathbreakers and Pioneers*, 153; see also Daniel Ellis Conner, *A Confederate in the Colorado Goldfields* (Norman: University of Oklahoma Press, 1970), 126–157, on Mace's Hole.

20. Baskin, *History of the Arkansas Valley, Colorado*, 775; see also Hoig, *Sand Creek Massacre*.

21. Hoig offers a general history of the Sand Creek massacre. The records of David Moffat, First National Bank of Denver, contain a list of subscriptions to finance the Colorado regiment led by Chivington against the Sand Creek settlement. The list of contributors reads like "Who's Who in Denver."

22. Hall, *History of the State of Colorado* 3: 454–456.

23. Ibid. 2: 214 (land values), 1: 507 (railroad); see also Robert Dykstra, *The Cattle Towns* (New York: Knopf, 1968), on the Kansas cattle towns.

24. Alvin Theodore Steinel, *History of Agriculture in Colorado* (Fort Collins, CO: State Agricultural College, 1929), 123–125; LeCompte, *Pueblo, Hardscrabble, and Greenhorn*, 40, on Goodnight; see also Baxter, vol. 6 (CoHi), on Goodnight's "law and order" boys.

25. County Commissioner records are in the Pueblo County Courthouse in Pueblo.

26. Baskin, *History of the Arkansas Valley, Colorado*, 776 (sale in 1869); County Commissioner proceedings (Pueblo Courthouse); *Colorado Chieftain* (weekly, Pueblo), 7 April 1870 (election).

27. *Colorado Chieftain*, 7 April 1870 reports the election. Baxter, although a candidate of the People's Party for municipal office, was the Republican candidate for county commissioner. As was the case in Greeley, the lines of partisan struggle were less easily defined than electoral rhetoric might suggest. Baxter represented the "people" because he was a long-term resident and "one of the largest property holders of Pueblo County." He also shared the boosters' interest in economic development, however, and was, among other things, half-owner of the Jewett Grist Mill (see Baskin, *History of the Arkansas Valley, Colorado*, 783).

28. *Colorado Chieftain*, 6 June 1870, 2 (license laws), 7 July 1870, 2, and 14 July 1870, 2 (weapons); see also 8 February 1872 (court records).

29. District Court records, State Archives in Denver.

30. Hall, *History of the State of Colorado* 3: 458; court records at State Archives in Denver; delinquent taxpayers were listed in the *Colorado Chieftain*, 7 April 1870.

31. *Colorado Chieftain*, 22 September 1870, 2.

32. Ibid., 18 April 1872, 2.

33. Ibid., 21 November 1872, 4.

34. Ibid., 10 March 1870.

35. Ibid.

36. Robert G. Athearn, *The Denver and Rio Grande Western Railroad* (Lincoln: University of Nebraska Press, 1977), 3–5.

37. Ibid., 5–15.

38. Ibid., 9–18, 23.

39. Ibid., 18–20.

40. Daniel J. Boorstin, *The Americans: The National Experience* (New York: Vintage Books, 1965), 161–168, discusses intertown competition more generally; Walter Prescott Webb, *The Great Plains* (New York: Grosset and Dunlap, 1931), 279, discusses railroads and land speculation more generally.

41. Athearn, *The Denver and Rio Grande*, 22–23.

42. Ibid., 23.

43. Ibid., 23–25.

44. Hall, *History of the State of Colorado* 2: 101; Athearn, *The Denver and Rio Grande*, 29; *Colorado Chieftain*, 28 November 1872 (railroad and special election).

45. Hall, *History of the State of Colorado* 2: 101–102; *Colorado Chieftain,* 5–12 December 1872.
46. *Colorado Chieftain,* 19 December 1872, 2.
47. Hall, *History of the State of Colorado* 2: 100–101; *Colorado Chieftain,* 23 January 1873.
48. *Colorado Chieftain,* 12 December 1872, 1.
49. Baskin, *History of the Arkansas Valley, Colorado,* 787–788, 806–807.
50. Frank Fossett, *Colorado* (1880; reprint ed., Glorieta, NM: Rio Grande Press, 1976), 167; these figures are considerably lower than those from 1874 (see Hall, *History of the State of Colorado* 2: 214).
51. Hall, *History of the State of Colorado* 3: 462–463.
52. Ibid., 3: 462–469; Baskin, *History of the Arkansas Valley, Colorado,* 781.
53. Baskin, *History of the Arkansas Valley, Colorado,* 866–868; Richard Goff and Robert H. McCaffree, *Century in the Saddle* (Boulder, CO: Johnson Publishing Co., 1967), 111–113.
54. Goff and McCaffree, *Century in the Saddle,* 111–115.
55. Hall, *History of the State of Colorado,* 3: 445; see also Steinel, *History of Agriculture in Colorado,* on sheep wars and the Prairie Cattle Company.
56. *Rocky Mountain News* (weekly, Denver), 28 April 1880, discusses the federal court cases.
57. Steinel, *History of Agriculture in Colorado,* 134, on illegal fences.
58. Carl Ubbelohde, Maxine Benson, and Duane Smith, *A Colorado History* (Boulder, CO: Pruett, 1972), 205.
59. Ibid., 246.
60. Baskin, *A History of the Arkansas Valley, Colorado,* 787–808.
61. Ubbelohde et al., *A Colorado History,* 298.

CHAPTER 7. CAÑON CITY

1. *Cañon City Times* (weekly), 15 September 1860; O. L. Baskin (ed.), *History of the Arkansas Valley, Colorado* (Chicago: Baskin, 1881), 627–629; Frank Hall, *History of the State of Colorado,* 4 vols. (Chicago: Blakely, 1889–1895) 3: 392–393. These accounts refer to a "lot-jumping" incident that seems to have been more apparent than real. Kroenig and Young had come to Cañon City in October 1859 with some of the Fountain City residents, but they constructed nothing to secure a claim. In March 1860, Kroenig and Young returned, having secured a commitment from the major wholesale trade merchants, and established Cañon City.
2. Hall, *History of the State of Colorado* 3: 400 (oil); Baskin, *History of the Arkansas Valley, Colorado,* 635–636 (brickyards and other improvements), 643–646 (ranches); Rosemae Welles Campbell, *From Trappers to Tourists* (Palmer Lake, CO: Filter Press, 1972), 27–29 (on Kroenig).
3. Land claim club records are in the Fremont County Courthouse, in Cañon City; see also *Cañon City Times,* 3 November 1860.
4. Claim club records (courthouse).
5. Claim club records.
6. *Cañon City Times,* 26 January 1861 published notice of sales.
7. Ibid., 29 September 1860, 3; p. 1 reports public meeting.
8. Ibid., 6 October 1860; see Jerome Smiley, *History of Denver* (Denver: Old Americana Publishing Co., 1901), 319, on the Provisional Territory estray law.
9. *Cañon City Times,* 22 December 1860 reports the Civil Code; 29 December 1860 edition reports the public meeting that established the criminal code.

10. Baskin, *History of the Arkansas Valley, Colorado*, 570.
11. *Cañon City Times*, 2 February 1861, 3.
12. Ibid., 4 July 1861; 8 August 1861 edition reports Hall's arrival; 12 August 1861 edition reports Pueblo Convention.
13. Baskin, *History of the Arkansas Valley, Colorado*, 565.
14. District Court, County Surveyor, and claim club records are in the Fremont County Courthouse, in Cañon City. Baskin, *History of the Arkansas Valley, Colorado*, 567 reports on County Commissioners.
15. Baskin, *History of the Arkansas Valley, Colorado*, 570–573.
16. Surveyor records (court house); Baskin, *History of the Arkansas Valley, Colorado*, 643–644.
17. Hall, *History of the State of Colorado* 3: 394.
18. Baskin, *History of the Arkansas Valley, Colorado*, 573.
19. Court and Commissioner records are in the County Courthouse; Frazier's court is discussed in Baskin, *History of the Arkansas Valley, Colorado*, 628.
20. Commissioner records from 1865 to 1870 are in the Fremont County Courthouse, in Cañon City.
21. County Commissioner records (courthouse); see Alvin Theodore Steinel, *History of Agriculture in Colorado* (Fort Collins, CO: State Agricultural College, 1929), 111, on territorial laws.
22. Hall, *History of the State of Colorado* 3: 400–401; Carl Ubbelohde, Maxine Benson, and Duane Smith, *A Colorado History* (Boulder, CO: Pruett, 1972), 301–302.
23. Baskin, *History of the Arkansas Valley, Colorado*, 596–597; G. M. Binckley and Frank Hartwell (eds.), *Southern Colorado* (Cañon City: Binckley and Hartwell, 1879), 59–60.
24. Baskin, *History of the Arkansas Valley, Colorado*, 599–600.
25. Hall, *History of the State of Colorado* 3: 395–396.
26. Baskin, *History of the Arkansas Valley, Coloardo*, 659; Frazier was enumerated in the 1870 census as a blacksmith, and his household was therefore included in the service industry.
27. Commissioner records (courthouse).
28. Town government records are in City Hall and are available on microfilm through the State Archives in Denver.
29. *Cañon City Times*, 1 August 1872, 3.
30. Territorial Prison Warden, Annual Reports to the Colorado Governor, available in Colorado State Archives, Denver.
31. *Cañon City Times*, 6 March 1873, 3.
32. Ibid., 15 May 1873, 2.
33. Binckley and Hartwell, *Southern Colorado*, 62–63; Baskin, *History of the Arkansas Valley, Colorado*, 599–600; Hall, *History of the State of Colorado* 3: 397.
34. Robert Athearn, *The Denver and Rio Grande Western Railroad* (Lincoln: University of Nebraska Press, 1977), 15–25.
35. Athearn, *The Denver and Rio Grande*, 25–27, 33–36 (popular criticism), 25 (forfeit bonds).
36. Ibid., 46.
37. Ibid., 25; Baskin, *History of the Arkansas Valley, Colorado*, 597, 618, on land sales; Binckley and Hartwell, *Southern Colorado*, 59, 65–66.
38. Athearn, *The Denver and Rio Grande*, 25–26; Hall, *History of the State of Colorado* 3: 397.
39. Hall, *History of the State of Colorado* 3: 397–398; Baskin, *History of the Arkansas Valley, Colorado*, 600–603; Binckley and Harris, *Southern Colorado*, 63.

40. *Cañon City Times,* 8 May 1873, 3.
41. Ibid., 9 July 1874 (quote), 4 April 1874 (bond election).
42. Athearn, *The Denver and Rio Grande,* 26 (possession of railroad), 43–48 (competition with A.T.&S.F.); Hall, *History of the State of Colorado* 3: 368–369 (Pueblo and Arkansas Railroad).
43. Athearn, *The Denver and Rio Grande,* 43–48.
44. Ibid., 51–54.
45. Ibid., 55–57.
46. Ibid., 58–60.
47. Ibid., 60–63.
48. Ibid., 63–65.
49. Ibid., 67–75, 95 (Supreme Court decision).
50. Ibid., 74–79.
51. Ibid., 79–83.
52. Ibid., 83 (quote), 84–86 (subsequent decisions).
53. Ibid., 85–87, 96.
54. Ibid., 242 (looting the D.&R.G.).
55. Figures from Frank Fossett, *Colorado* (Glorieta, NM: Rio Grande Press, 1976), 578–579.
56. Figures from ibid., 580; Campbell, *From Trappers to Tourists,* 98, on Teller.
57. Fossett, *Colorado,* 580–581.
58. Such local histories are offered by Ralph Mann, *After the Gold Rush* (Stanford, CA: Stanford University Press, 1982) and reviewed by Robert Dykstra and William Silag, "Doing Local History: Monographic Approaches to the Smaller Community," *American Quarterly* 37, (3): 411–425. An extended version of this critique is offered in Richard Hogan, "Carnival and Caucus: A Typology for Comparative Frontier History," *Social Science History* 11 (2) (summer 1987): 139–142.

CHAPTER 8. THE ENDURING LEGACY
OF THE AMERICAN FRONTIER

1. Lyle Dorsett, *The Queen City: A History of Denver* (Boulder, CO: Pruett Publishing Co., 1977), is an excellent example of this consensus tradition, as is D. H. Doyle, *The Social Order of a Frontier Community* (Urbana: University of Illinois Press, 1978). Ralph Mann, *After the Gold Rush* (Stanford, CA: Stanford University Press, 1982), and Carl Abbott, *Boosters and Businessmen: Popular Economic Thought and Urban Growth in the Antebellum Middle West* (Westport, CT: Greenwood Press, 1981), offer more compelling analyses because they compare the experience of distinctive communities and, to some extent, recognize conflicting (or competing) interests in economic and political development. Stephen Leonard's doctoral dissertation, "Denver's Foreign Born Immigrants, 1859-1900" (Claremont Graduate School, History, 1971), focuses on ethnic differences and conflicts but does not deal explicitly with their relation to class conflicts more generally, although both he and Dorsett explore the class-based support that the Colorado Democrats attempted to secure through race-baiting.

2. The conflict tradition is a combination of revisionist approaches, some of which are neo-Marxist. In local history, Allan Bogue, "Social Theory and the Pioneer," *Agricultural History* 34 (1960): 21–34, offers an early critical (but not Marxist) perspective. His paper, "The Iowa Claim Clubs: Symbol and Substance," in Stephen Salisbury (ed.), *Essays on the History of the American West* (Hinsdale, IL: Dryden Press, 1975), 342–359, provides an excellent example of this early conflict tradition that distinguishes the

interests of farmers and speculators but does not deal, directly, with the concept of exploitation. Robert Dykstra, *The Cattle Towns* (New York: Knopf, 1968), explores the conflicting interests of ranchers and farmers and the extent to which local boosters represent the interest of the ascendant industrial classes. He also deals, more directly, with the significance of relations with eastern capital—in his case, the Chicago meat-packing interests and the railroads. In this regard, Paul E. Johnson, *A Shopkeeper's Millenium* (New York: Hill and Wang, 1978), offers an outstanding analysis of how capitalization affects local class relations and how ethnic and religious distinctions are exploited in efforts to segment the laboring classes.

Among historians who focus on the process of economic and political development from a national (or, at least, nonlocal) perspective, John Denis Haeger, *The Investment Frontier* (Albany: State University of New York Press, 1981) and Malcolm J. Rohrbough, *The Land Office Business: The Settlement and Administration of American Public Lands, 1789–1837* (New York: Oxford University Press, 1968), offer exceptionally insightful analyses of relations between speculators and farmers, on the one hand, and government, on the other. Nevertheless, neither explicitly addresses the relationship between national capital investment and local class structure, nor do they frame their arguments in terms of class conflict more generally.

Richard Franklin Bensel, *Sectionalism and American Political Development, 1880–1980* (Madison: University of Wisconsin Press, 1984), applies world system theory in explaining how the financial, commercial, and industrial core (essentially, the Northeast) exploited the largely agrarian and extractive industries of the South and West, but he ignores class structure and class conflict, both in the core and in the periphery. Stephen Skowronek, *Building a New American State: The Expansion of National Administrative Capacities, 1877–1920* (New York: Cambridge University Press, 1982), offers a structural model, essentially explaining the increase in federal administrative capacity by the increasing complexity of the national political economy. He, like Theda Skocpol, in *States and Social Revolution* (New York: Cambridge University Press, 1979), and "Political Response to Capitalist Crisis," *Politics and Society* 10, no. 2 (1980), 155–201, views the state as a relatively autonomous political structure that is more or less capable of accommodating the challenges of governing in a national or international political economy.

3. Eric Olin Wright, *Classes* (London: New Left Books, 1985), offers a neo-Marxist theory of class that self-consciously avoids commercial relations or anything that cannot (however obliquely) be reduced to exploitation. In this regard, I prefer the less structural, more interactive model employed by William Finlay, "One Occupation, Two Labor Markets," *American Sociological Review* 48, no. 3 (1983) 306–314. Michael Burawoy, *The Politics of Production* (New York: Verso, 1985), also offers an interesting, interactive model of structure and process, which focuses on the political struggles at the workplace.

4. Wright, *Classes*, offers the best example of a theory that focuses on exploitation and ignores commercial relations. Bensel, *Sectionalism and American Political Development, 1880–1980*, offers the opposite extreme, focusing on market forces and ignoring class structure. Eric R. Wolf, *Europe and the People without History* (Berkeley: University of California Press, 1982), offers a useful corrective, in suggesting that world system theory attempts to bring the people back into the analysis. In this regard, Barrington Moore, *The Social Origins of Dictatorship and Democracy* (Boston: Beacon Press, 1967), offers an outstanding model for dealing with the interplay of class structure and economic and political development efforts.

5. Fred Block, "The Ruling Class Does Not Rule," *Socialist Revolution* 33 (1977): 6–28, and "Beyond Corporate Liberalism," *Social Problems* 24 (1977): 352–361, argues

that state officials are functionally independent from the capitalist class and serve as managers of the crises of capitalism. Skocpol, "Political Response to Capitalist Crisis," argues that Block does not go far enough in asserting the autonomy of the state.

6. Jeffery Paige, *Agrarian Revolution* (New York: Free Press, 1975), essentially ignores political experience and organization in his structural analysis of revolution or reform. In this regard, I am inclined to follow Charles Tilly, *From Mobilization to Revolution* (Reading, MA: Addison-Wesley, 1978), who is more concerned with organization and experience as intervening variables in the relation between class structure and political struggle.

7. At the Social Science History Meetings in Chicago in 1988, Steve Rytina suggested that partisan affiliation is, by definition, cooptation. Although I certainly see the merits of this argument as well as the benefits of extrainstitutional struggle, *cooptation* has negative connotations, suggesting that partisan politics are irrational. I am more inclined to see class-based partisanship as short-term rationality within the limits of available experience and resources, particularly since some segments of the laboring classes later adopted more radical tactics.

8. Anthony Giddens, *Profiles and Critiques in Social Theory* (Berkeley: University of California Press, 1982), uses the term *double hermeneutic* to describe the relationship between social scientist and social reality. This might be a useful way of considering the relationship between economic circumstance and political struggle as they relate to the interpretation of the oral history of a class. In any case, the class is viewed here as neither an objective nor a subjective reality but as an ongoing dialectic, involving objective constraint and resistance based on subjective experience and the interpretation of past and present circumstance. The vision of the future is, of course, more problematic.

9. Scott G. McNall, *The Road to Rebellion: Class Formation and Kansas Populism* (Chicago: University of Chicago Press, 1988) offers a similar perspective on class as process (rather than structure) and also offers an excellent review of the debates surrounding this concept of class, particularly as it relates to class-based political struggle.

10. Patrick H. Mooney, *My Own Boss? Class, Rationality, and the Family Farm* (Boulder, CO: Westview Press, 1988), argues that American farmers occupy one of four distinct class locations, depending on their economic resources (market position) and attachment to craft versus pursuit of profit. McNall, *The Road to Rebellion*, argues that farmers (at least in Kansas) were petty-bourgeois. Allan Kulikoff, "The Transition to Capitalism in Rural America," *William and Mary Quarterly* 46 (January 1989), 3rd series: 120–144, distinguishes farmers as members of the "yeoman class," who struggled within a capitalist system to maintain quasi-independence (both economic and political) through communal exchange networks and food production for family subsistence. To some extent, I borrow from each of these perspectives, producing a simple distinction between laboring and nonlaboring classes that is production-based (unlike Mooney) but at the same time viewing class as a process (like McNall) and a struggle to maintain relative autonomy (like Kulikoff). Perhaps the concept of *yeoman* would be preferable to *artisan*, although it might seem less appropriate when applied to miners and crafts.

11. *Weekly Register* (Central City), 2 January 1880, 2, reports the coal miners' strike and reports the strikes in Denver in the 25 June 1880 edition (p. 4); *Rocky Mountain News* (weekly, Denver), 11 February 1880, 4, reports the printers' strike; the Greenbackers' platform is published in the *Denver Weekly Times*, 2 June 1880, 1.

12. *Greeley Tribune* (weekly), 24 September 1873, 2.

13. This interpretation is based on Michael Schwartz, *Radical Protest and Social Structure: The Southern Farmers' Alliance and Cotton Tenancy, 1880–1890* (1976; reprint ed., Chicago: University of Chicago Press, 1988).

14. This interpretation is based on Lawrence Goodwyn, *The Populist Moment* (New York: Oxford University Press, 1978); Leadville population figures are from Frank Fosset, *Colorado* (1880; reprint ed., Glorieta, NM: Rio Grande Press, 1976).

15. This interpretation is based on McNall, *The Road to Rebellion;* a more detailed review of all three interpretations is offered in my "Three Pieces of the Populist Puzzle," *Sociological Forum* (forthcoming).

16. Carl Ubbelohde, Maxine Benson, and Duane Smith, *A Colorado History* (Boulder, Co: Pruett, 1972), 254–256, discuss the violent struggles between miners and mineowners in the early twentieth century.

17. Schwartz, *Radical Protest and Social Structure,* describes the radical struggles of the Southern Farmers' Alliance in terms of "structural power" and "extra-institutional tactics." His concepts and his general theory of radical protest are essentially reproduced here, although I do not conclude that the laboring classes were coopted.

18. H. William Axford, *Gilpin County Gold* (Chicago: Swallow Press, 1976), 13–14, discusses these efforts by the Cornish miners of Central City.

19. Ubbelohde et al., *A Colorado History,* 160, reports discoveries and difficulties of 1873; *Weekly Register,* 8 June 1878, 3, miners' meetings; 25 July 1879, 4, claim-jumping; 2 January 1880, 2, defying local courts.

20. *Rocky Mountain News,* 16 March 1870, on strike; *Weekly Register,* 6 August 1880, on "bears" of Wall Street.

21. *Weekly Register,* 18 June 1880, 2, on Typographical Workers Union; *Rocky Mountain News,* 9 June 1880, 6, on intimidation; 23 June 1880, 8, on Mooney in Denver and Greenbackers; see also *Denver Weekly Times,* 16 June 1880, 2, warning to Denver brickmakers.

22. Fossett, *Colorado,* 171, on wheat production.

23. *Greeley Tribune,* 2 October 1878, 2, quote; 16 October 1878, 3, vote in Erie and Greeley. It is likely that in 1880 the farmers of Larimer County were struggling against debt, since the county was primarily settled after 1875 when land prices once again began to boom and capital investment began to increase dramatically (see Fossett, *Colorado,* 157, on population growth). In this regard, the Larimer County farmers were like the indebted Central Kansas farmers, who supported the Populist Party (see McNall, *The Road to Rebellion*).

24. Fossett, *Colorado,* 579, on coal production.

25. Ibid., 590, on county vote, 1876–1878.

26. *Denver Weekly Times,* 18 February 1880, 3 (quotes).

27. See chapters 5–7 on the exploitation of wage labor in these Caucus towns; Frank Hall, *History of the State of Colorado,* 4 vols. (Chicago: Blakely, 1889–1895) 3: 462–469, and O. L. Baskin, ed., *History of the Arkansas Valley, Colorado* (Chicago: Baskin, 1881), 781, describe industrialization and immigration in later years of Pueblo.

28. *Weekly Register,* 2 January 1880, 2, on coal strike; *Rocky Mountain News,* 23 June 1880, 1, on settlement of Leadville strike.

29. On Leadville's partisan political shifts see *Denver Weekly Times,* 14 April 1880, 2; 5 May 1880, 8; 9 June 1880, 3.

30. Ubbelohde et al., *A Colorado History,* 243–256.

31. On capitalization and segmentation, see Eric Wright and Bill Martin, "The Transformation of the American Class Structure, 1960–1980," *American Journal of Sociology* 93, no. 1 (July 1987): 1–29. The sociological literature on labor market segmentation in contemporary society is reviewed by Randy Hodson and Robert L. Kaufman, "Economic Dualism: A Critical Approach," *American Sociological Review* 47 (1982): 727–739. The political consequences of segmentation are discussed by David Gordon, Richard Evans, and Michael Reich, *Segmented Work, Divided Workers* (New York: Cambridge University Press, 1982).

BIBLIOGRAPHY

ARCHIVAL SOURCES

Colorado Territorial District Court and United States Surveyor General records (1862–1876) are in the Denver Federal Records Center. Microfilmed copies of the Eighth (1860) United States Bureau of the Census Population Reports for Arapahoe County, Kansas Territory, as well as the Ninth (1870) and Tenth (1880) Census Population Reports for Colorado are also available at the Denver Federal Center. Colorado state government records, including Colorado State District Court records and annual reports to the governor from the penitentiary warden (1874–1878) are in the State Archives at Denver. The State Archives also contains many county, Justice of the Peace, and Police Court dockets (except as indicated below).

City Council (Aldermen, or Trustees) and County Commissioner proceedings are in the city and county offices for each of the six towns (except as indicated below). Most of the documents not found in the federal, state, county, or municipal offices were located in either the Colorado Historical Society in Denver or in the Western History Department of the Denver Public Library. The Colorado Cattlemen's Association records are in the Colorado Historical Society. Records of the Union Colony are in the Greeley Municipal Museum.

Denver and Arapahoe County

Auraria Town Company Records (30 October 1858–5 May 1860) are in the Colorado Historical Society in Denver. Denver City (31 December 1858–11 March 1861) and Saint Charles (24 September 1858–5 November 1858) records are in the Western History Department of the Denver Public Library. No records of the first municipal government have survived, but proceedings of the second City Council (8 October 1860–29 December 1863) are in the Colorado Historical Society in Denver. The first meeting of this council and the meetings of the Governor's Guard (presumably the Jefferson Rangers) are on microfilm in the Western History Department of the Denver Public Library (M34-1245). Legislative records from later years are in the city and county offices, and court records are in the state and federal archives.

The only surviving official record of the Arapahoe County Land Claim Club is the claim of the Denver City Town Company, certified by the club's secretary in 1859, preserved in the Colorado State Historical Society. The First National Bank records, in the Colorado Historical Society in Denver, contain the list of subscribers who funded the Colorado Regiment responsible for the Sand Creek Massacre.

Central City and Gilpin County

Gilpin County Courthouse has mining district claim and court records dating from 1859 but no county commissioner records predating 1886. The Western History Department of the Denver Public Library has copies of many of these mining camp records. The Central City Clerk's office has Council minutes from 1871. Colorado State Archives has Mayor and City Council administrative proceedings (from 1870) as well as court records.

Greeley and Weld County

Saint Vrain Claim Club records (6 October 1859–3 November 1860) are in the Colorado Historical Society. The Greeley Municipal Museum contains early records of the Union Colony (dating from April of 1870), including proceedings of the executive committee, lists of shareholders, and membership applications. The museum also has one Justice of the Peace Judgement Docket, 1871–1876. County Commissioners minutes (from 1863) and District Court dockets (from 1867) are in the Weld County Courthouse at Greeley. Some of these records have been removed from the courthouse and stored in a local grain silo.

Golden and Jefferson County

The Mechanics Mining and Trading Company (also known as "the Boston Company") records are in the Colorado Historical Society. Junction District Claim Club records (from 1860), Justice and District Court judgement dockets (from 1862), and County Commissioner proceedings (from 1862) are in the Jefferson County Building. Municipal Trustees records (from 1871) are in City Hall.

Pueblo City and County

Arkansas Valley Ditch Company records (from 1864) and George Baxter's papers, including a history of Pueblo in volume 6, are in the Colorado State Historical Society in Denver. County Commissioner proceedings (from 1862) are in the Pueblo County courthouse. Municipal Trustees records (from 1871) are in City Hall. District Court records are in the state and federal archives. No official Justice of the Peace or Police Court records have survived.

Cañon City and Fremont County

Arkansas Valley and Cañon City Land Claim Club records (from 1860), Probate and District Court records (from 1865), and County Commissioner minutes (from 1865) are in the Fremont County Courthouse. City Council minutes and ordinances (from 1872) are available on microfilm from the State Archives in Denver. The Territorial District Court records are in the Denver Federal Center.

Published Books and Articles

Abbott, Carl. 1976. *Colorado: A Centennial History*. Boulder: University of Colorado Press.

———. 1981. *Boosters and Businessmen: Popular Economic Thought and Urban Growth in the Antebellum Middle West*. Westport, CT: Greenwood Press.

Athearn, Robert G. 1977. *The Denver and Rio Grande Western Railroad*. Lincoln: University of Nebraska Press.

Axford, H. William. 1976. *Gilpin County Gold*. Chicago: Swallow Press.
Baskin, O. L. (ed.). 1881. *History of the Arkansas Valley, Colorado*. Chicago: Baskin.
Bensel, Richard Franklin. 1984. *Sectionalism and American Political Development, 1880–1980*. Madison: University of Wisconsin Press.
Binckley, G. M., and Frank Hartwell (eds.). 1879. *Southern Colorado*. Cañon City: Binckley and Hartwell.
Block, Fred. 1977. "Beyond Corporate Liberalism." *Social Problems* 24:352-361.
———. 1977. "The Ruling Class Does Not Rule." *Socialist Revolution* 33:6–28.
Bogue, Allan. 1960. "Social Theory and the Pioneer." *Agricultural History* 34:21-34.
———. 1975. "The Iowa Claim Clubs: Symbol and Substance." In Stephen Salisbury (ed.), *Essays on the History of the American West*, 342–359. Hinsdale, IL: Dryden Press.
Boorstin, Daniel J. 1965. *The Americans: The National Experience*. New York: Vintage Books.
Boyd, David. 1890. *A History of Greeley and the Union Colony of Colorado*. Greeley: Greeley Tribune Press.
Burawoy, Michael. 1982. "Introduction." In Michael Burawoy and Theda Skocpol (eds.), *Marxist Inquiries*, supplement to *American Journal of Sociology* 88:S1–S32.
———. 1985. *The Politics of Production*. New York: Verso.
Burg, B. Richard. 1968. "Administration of Justice in Denver People's Courts: 1859–1861." *Journal of the Old West* 7 (4 Oct.):510-521.
Burt, S. W. and E. L. Berthoud. 1861. *Rocky Mountain Gold Regions*. Denver: Rocky Mountain News Publishing Co.
Campbell, Rosemae Welles. 1972. *From Trappers to Tourists*. Palmer Lake, CO: Filter Press.
Colorado School of Mines. 1974. "Gold Placers in Colorado." *Quarterly of the Colorado School of Mines* 69(3–4):3–4, 69.
Conner, Daniel Ellis. 1970. *A Confederate in the Colorado Goldfields*. Norman: University of Oklahoma Press.
Dorsett, Lyle. 1977. *The Queen City: A History of Denver*. Boulder, CO: Pruett Publishing Co.
Doyle, D. H. 1978. *The Social Order of a Frontier Community*. Urbana: University of Illinois Press.
Dykstra, Robert. 1968. *The Cattle Towns*. New York: Knopf.
Dykstra, Robert, and William Silag. 1985. "Doing Local History: Monographic Approaches to the Smaller Community." *American Quarterly* 37(3):411-425.
Elkins, Stanley and Eric McKitrick. 1954. "A Meaning for Turner's Frontier." *Political Science Quarterly* 69:321–353, 565–602.
Finlay, William. 1983. "One Occupation, Two Labor Markets." *American Sociological Review* 48:306-314.
Fosset, Frank. 1976. *Colorado*. 1880. Reprint. Glorieta, NM: Rio Grande Press.
Friedland, William H., Amy E. Barton, and Robert J. Thomas. 1981. *Manufacturing Green Gold*. New York: Cambridge University Press.
Giddens, Anthony. 1982. *Profiles and Critiques in Social Theory*. Berkeley: University of California Press.
Goff, Richard, and Robert H. McCaffree. 1967. *Century in the Saddle*. Boulder, CO: Johnson Publishing Co.
Goodman, Robert. 1979. *The Last Entrepreneurs: America's Regional War for Jobs and Dollars*. Boston: South End Press.
Goodwyn, Lawrence, 1978. *The Populist Moment*. New York: Oxford University Press.

Gordon, David, Richard Edwards, and Michael Reich. 1982. *Segmented Work, Divided Workers*. New York: Cambridge University Press.
Guice, John. 1972. *The Rocky Mountain Bench*. New Haven, CT: Yale University Press.
Haeger, John Denis. 1981. *The Investment Frontier*. Albany: State University of New York Press.
Hafen, Leroy (ed.). 1948. *Reports from Colorado*. New York: Lewis Historical.
Hall, Frank. 1889–1895. *History of the State of Colorado*, 4 vols. Chicago: Blakely.
Hall, Thomas, 1986. "Incorporation into the World System: Toward a Critique." *American Sociological Review* 51:390–402.
Hodson, Randy, and Robert L. Kaufman. 1982. "Economic Dualism: A Critical Approach." *American Sociological Review* 47:727–739.
Hogan, Richard. 1985. "The Frontier as Social Control." *Theory and Society* 14(Jan.): 35–51.
———. 1987. "Carnival and Caucus: A Typology for Comparative Frontier History." *Social Science History* 11(2):139–167.
———. Forthcoming. "Three Pieces of the Populist Puzzle." *Sociological Forum*.
Hoig, Stanley. 1961. *The Sand Creek Massacre*. Norman: University of Oklahoma Press.
Hollister, Ovando J. 1867. *The Mines of Colorado*. Springfield, MA: Samuel Bowles.
Johnson, Paul E. 1978. *A Shopkeeper's Millennium*. New York: Hill and Wang.
Kemp, D. C. 1949. *Colorado's Little Kingdom*. Denver: Sage Books.
King, Joseph E. 1977. *A Mine to Make a Mine*. College Station: Texas A&M Press.
Krakel, Dean Fenton. 1954. *South Platte Country*. Laramie, WY: Powder River Publishers.
Kulikoff, Allan. 1989. "The Transition to Capitalism in Rural America." *William and Mary Quarterly*, 3rd series, 46 (Jan.):120–144.
LeCompte, Janet. 1978. *Pueblo, Hardscrabble, and Greenhorn*. Norman: University of Oklahoma Press.
Leonard, Stephen. 1971. *Denver's Foreign Born Immigrants, 1859–1900*. Doctoral dissertation, Claremont Graduate School, History.
Logan, John R., and Harvey Molotch. 1987. *Urban Fortunes*. Berkeley: University of California Press.
McNall, Scott G. 1988. *The Road to Rebellion: Class Formation and Kansas Populism*. Chicago: University of Chicago Press.
Mann, Ralph. 1982. *After the Gold Rush*. Stanford, CA: Stanford University Press.
Marshall, Thomas Maitland. 1920. *Early Records of Gilpin County, Colorado*. Boulder, CO: University of Colorado Press.
Merk, Frederick. 1978. *History of the Westward Movement*. New York: Knopf.
Mooney, Patrick H. 1988. *My Own Boss? Class, Rationality, and the Family Farm*. Boulder, CO: Westview Press.
Moore, Barrington. 1967. *The Social Origins of Dictatorship and Democracy*. Boston: Beacon Press.
Mumey, Nolie. 1962. *Laws of Nevadaville*. Boulder, CO: Johnson Publishing Co.
Paige, Jeffery. 1975. *Agrarian Revolution*. New York: Free Press.
Rohrbough, Malcolm J. 1968. *The Land Office Business: The Settlement and Administration of American Public Lands, 1789–1837*. New York: Oxford University Press.
Roy, William G. 1983. "The Interlocking Directorate Structure of the United States." *American Sociological Review* 48:248–256.
Rubenstein, Richard E. 1970. *Rebels in Eden*. Boston: Little, Brown and Co.
Ryder, Eugene Frank. 1971. *The Denver Police Department*. Doctoral dissertation, University of Denver, History.

Schwartz, Michael. 1988. *Radical Protest and Social Structure: The Southern Farmers' Alliance and Cotton Tenancy, 1880–1890.* 1976. Reprint. Chicago: University of Chicago Press.
Skocpol, Theda. 1980. "Political Response to Capitalist Crisis." *Politics and Society* 10(2):155–201.
———. 1979. *States and Social Revolution.* New York: Cambridge University Press.
Skowronek, Stephen. 1982. *Building a New American State: The Expansion of National Administrative Capacities, 1877–1920.* New York: Cambridge University Press.
Smelser, Marshall. 1968. *The Democratic Republic, 1800–1815.* New York: Harper and Row.
Smiley, Jerome C. 1901. *History of Denver.* Denver: Old Americana Publishing Co.
Smith, Duane. 1974. *Rocky Mountain Mining Camps.* Lincoln: University of Nebraska Press.
Sprague, Marshall. 1976. *Colorado: A Bicentennial History.* New York: Norton.
Steinel, Alvin Theodore. 1929. *History of Agriculture in Colorado.* Fort Collins, CO: State Agricultural College.
Teaford, Jon. 1984. *The Unheralded Triumph.* Baltimore: Johns Hopkins University Press.
Thompson, E. P. 1966. *The Making of the English Working Class.* New York: Vintage.
Tilly, Charles. 1978. *From Mobilization to Revolution.* Reading, MA: Addison-Wesley.
Turner, Frederick Jackson. 1972. "The Significance of the Frontier in American History." Reprinted in Rogers Taylor (ed.), *The Turner Thesis.* Lexington, MA: D. C. Heath & Co.
Ubbelohde, Carl, Maxine Benson, and Duane Smith. 1972. *A Colorado History.* Boulder, CO: Pruett.
Wallerstein, Immanuel. 1988. *The Modern World System III: The Second Era of Great Expansion of the Capitalist World Economy, 1730–1840s.* San Diego: Academic Press.
Webb, Walter Prescott. 1931. *The Great Plains.* New York: Grosset and Dunlap.
Wharton, Junius E. 1866. *History of the City of Denver.* Denver: Byers and Dailey Printers.
Whittaker, Milo E. 1917. *Pathbreakers and Pioneers of the Pueblo Region.* Pueblo: Franklin Press.
Willard, James F. 1918. *The Union Colony at Greeley, Colorado: 1869–1871.* Denver: W. F. Robinson Printing Co.
Wolf, Eric R. 1982. *Europe and the People without History.* Berkeley: University of California Press.
Wright, Eric Olin. 1985. *Classes.* London: New Left Books.
Wright, Eric, and Bill Martin. 1987. "The Transformation of the American Class Structure, 1960–1980." *American Journal of Sociology* 93(1):1–29.
Wright, Gavin. 1978. *The Political Economy of the Cotton South.* New York: W. W. Norton.

COLORADO NEWSPAPERS

Cañon City Times (weekly, Cañon City) 15 September 1860–7 October 1861; 7 March 1872–3 May 1877.
Colorado Republican (weekly, Denver) 25 May 1861–26 June 1862.
Colorado Chieftain (weekly, Pueblo) 1 June 1868–12 June 1873.
Colorado Transcript (weekly, Golden) 19 December 1866–1 June 1881.
Colorado Tribune (weekly, Denver) 15 May 1867–3 January 1872 (renamed *Denver Tribune* in February 1871).

Denver Weekly Times 19 February 1873–8 March 1889.
Greeley Tribune (weekly) 19 April 1871–9 April 1884.
Rocky Mountain Gold Reporter (weekly, Mountain City) 6 August–17 September 1859.
Rocky Mountain Herald (daily, Denver) 1 May 1860–24 May 1861.
Rocky Mountain Herald (weekly, Denver) 5 May 1860–18 May 1861.
Rocky Mountain News (weekly, Denver) 23 April 1859–29 December, 1880.
Triweekly Miners' Register (Central City) 28 July 1862–20 August 1863.
Weekly Register (Central City) 30 July 1868–31 December 1880 (renamed *Weekly Register-Call* in June 1878).
Western Mountaineer (weekly, Golden) 7 December 1859–20 December 1860.

INDEX

Arapahoe County, 24, 27, 63
Arkansas Valley Ditch Company, 158

Bakers, 35
Bent and Saint Vrain, 79, 151
Berthoud, E. L., 122, 140
Black Hawk ore reduction mill, 59, 61, 62, 66–67
Blacksmiths, 35
Board of Immigration, 43, 104
Boosters, 3, 5, 6, 12, 208
  Cañon City, 194
  Central City, 49, 70
  Denver, 19, 40, 48, 57
  Pueblo, 151, 166
  See also under Class: class-based interests, merchants and speculators
Boston and Colorado Smelting Company, 73
Boston Company, 123
Bummers, 28, 223n23
Byers, William, 26, 32, 36–37, 71, 79, 84

Cañon City, 189–190
  and the Civil War, 184
  decline, 184–185
  economy of 1870, 189–191
  establishment, 179
  Law and Order Committee, 181
  local government, 181–183, 186–187
  national incorporation of coal, 188, 203, 204
  national incorporation of petroleum, 188
  national incorporation of railroads, 196–203
  resistance by farmers to national incorporation, 195, 205–206
  revitalization, 186
  and the State Penitentiary, 189
  town chartering of, 193
  versus county, 195, 198–199
Carter, Eli, 122, 127, 133, 135
Cattlemen's Association, 81, 111
  and cattle thieves, 111
Central City
  Board of Aldermen, 70, 73, 76
  capital for, 71

charter, 63
and Civil War, 60, 63
local economy, 54, 67
local government, 57, 58, 60, 65, 66, 70
Opera House, 73
Central Colorado Improvement Company, 83, 124, 188, 197, 204
Chinese labor, 42, 63
Chinese riot, 46–47, 77
Cibola Hydraulic Company, 124
Civil War, 35, 60
  and Pueblo, 158–159
  and speculation, 60
  and water rights, 158
Claim clubs, 7
  Arapahoe County Land Claim Club, 7, 25, 36, 37
  Cañon City and Arkansas Valley Land Claim Club, 180
  Golden Gate Land Claim Club, 134
  Junction District Land Claim Club, 136
  St. Vrain Claim Club, 80–81
Clark, J. Max, 43, 104, 109, 112–113
Classes
  distinguished, 6–8
  divisions among, 211, 218, 239nn6–10
  organization of, 211–215
  See also strikes
Class-based interests, 7–9, 12–13, 34–35
  and gold miners, 57–58, 209
  and resistance to national capital, 14–15, 208, 214
  of farmers, 2, 219
  of laboring people, 12, 214
  of merchants and speculators, 2, 12, 29–30, 70
  of nonlaboring people, 12
  of silver miners, 219
Class consciousness, 208–209
  and Greeley farmers, 90, 109, 111–112
  as a bar to organizing, 219, 220
Coal mines, 115, 188, 204
Colorado Coal and Iron Company, 174, 177, 204
Colorado Stockgrowers Association. *See* Cattlemen's Association

247

248   Index

Colorado Territory, 38, 63–66, 137
Conflict perspective, 5–7, 12, 207, 237n1
Consensus perspective, 5–7, 207, 237n1
Consolidated Ditch Company, 59, 124
Cornish miners, 73, 75
Courts and criminal dockets
   for Cañon City Probate Court, 186
   for Cañon City District Court, 194
   for Central City District Court, 74, 76
   for Central City Justice of the Peace courts, 64, 70, 75
   for Central City territorial courts, 70, 75
   for Denver Justice of the Peace courts, 44
   for Denver People's Court, 24
   for Denver Vigilance Committee, 28
   for Golden People's Court, 132
   for Golden Citizen's Courts, 127
   for Golden District Court, 143, 144
   for Golden Justice of the Peace courts, 139, 143, 145
   for Golden People's Court, 128, 130
   for Greeley Justice of the Peace Courts, 101, 115
   for Greeley territorial courts, 102–115
   for Pueblo District Court, 156, 165, 166
Crime. *See* Courts and criminal dockets

Democratic Party, 4, 45–47, 114, 166–167, 217
Denver, 20, 40
   and provisional government of Jefferson Territory, 26, 34
   establishment of, 19
   frontier economy of, 20–24
   local government of, 27, 29
   City Council of, 36
   frontier government of, 29–35
   People's government of Denver City, 33 (*see also under* People's Court: Denver)
   transition, 39–42
Denver Board of Trade, 40
Denver Land Company
   and the Union Colony, 81–84
Denver, Mount Vernon, and Gregory Diggings Wagon Road Company, 134

Evans, John, Governor, 39–40

Farmers, 43–44
   and class consciousness, 43–44, 109–112
   division among, 112–113, 219
   in Cañon City, 191–192
   in Greeley, 92–93, 97, 106–107, 109–112
   in Pueblo, 161–163
   versus merchants, 97

Fences
   for Greeley, 103
   illegal, 175–177
Fountain City, 152
   and support of provisional government, 153, 154
Fremont County, 185–186

Gilpin County, 64
Golden, 139
   as territorial capital, 138
   businesspersons, 124–125, 142
   comparison to Denver and Central City, 125–126
   establishment, 121–122
   local economy, 123–124, 140–141
   local government, 129, 137–139, 143, 145
   national incorporation and local control, 143, 149–150
   national incorporation and the railroad war, 146–149
   national incorporation through transportation, 140
   People's Court, 130–132
   wagon road companies, 134
Golden City Association
   and establishment of Golden, 123
   and municipal government, 126
   and state government, 133
Gould, Jay, 40, 71, 148
Grange, 1, 8, 109, 111, 113, 214
   in Greeley, 109, 114
Greeley, Horace, 82
Greeley
   and temperance, 82, 90, 99, 116
   as county seat, 108–109
   farmer's club, 106–107
   local economy of, 91–93
   Board of Trustees, 100
   Colony versus municipal government, 100–101, 106
   elections, 94, 95, 96–97
   establishment, 89
   issues, 90, 95, 100
   See also Union Colony
Greeley Farmers' Club, 106–107
Greenbacker Party, 1, 4, 111, 114, 213, 214, 216, 218
Gregory, John H., 49, 53, 61
Gregory Diggings
   and Consolidated Gregory Company, 61
   and control of production, 52
   and legislation, 51, 52–53
   and profitability, 62
   discovery of, 49–50
   and mountain versus gulch, 51
   newcomers versus oldtimers, 50–51

Herd law, 90, 101–102, 103
Homestead Act, 2, 37

Irrigation conventions
  Denver, 1873, 104–105
  Denver, 1879, 109
  Weld County, 104
Irrigation districts, 110

Jefferson County
  and transportation, 143
  elections, 133–134
  organization of, 127

Lot jumping, 8, 19, 27, 37–38, 154
Loveland, W. A. H., 45, 122, 147, 148

Mechanics Mining and Trading Company, 121
Meeker, Nathan C., 82
Mexican Americans
  in Cañon City, 192
  in Greeley, 116
  in Pueblo, 154, 163
Miners, coal, 115
  and Greenback vote, 115, 216–217
Miners, gold
  interests of, 7, 51–52, 57–58
  versus merchants, 56
  opposition of to provisional government, 58
Miners, silver, 218–219
Mining camp laws
  and municipal government, 64, 75
  Central City, 57, 75
Mining districts, 7, 52, 59–60 (see also Gregory Diggings)
Monopoly capital, 1, 3–4, 11–12
  and mining, 53
  and railroads, 39
  as threat to local autonomy, 230n1
  definition of, 15
  hindrances to, 214–215
  and national monopoly class, 6
  resistance to, 3, 15, 120, 212, 220

National Farmers Alliance, 111

Palmer, William J., 169, 170, 196–201, 205
Panic of 1873 and the railroad war, 147
People's Court
  and crimes against persons, 30
  Denver, 24–25, 28–30, 32, 36
  Golden, 130–132
  Pueblo, 156
Populists, 111
Price fixing, 34, 35, 56, 210, 224n35

Printers, 35, 45
Proletarianization, 8–9, 15, 24
  and caucus towns, 119
  and labor discipline, 42
  and strikes, 42
  and impact of Chinese workers, 42, 46
Provisional government of Jefferson Territory, 26, 58, 126, 133, 153
  and Cañon City, 182, 184
  and Central City courts, 65, 70
  and Central City miners, 63–64
  and charters, 133
  and courts, 45
  and county elections, 133
  and Denver, 33
  and Ditch War, 59–60
  and eventual acceptance by Golden, 137–138
  and frontier vice, 38
  and Greeley, 81
  and irrigation, 133
  and lack of laboring class support, 136
  and local Golden autonomy, 137
  and Pueblo, 155
  and Jefferson Rangers, 27
  miners' opposition to, 58
Public and private government
  Carnival definition, 3, 9–10
  Carnival overview, 18
  Caucus definition, 3, 10
Pueblo
  Board of Trade, 166
  and cattle trade, 161
  during Civil War, 155–159
  and commercial enterprise, 159
  county commissioners, 164
  in 1879, 174
  elections, 157
  establishment of, 153
  farmers, 161–163
  frontier economy, 153–154
  and the Indian question, 155
  land rights, 157–158
  local government, 154, 156, 163, 165
  national incorporation, 163, 175, 177
  national incorporation and the railroad, 169–173
  renewed prosperity, 159–162
  organizing of, 164
  and support of territorial government, 155, 159
  versus county, 166–167
Pullman, George, 61

Railroads
  Atchison, Topeka and Santa Fe, 172, 197
  Cañon City and San Juan Railroad, 199

Railroads, *continued*
  Colorado Central and Pacific Railroad, 140
  Colorado Central Railroad, 39, 72, 146
  and the Colorado railroad war, 146–149
  Denver and Rio Grande Railroad, 169, 197
  Denver Pacific, 40, 84, 146, 147
  and funding, 39, 40, 72, 81, 171–173, 197–198
  Kansas Pacific, 39, 146, 169
  Union Pacific, 39, 72, 146
Republican Party, 4, 45–47, 77, 112–113, 114, 166–167, 217
Rockefeller, John D., 177

Sage, Russell, 148, 202
Saint Vrain, Golden City, and Colorado Wagon Road Company, 124
Sand Creek Massacre, 159
Statehood, 1
  and attracting of capital, 71
  and constitutional convention, 72, 133
  defeat of, 26
  organizing of, 25–26
Strikes, 212, 216
  Clear Creek, 42, 215
  coal miners, 1
  Cripple Creek, 47, 213
  Denver bricklayers, 1
  Denver carpenters, 1
  Denver printers, 1, 45
  Leadville, 45–46
  Ludlow Station, 47, 213
  miners, 42

Teller, Henry M., 66, 71, 73
Town companies, 2, 7
  Auraria Town Company, 7, 19, 25, 123
  Cañon City, 181
  Central City (lack of), 53
  Denver Town Company, 8, 19, 27, 37
  Golden City Association, 122
  Golden Gate Town Company, 135
  Greeley (*see* Union colony)
  Pueblo, 154
  Saint Charles Town Company, 19, 123

Union Colony (Greeley), 94
  and fences, 103, 108
  and foreign capital, 98
  organization, 82–83
  and purchase of land, 84, 85–86, 95
  raising of revenue, 94
Unions, 212
  Denver, skilled trades, 47
  hindrances to, 213

  opposition by political parties to, 45–46, 217
  printers, 35, 45
  and silver miners, 220
  Western Federation of Miners, 44, 47

Vice
  in Cañon City, 193
  in Central City, 57, 74
  in Denver, 36–37, 38
  in Golden, 145
  in Greeley (temperance), 101, 116
  in Pueblo, 166
Vigilance committees
  and defense of law and order, 75, 126–127, 168
  and defense of property, 30, 155
  Denver Vigilance Committee, 26, 28, 30, 31, 223n23, 224n25, 31
  in Golden, 126, 130
  in Pueblo, 155, 156, 168

Wall, D. K., 121–122
Water rights, 1, 59
  and the Union Colony, 91, 101, 103–105, 109
  and the Poudre River District, 109–110
  and Central City Consolidated Ditch Company, 59
  and Denver irrigation, 43
Weld County
  as county seat, 108–109
  organizing of, 81
World system theory, 5, 207, 238n4

www.ingramcontent.com/pod-product-compliance
Lightning Source LLC
Chambersburg PA
CBHW070758230426

43665CB00017B/2402